C0-DVG-549

Management of Industrial
Construction Projects

Contents

Preface

This book should satisfy the basic needs of engineers and managers who require a sound introduction to this complex subject.

The material has been selected on the basis of twenty years of professional experience with international consultants, contractors and promoters in many industrial construction projects. Some of it is very straightforward and simply presented: some is more complex. In any case, it is intended to be readable, practical and informative.

The structure is as follows:

- Chapter 1 is a general introduction.
- Chapters 2, 3, and 4 are about planning and scheduling. They assume no prior knowledge and provide a good working basis of bar charts, networks and practical computer applications. They represent a solid foundation.
- Chapters 5, 6 and 7 develop the background to estimation of costs and prices. They are aimed at project level and do not deal with the detail of clerical techniques.
- Chapters 8 and 9 lead on naturally from cost estimation to cost control. Again, the discussion is at project level and provides an understanding of overall concerns and practices.
- Chapter 10 is about quality – a very topical subject, often misunderstood and misinterpreted. The chapter gives practical advice, based on experience, on *what* is important, and *why* it is important, in achieving a quality result.
- Chapter 11, 'Performance', brings together the conclusions of the foregoing chapters and could be called 'Total quality'.
- Chapter 12, 'Organization', is both general and specific. The general view concerns fundamentals; the selected specific views are on culture, systems and team management.

- Chapter 13 treats procurement as a separate topic because procurement affects practically everything in a project.
- Chapter 14 deals with the basic legal aspects of contracts and project construction work.

These represent, together, a fairly comprehensive treatment. However, the book is by no means exhaustive and will not satisfy all requirements. A reading list is included for the benefit of those who want to pursue certain aspects of project and general management further.

For convenience only, the male gender has been used throughout this book. Non-technical definitions have been based on the *Concise Oxford Dictionary*.

J.J. O'Neill

Acknowledgements

To all who contributed in any way to the preparation and publication of this book – thank you.

Very special thanks are due to
- my wife and family, friends and relatives for all their help and encouragement.
- Terry Donnelly, of DuPont Maintenance Painting Services, for spending hours on various drafts.
- Dennis Lock, for a comprehensive review of the basic draft work.
- Mary Ann Ostroff, of DuPont Project Engineering Division (PED), for reviewing the chapters on estimating and cost control.
- Hugh Beaton, of DuPont PED, for an encouraging review and comment on the 'planning' chapters.
- Bill Hovis, of Dupont PED, for comments on the 'Quality' chapter.
- Ernie Bond, for after-hours assistance in preparing the 'computer applications' figures.
- Dr Roy Bailey, Dr Charles Margerison and Dr Dick McCann, for advice on the team-management section in Chapter 12.
- Joel Koppelman, of Primavera Systems, Inc, for reviewing the material on computer applications in Chapter 4.
- DuPont colleagues at Maydown, Northern Ireland, as well as those in Europe and especially Pete Richmond in the USA.

For permission to reproduce printed material, I am grateful to
- DuPont Company, for many of the figures and for references to the Project Engineering Division's project system.
- Primavera Systems, Inc, and the DuPont Company, for the computer plots in Chapter 4.
- E & FN Spon Ltd and Davis, Belfield and Everest, for Figure 86.
- Dr Charles Margerison, for himself, Dr Dick McCann and MCB University Press for the figures on team-management.

• Penguin Books Ltd, for permission to use Dr Charles Handy's material on 'culture' in Chapter 12.

Extracts from British Standards are reproduced with the permission of the British Standards Institution. Complete copies of the documents can be obtained by post from BSI Sales, Linford Wood, Milton Keynes, Bucks. MK14 6LE.

1

Introduction

Projects always have a start and an end – otherwise they do not exist as projects. This fundamental is often overlooked, incredibly, by the very people who should know better – those who pay, either directly or indirectly, and those who suffer or benefit, either directly or indirectly.

Can you imagine a client who decides to build a new airline catering unit, engages a consultant, agrees a completion time of 3 years and who, years later, still does not have a new facility and has thrown away millions of dollars on useless design works? It happened. Another client invested 20 million of his own dollars in a $50 million plant, which was successfully designed and built in an incredibly tight 2-year programme. He was then taken over by an asset-stripper when start-up costs drained him.

Of course, there are also clients who start projects, budget enough money and a little more, enough time and a little more, give the project enough effort and control and a little more – and, sure enough, get what they want – and a little more, with budget cash left and time to spare. How do they do it? And how do they keep doing it?

The direct answer is that they manage the project! They know, from start to finish, that they have a project on hand – with real start dates, real end dates, real objectives in terms of quality, money spent and value earned – and, above all, a realistic project attitude. The failures, on the other hand, at some stage, become blinded by what is going on and lose sight of reality. How do they do it? The direct answer is that they fail to manage the project. Generally, those involved pay the inevitable price of failure – one way or another.

So what are the real lessons? The first is that nature imposes her own laws on any situation – and man must either control nature or accommodate it. Consequently, he must be able to recognize when a situation is desirable or undesirable and know how to move from bad to good.

The second is that realism, at the start of a project, does not examine a proposed task with emotion or even optimism. It *demands* to know — is this practical and achievable within the necessary time-scale for success? At the right price? With the necessary performance standards? If you decide to undertake this project, why, where, when and how will you measure its progress? How will you know that it is on track? Can you live with failure at any stage? How can you be sure of success?

Types of projects

A project is an undertaking to achieve specific objectives in a certain time. This is a broadly based definition, illustrated by referring to *types* of projects as follows:

- *Creative* projects such as research and development, writing a book or painting a picture. The main feature of this type of project is the intrinsic satisfaction necessary to the participants. For example, an artist might produce an outstanding work for little material cost — yet his work could be priceless. Similarly, a team of dedicated researchers with a low budget might produce better results than a highly paid team working with unlimited resources on the same problem.
- *Rule-book* projects such as financial auditing, inspecting materials on a construction job or acting as judge in a court case. The main feature of this type of project is that rules of conduct exist and these may be interpreted to the benefit or detriment of the project. For example, a referee must make decisions within the rules of play and yet allow a game to get along by *effectively* applying those rules.
- *Team* projects such as designing and constructing a chemical plant, organizing a big conference or conducting an orchestra at a public performance. The main feature of this type of project is that a diverse range of high-level skills and training may be required to contribute to the execution of the project. For example, the team required to carry out the chemical-plant project might include accountants, engineers of many disciplines, lawyers, chemists and other scientists, environmental experts and operations/manufacturing people.
- *Task* projects such as building houses, digging trenches or carrying out military operations. The main feature of this type of project is that physical work is involved, often against a strict time-table. For example, in digging trenches, the units of measurement may be in cubic metres per man-day and those involved will be expected to achieve the target rates.

Table 1. Project types and key management styles.

Project type	Key management style
Creative	Encouraging
Rule-book	Applying rules effectively
Team	Directing, team leadership
Task	Commanding, asserting authority

These project types have much in common and complex industrial projects have elements of them all. However, the differences are more apparent if the key styles of management for particular project types are considered. These are outlined in Table 1. This is an overview of project features rather than an absolute way of putting projects into category boxes. It shows the contrast in the project environment which, if understood, can help towards overall success. For example:

- In a research project, you would not expect to find a manager who makes his own decisions and achieves results by direct orders – you would, however, find that the style has its place on a building site or on a military exercise.
- A team leader on a financial or safety audit may encourage, direct or even command his team members in the process. The results, however, will have more to do with whether or not the relevant bureaucratic rules are effectively applied in the project circumstances.
- The designers on an engineering project have to apply the rules effectively and work within the relevant codes of practice for their discipline. However, the creative requirement of their design work may be served best by an encouraging style in a team atmosphere.

Project management

The development of project-management methods has taken place mainly in the past few decades, in line with the growth in general management knowledge and practices. If 'management' is defined as '*the control of resources*', then 'project management' may be defined as '*the control of resources in a temporary arrangement to achieve project objectives*'.

In this context, the project manager acts as a general manager for the duration of the project. Consequently, the *control* of the project crucially depends upon his understanding how time, money and other resources are related and can interact for the achievement of the required project results and objectives.

Project results

The unsuccessful project never has a satisfactory end, even though it may have an exciting start and a satisfactory middle. Conversely, the successful project greatly benefits from early successes but the secret of its eventual success may lie in or towards its end. So what is the difference and how do you know if you are on the road to final success or failure?

Generally speaking, a project may be classified as successful only when measured against objective criteria *at completion*. Ideally, the criteria used for final measurement are the same as those used in the initial decision framework. However, this is not an essential condition because criteria changes, whether internally or externally generated, might occur during a project life-cycle.

Therefore, the control and monitoring of the potential or achievable *end results* against most likely *end criteria* in the project are of fundamental and continuing importance all along. The direct analogy is that of the static or moving target as shown in Fig. 1(a) and (b). Fig. 1(a) represents a straightforward 'ready, aim, fire, follow the path, arrive at the target' situation. Fig. 1(b) represents the more complex situation where a target has first been presented but, in the course of reaching the target, you find that the target has shifted. In the project situation it is the same as changing the criteria.

The basic differences in approach can be seen at a glance. Project (b) – reach a moving target – requires different actions than project (a), because the criteria can change. The primary and continuing question, at all times, must therefore be related directly to the task:

- What is the task?   Define it.
- What are the main subtasks?   Define them.

These questions appear obvious. However, experience shows that the answers differ widely depending on individual perception. For example, a manufacturing company might intend to expand facilities for a new product. Under the leadership of the project manager (individual or team or committee), a substructure of line specialists will be involved, each with a diferent contribution to make. The finance manager will see the project in terms of cash flows, budgets, bank dealings, loans, etc.

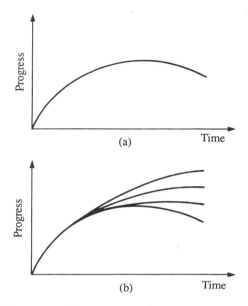

Figure 1. *Changing criteria in a project.*

The technical managers will see it as a civil-, architectural-, mechanical- or electrical-engineering project. The manufacturing manager will see it as an industrial-engineering project, with selection of equipment, capacities, layout, process flows, etc., as key aspects. The marketing manager will see the project in terms of market projections, quality of product, pricing policies, delivery times, etc.

Each individual will be right within his own parameters. However, the total project demands will consist of elements of all these functions and the state of balance required for eventual success. Therefore, the definition of the real task must be an overriding consideration. Further, it must continue throughout the project life-cycle, as differing interests may need to predominate at various cycle points.

The essence of this project management, therefore, is not limited to the management of the project. Rather, it must be primarily directed at the management and control of the resources, including the time, people, knowledge and money within the project framework as required by changing circumstances. The key feature lies in balancing the shifts in emphasis at each stage and this demands continuous redefinition of the specific tasks at hand.

To consider this example further, the initial *statement of objectives* may be in the form:

The project requires the design and construction of a manufacturing plant within 2 years at a cost not exceeding £20 million. The project will be financed by organization cash and long-term bank loans. The market has a projected growth rate of 20 per cent per annum. Present capacity will be insufficient in 2 years time. Market share will then suffer until the new plant comes on-stream. The product must have characteristics according to predetermined specifications.

The project manager appointed to organize this project will not have full autonomy (unless he is the owner). Instead, his activities will be monitored by supervisors and his results must therefore be in line with their definition of the task.

The primary purpose of the statement of objectives is to permit the development of an appropriate strategy. Strategy, in this case, means bringing about the conditions most favourable to success and, in project management, decision-making should always be within a strategic framework. For example, successful results in a project could depend on targets achieved at intermediate points and the effective strategy must acknowledge these key elements. In relation to the project example, the main and subtasks are developed as follows:

- Main task: to produce a marketable product within 2 years within a budget of £20 million.
- Main subtasks:
  (a) Develop strategy based on the time-scale, the present resources and the performances required. Know the critical factors for success.
  (b) Develop tactical considerations from the strategy. Ask why, what, where, how, who, when?
  (c) Implement and control.

Before examining the nature of the different actions required, take a closer look at the initial target, i.e. the project objectives.

Project objectives

Any project will have objectives in these spheres:

- Time – completion is required within a certain time.
- Costs – expected project costs versus benefits will enable rewards or profits to be made.
- Quality – completion is required within criteria which measure standards achieved against standards required or specified.

- Performance – project performance is required to satisfy the time, cost and quality parameters.

These are not necessarily presented in order of importance for every project but do reflect, nevertheless, the natural order:

If you do not have the time, you will not.
If you do not have the money, you cannot.
If you do not know what you want, you will never get it.

Each of these is developed in more detail later and the tools (techniques) which could be used are introduced. But at this stage it is helpful to outline each area for an initial understanding.

Take time first. Probably you have heard of plans and planning – you may have even prepared or taken part in some. So what is the mystery element or elements which distinguish successful plans from unsuccessful? The only true answer is that the successful plan works. The likely explanation is that the plan is recognized as being one of the main factors for success – the others being both derived from and included in the plan and covering, perhaps, the allocation and effective use of resources, cost control and the means for achieving the agreed standards.

Details of planning and scheduling are developed later but an understanding of planning begins with an understanding that planning has to allow for its own imperfections. Since the plan is drawn up by people and will be carried out by people, all those involved have to understand and believe in those elements of the plan where they have direct responsibilities.

You cannot manage time – but you can manage your own efforts in a time framework. This is the cornerstone of all planning, where you talk about moving from situation A to situation B and the steps necessary for that movement. The plan needs to look at the steps in this way:

The *broad* plan showing the major steps required on a calendar-type layout, with definite start and end dates. The steps need not contain much detail but must state, or show, that if a particular sequence of main activities is followed on intermediate dates, a desired result will emerge at a later date. Its primary purpose is to show management what can be achieved and if it is being achieved during execution of the project.

The *project* plan is a detailed enlargement of the broad plan and provides further infill activities and dates derived from the broad plan. Its primary purpose is to provide initial project management and direction. Actual events will mean revising and updating the plan to accommodate changes. This plan level should spell out resources to be used and generally indicate how they should be used. A 'critical path (or paths)' can usually be developed to show those activities which require the most management effort if end dates are to be met.

More detailed plans are further derived from the project plan or a revised project plan and and show activities on a monthly, weekly, daily or even hourly time-scale depending on the nature of the project. These plans can show resources in greater detail and deal with small unit activities. Their usefulness is mainly directed to the day-to-day management of the project and they are best drawn-up in an easily followed bar chart.

These are the main frameworks available for project planning. However, in this introduction, the main points to bear in mind are:

- Plans are made up by people; they are therefore open to challenge in varying degrees relevant to the experience of the planners and the nature of the project.
- People and their plans are generally optimistic and it pays to maintain a healthy scepticism.
- If you can accept a particular plan, then accept it as if it were your own and do everything possible to make it work.
- If you have to make a plan, get assistance from the people who will be involved. This is frequently the most challenging aspect of putting a plan together and making it work.

Take costs next – everybody knows what money is and what can be done with it. In project considerations, though, the focus is on particular aspects of the use of money and you will deliberately plan and try to get something for a certain price – you negotiate each step of the way. The cost aspect is thus broken down into three project areas:

- estimating,
- accounting,
- control.

Estimating, in principle, is guessing. However, there are degrees of guessing. These range from the uneducated guess to the sophisticated accumulation of data and number-crunching probability analyses. Jargon names like 'ball-park figure' have a place here and these may be further adjusted by 'contingency' factors which allow for mistakes – provided they occur within a percentage range plus or minus.

Preparing an estimate obviously takes both time and money. The results depend upon these factors as well as the skill and experience of the estimators and the brief to which they work. Because of the possible variations from planned expenditure, estimates may be regarded as belonging to a class, e.g. a class-one to a class-four quality.

Typically, a class-one estimate may be in the range of predicted accuracy of ± 5 per cent while a class-four example may be ± 50 per cent. What matters is the use to which the particular estimate is put and the assumptions upon which it has been based. During progress of the project, it is necessary to re-examine an estimate periodically. This can lead to adjustments which will be more reliable as hard project data is generated.

Project accounting is essentially the book-keeping exercise. It records expenditures into predetermined account codes and classifies them into categories such as capital funds, indirect/direct overheads, materials, field labour, plant, etc. It differs from both estimating and cost control mainly because it takes no action other than providing historical records.

Project cost control, on the other hand, is the most dynamic aspect of the project cost arena. Essentially, it combines the estimate of time and money together with the accounting record for the expressed purpose of control, i.e. taking action. Since a project is never static, this control function looks for reliable data, analyses it against desired objectives, shows or predicts values earned against targets, examines the trends and indicates possible courses of action.

Take quality next. This is frequently mentioned in the form:

We are going to build something for the right price, in the right time at the right quality.

But, in this context, while *x* years and *y* pounds are acceptable the stand-alone word 'quality' is not sufficiently precise to be a project objective. Rather, what is required is an objective in the form:

. . . to a predetermined quality standard.

In this overall context, quality may generally be regarded as 'complying with requirements' and the degree of quality achievement may be taken as the degree of compliance or non-compliance with those requirements.

Quality compliance will be included in the price and schedule if an enterprise operates a proven quality programme. Otherwise, the cost of reaching or exceeding quality standards may exist as a penalty-producing exercise which prevents achievement of the costs and time objectives. At the end of the day, a project will be judged unsuccessful if the quality standards exceed requirements and cost too much or take too long to achieve, thereby jeopardizing other down-stream activities.

Performance is the final issue for comment at this stage. In the project environment, performance is tangible and can therefore be measured. It is the ratio of actual results to optimum results in terms of the project objectives.

Apart from the time, quality and cost aspects, the project objective(s) must describe *all* the desired results after a transformation process. Consequently, personal assessments of project performance must be reduced to the extent that they can be supported by the measurement of relevant data. Performance in any area will then be subject to performance index measurements which can indicate where action is necessary for the project direction. These may be taken and used to keep the project on course.

Performance in this context means looking at:

- The baselines for the measurement of performance, including time, costs and quality standards.
- The areas of productivity. (What does it mean to be productive?)
- How resources are allocated, monitored and controlled, including the necessary reporting and reviewing.

The qualitative methods available for measuring cost performance indices, schedule performance indices and trend analysis are described later.

Project perspective

Apart from the case where a project is carried out completely 'in-house', a project will normally involve a number of different organizations. For example, construction projects often involve the following:

- a promoting organization – the owner(s) or initiator,
- a technical consultant(s),
- a contractor(s).

Each of these parties will have its own individual project set-up and so the project perspective will be different for each of them. Given the project battles against time, costs, quality of results and overall performance, additional conflicts may arise due to the differing levels of interests or expectations of the involved parties. This is shown in Fig. 2. This schematic shows a streamlined shape where the interests of each party overlap, suggesting a degree of mutual interest. It is easy to visualize the situation where one party's interests diverge – with the resulting imbalance threatening the stability of the system.

Consequently, the promoter, with the primary project interest, must adopt a strategy which results in the best 'fit' of interests and permits control of the project. It follows that the promoter who understands and applies project-management methods has a much better chance of selecting and using an appropriate strategy than the one who does not.

The development of project strategy

The object of strategy is to bring about conditions most favourable to success. The project manager, therefore, must habitually analyse the project situation against the strategic requirements and define, acknowledge and implement corrections required either in refining the strategy or in tactical actions to maintain strategic momentum.

The resource to be utilized here is knowledge:

- Knowledge of the project task and its definition.
- Knowledge of the resources available[1] and required.[2]
- Knowledge of the environments in which the project will operate.

Application of the knowledge resource is of such fundamental importance that it cannot be overstated. Project management is not based on gambling. Neither are its actions normally based on absolute certainty. However, realism demands objectivity, particularly at the strategic level, and seeks to reduce subjectivity. Hence facts and figures, based on past and present experiences, have more relevance in project analysis than optimism or any other emotional guide-line.

Knowledge people, making contributions at every step of the project process, will have a significant involvement from the early stages. In looking at the project task, therefore, the project manager, alone or with others, must analyse the knowledge contributions required. This is nowhere more important than in the development of the project strategy and in the design or selection of the systems to be used for project execution and control. Thus the initial planning is crucial and the strategy must form a written plan of action for maximizing the efficiency and effectiveness of the resources in line with the available or future opportunities for achieving project objectives.

---

[1] Knowledge itself is here included as a resource. Hence the substatement 'knowledge of the knowledge available and required' is compatible within this context.

[2] 'And required' is not a necessary precondition as resources, like energy, exist in different forms. The mobilization of time and energy in the project dimension may result in the later application of physical labour to a particular task. However, the labour resource has not been acquired or created. It already existed, and its use has been gained by the exchanges of time and money in the project conversion process.

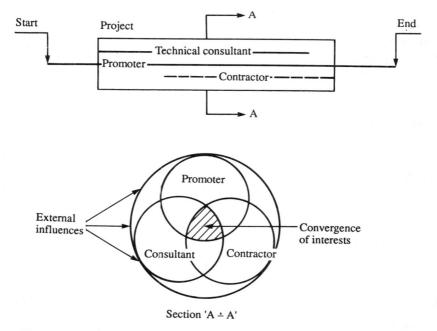

Figure 2. *The project perspective for different organizations.*

The written plan of action, which could apply to the project previously described, must be derived from at least the following:

The project

- What is the project task?
- What are the main subtasks?
- What will be the project environment?
- Are government agencies or regulations involved? Where, when, to what extent?
- What are the fundamental assumptions? Are they based on realism?

The objectives

- What is the time-scale for achieving the main tasks?
- What time-scales can be developed for the main subtasks?
- What is the total budget?
- How has it been derived?

- What is the main phasing of expenditure?
- What results are expected in line with the spending of time and money?
- What development effort is required?
- What are the assumptions for its success?

The resources

- What knowledge resources are required?
- Are they available or must they be acquired?
- When? In what quantity? How will their output be controlled?
- What technical effort is required?
- How will it be achieved?
- What capital equipment will be required? When?
- How will it be acquired?
- What physical effort, plant or equipment is required? Where? When? Will it be available? How will it be controlled?

The quality

- What does 'quality' mean for the project?
- What quality objectives can be established?
- Can these be achieved?
- What is necessary for this achievement?

The performance

- How can you measure or control the resource effort or expenditure against progress on all these objectives?

These items constitute the main project framework. Their development, analysis and execution must take place within an ordered system and many medium and all large organizations will possess project systems. However, the existence of a defined project system within an organization is neither a pre-condition nor a *sine qua non* for project success.

Many organizational systems tend to impose their system requirements on every project to the extent that project objectives become subordinate to the system requirements. What is required here is a *selection* of the elements of an existing system or systems and the effective integration of those elements into an executive plan for the particular project.

The project manager, therefore, if he is to be judged by his project results, must make an existing system subordinate to the project requirements. Strategic planning, in consequence, has to take this into account and be able to stand alone in its selective use of existing systems. If they do not exist already in the particular project environment, then they must be created.

2

The planning effort and the effort in planning

Knowledge of planning and scheduling is essential for the project manager. Planning is about selecting the activities and their dependencies relevant to the project execution; scheduling is about putting the activities on a time-scale. This chapter and the subsequent chapters expand on bar charts, networks and computer applications so that the reader may select the area most suited to his particular interest.

The bar chart

The plan is '*a detailed table showing times, durations, dates and so on of intended proceedings – a scheme of arrangement*'. The operative word in this definition is 'intended', i.e. has not yet happened. Project managers are concerned with the ordering of future events and this dictates the requirement for a 'plan'.

The most elementary and widely used plan presentation is the bar chart, examples of which are shown in Fig. 3(a) and (b). Fig. 3(a) has been deliberately drawn incorrectly; the intention is to provoke the reader to re-pattern the suggested sequence to that shown in Fig. 3(b). This exercise shows the basic simplicity of the bar chart and the following comments will normally apply:

- A series of activities is plotted on a time-scale.
- Each activity has an assumed definite start, duration and end.
- Activities could be either related or independent.
- All activities must be complete before the total project is complete.
- The level of detail could be enlarged or reduced.

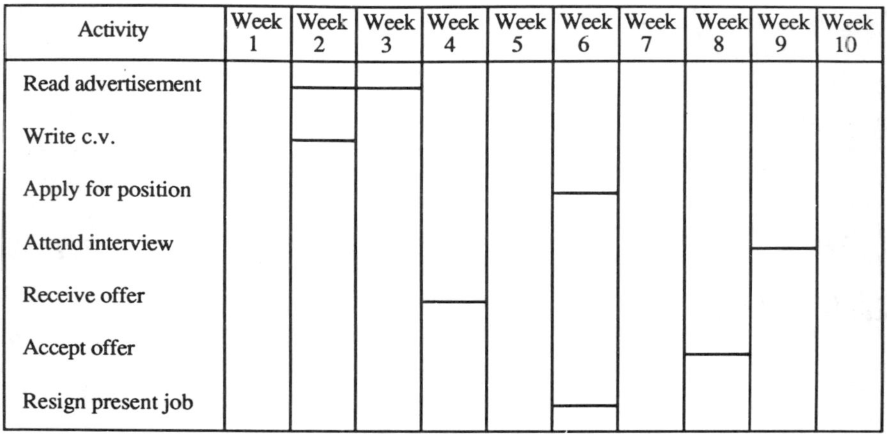

Activity	Week 1	Week 2	Week 3	Week 4	Week 5	Week 6	Week 7	Week 8	Week 9	Week 10
Read advertisement		▬								
Write c.v.		▬								
Apply for position						▬				
Attend interview									▬	
Receive offer				▬						
Accept offer								▬		
Resign present job						▬				

(a)

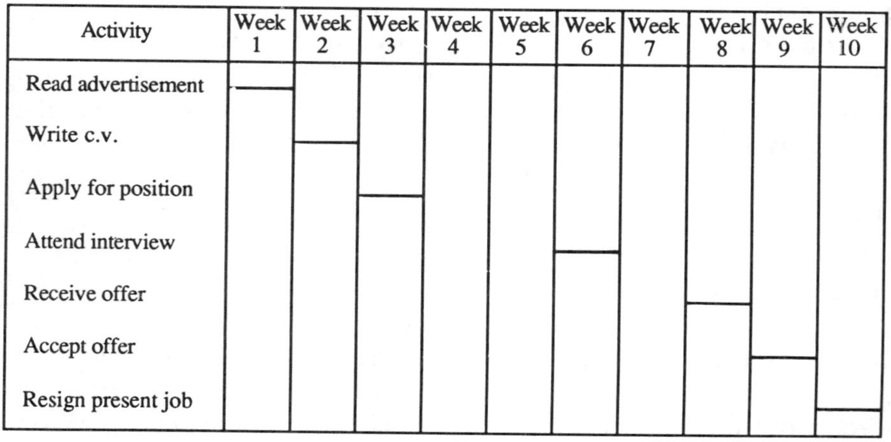

Activity	Week 1	Week 2	Week 3	Week 4	Week 5	Week 6	Week 7	Week 8	Week 9	Week 10
Read advertisement	▬									
Write c.v.		▬								
Apply for position			▬							
Attend interview						▬				
Receive offer								▬		
Accept offer									▬	
Resign present job										▬

(b)

Figure 3. *Bar chart for changing jobs.*

- The completion date could move backwards or forwards depending upon intermediate results.
- Progress could be shown against each activity
- The plan could be reviewed from time to time and the logic might be altered to suit changed conditions.

The bar-chart plan may then be taken as representing a series of subtasks which results in a completed main task or project. It forms a basis for communicating the ideas or requirements of one person to another. It also focuses attention on the importance of *managing* relevant activities to maintain a desired sequence. The endorsed plan represents the basis of authority and accountability for results and, as such, can function as a control document.

Activities and level of detail

The selected activities and the amount of detail must be decided at a strategic level. They should be appropriate to the nature, size and complexity of the project as well as to the intended use of the plan. The best plan will consequently be based on:

- Realistic assumptions.
- A practical level of detail.
- Realistic activity time periods.
- A commitment to action from each concerned party.

A managing director, reviewing plans for a new manufacturing plant, requires a broader-based activity display than a maintenance foreman's

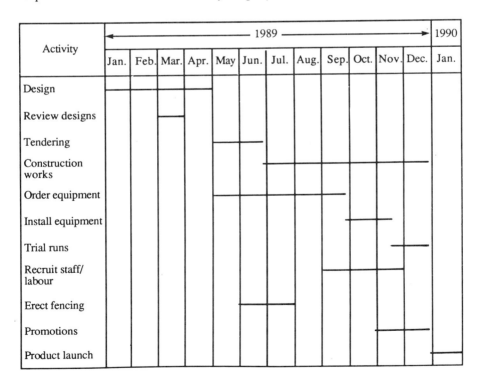

Figure 4 *Bar chart for a new manufacturing plant.*

display of activities for a plant shut-down and restart. Examples of bar-charts for these projects are shown in Figs. 4 and 5.

Comment on Fig. 4.

Activity	Recruit staff/labour
Start	Sep. 1989
Duration	3 months
End	Nov. 1989

This activity is relevant to the project success and will stimulate comment such as:

- How many staff will be needed?
- Who will initiate and control the recruitment?
- Can the personnel manager handle this assignment or will management consultants be required?
- Are the appropriate skilled personnel available?
- What happens if . . . ?

The timing and duration of this activity depend on later circumstances and they will be subject to review and report before, during and after execution.

Conclusion The level and detail are appropriate to this plan. The activity 'erect fencing' is not.

Comment on Fig. 5.

Activity	Acid- dip extrusion nozzles
Start	12.00
Duration	3 hours
End	15.00

This activity must be executed as it is essential for this project. Questions generated might include:

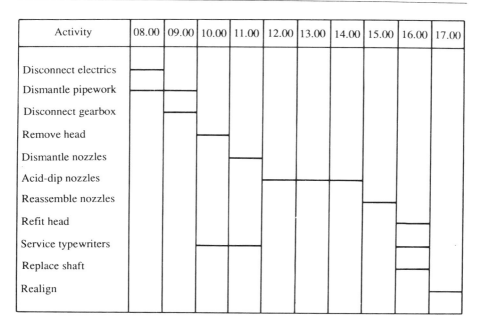

Activity	08.00	09.00	10.00	11.00	12.00	13.00	14.00	15.00	16.00	17.00
Disconnect electrics										
Dismantle pipework										
Disconnect gearbox										
Remove head										
Dismantle nozzles										
Acid-dip nozzles										
Reassemble nozzles										
Refit head										
Service typewriters										
Replace shaft										
Realign										

Figure 5. *Bar chart for maintenance/shut-down works.*

- Is the acid bath available?
- Are extra safety precautions needed? Protective clothing? Ventilation?
- Is sufficient acid in stock?
- Is periodic examination necessary? Every ½ hour?

The timing and duration of this activity may depend on the speed with which fitters can dismantle other equipment, the accumulation of process materials on the nozzles and the strength of the acid. If this type of activity is frequently carried out, experience will be the guiding factor in estimating the timing and duration.

Conclusion: The level and detail are appropriate to this plan. The activity 'service office typewriters' should not appear.

Float

The bar charts so far show activities starting, continuing and ending in a straight-line sequence. This is not always the case and in more detailed planning considerations, activities may have certain constraints or freedoms. For example, perhaps an activity cannot start before a particular date and must finish before another date. This is shown in

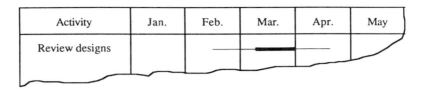

Figure 6. *An activity with float.*

Fig. 6. This activity, 'Review designs' (taken from Fig. 4), is now bounded by assumed conditions:

● It cannot start before mid-February.
● It must be completed by mid-April.
● It will take about 4 weeks to complete.

The single lines are used to show the amount of free time available; the heavier line shows the duration of the activity once it has started. Actual developments could result in a bar chart generated in February showing either of the situations in Fig. 7(a) or (b). From Fig. 7(a) it appears that design will be at the stage where management review may commence at the end of February; from Fig. 7(b) it appears that the designer will not be ready until later. The available free time is thus

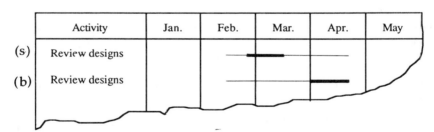

Figure 7. *Different uses of float.*

shown to be used differently in each of these cases. Fig. 8 shows the plan from Fig. 4 accounting for the assumed discretion in the use of float.

The term 'float' implies that the activities have certain freedoms. Nevertheless, freedom itself involves responsibility and the project manager must learn that float time is not free time, as the approach to managing float time can influence the project attitude.

In practice, it is necessary to have a policy such as:

● A definite start date will be established or projected in the reporting period prior to using float on an activity.

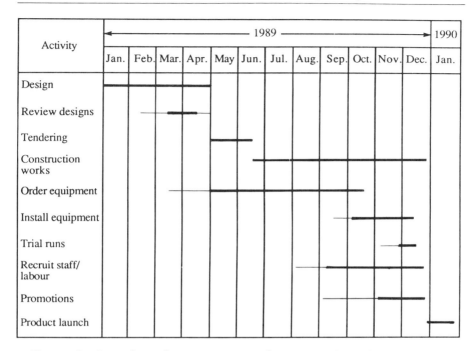

Figure 8. *Bar chart for a new manufacturing plant showing float.*

• Consumption of float will be regarded as consumption of a resource and will therefore be subject to acceptable explanation.

Recent developments in planning techniques allow activities to be manipulated within float periods. These techniques have been evolved to permit computer handling of data in network analysis and are covered later.

Relationships between activities

All activities selected to appear on a plan are interrelated to some degree or other. The relationship may be in direct support of the main task or a subtask or be a factor in either. Plans, developed for communicating intentions or requirements, are for controlling activities and require consideration of the harmony in which the activities best function.

Relationships between activities may be of many different forms. These include direct sequence conditions in time as well as resource-related conditions. For example, two otherwise unconnected items may use a common type of resource and restrictions regarding these activities may be based on resource availability.

The project plan should therefore attempt to illustrate the relationship between activities and the planner must decide where and how to do this. Some effects of possible relationships are shown in Figs. 9–11. Fig. 9 represents a project where each main subactivity is in direct follow-on relationship to its predecessor. The preceding activity must

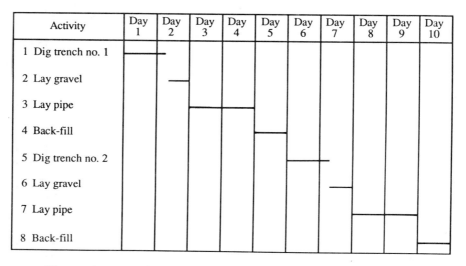

Figure 9. *Bar chart for pipe laying – one person involved.*

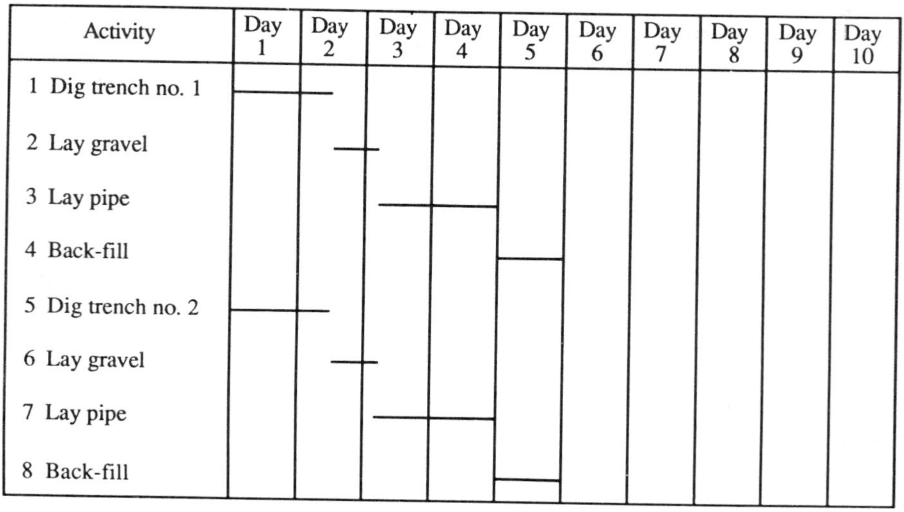

Figure 10. *Bar chart for pipe laying – two persons involved.*

be complete before the successor commences and so on through the sequence.

If two persons are involved, the activity sequence may be adjusted to that shown in Fig. 10. In this case, activities 5, 6, 7 and 8 occur in parallel to activities 1, 2, 3 and 4. The activities themselves have not changed, but their *relationship* has changed so that the overall project has a shorter time-period. If some activities have longer durations, as shown in Fig. 11, the total project duration alters once again.

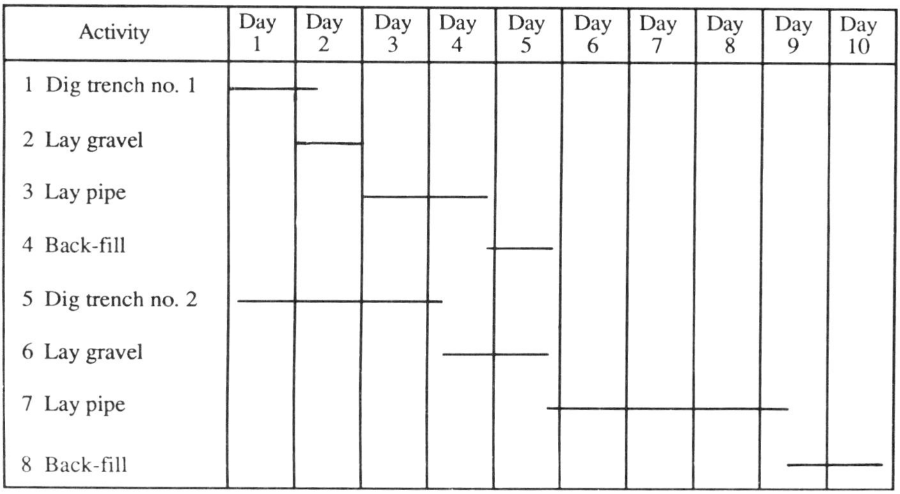

Activity	Day 1	Day 2	Day 3	Day 4	Day 5	Day 6	Day 7	Day 8	Day 9	Day 10
1 Dig trench no. 1	────	─								
2 Lay gravel		────	─							
3 Lay pipe			────	────	─					
4 Back-fill					────	─				
5 Dig trench no. 2	────	────	────	─						
6 Lay gravel				────	─					
7 Lay pipe						────	────	────	─	
8 Back-fill									────	─

Figure 11. *Bar chart for pipe laying – different activity durations.*

It can be seen that the *relationships* between activities have a fundamental bearing on the overall project objectives, in this case the total time period. The argument extends to performance criteria where the *quality* of the effort may have an effect on the end result. For example, if A is more skilled than B, then the result in Fig. 9 will be a function of A's skill alone. The results in Figs. 10 and 11, however, will be a composite of the skills of A and B.

The skills are mixed not only in producing the effect on each proposed activity in the allotted time-periods but also in the quality result for each activity. For bar-chart considerations, however, comments will be confined to the effects of relationships only on intermediate and overall times.

The bar chart suffers from a drawback in this area, as it is not a convenient vehicle for displaying interrelationships, particularly when project activity groups run into hundreds or thousands of subtasks. For that reason, it should be used primarily where the number of activities displayed is within manageable proportions, say not exceeding fifty.

Notwithstanding these points, the broad-plan bar chart may be constructed in a logical sequence which *implies* the interrelationship of activities. The basic elements of these relationships in time are as follows:

- An activity (successor) requires its predecessor to be complete before it can start (Fig. 12).

Figure 12. *A finish-to-start relationship (conventional).*

- Two activities must be complete before a successor can start. The two activities run in parallel (Fig. 13).

Figure 13. *A finish-to-finish relationship.*

- An activity may start at the same time as another (Fig. 14).

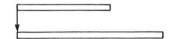

Figure 14. *A start-to-start relationship.*

Incorporating events in a bar chart

The activities shown on the bar charts examined so far are generally line representations of those activities which come under direct project control. External events can be represented as shown in Fig. 15. These events are different from project activities in that they represent single-point occurrences on the calendar time-scale. They can be usefully integrated into the bar chart, where relevant, for management information and control.

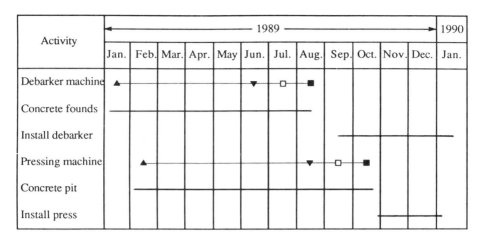

Figure 15. *Events and activities on a bar chart:* ▲ *, order placed;* ▼ *, manufacturing complete – goods despatched from vendor;* □ *, shipping complete – goods arrive in dock;* ■ *, customs clearance complete – goods arrive on site.*

The primary purpose of displaying such events, known as milestones, is to show the effects of either achieving or missing the event-indicated date. For example, if project success depends upon timely delivery of a piece of equipment so that installation and commissioning activities can be managed, the project activity directly depends on the event taking place on or before the expected date.

In an ideal world, if the orders were issued exactly when required, manufacturing ran exactly as promised, shipping dates and times did not change and customs formalities were in order, the events would not require project management interference or comment. But this is not an ideal world and external events can have a negative effect on project activity timings. Hence the purpose of displaying the events on the bar chart is to call attention to their importance in the overall scheme of arrangement.

Generally, therefore, resources must be allocated to manage external activities, for example, by visits to vendors' premises to inspect and report on quality and progress. It follows that the selection of events to be so managed must conform to the selection criteria for activities and must be decided at a strategic level (see Chapter 13).

Resources on a bar chart

Activities shown on a bar chart represent conversion of project resources over time. For example, from the bar chart in Fig. 16 the line 'excavate foundation' over a 2-week period indicates an exchange of time and effort to complete an activity. As plans represent the ordering of future proceedings, it can be inferred from this activity line that:

- The estimated time to excavate foundations depends upon two men working continuously over a 2-week period.
- The excavation units represent a quantity of work equal to the output of two men for 2 weeks.
- If the allocated resources varied, the quantity of work was greater or less than that expected or an external influence, such as rainy weather, affected the activity, then the line representing time would change. For example, if four men were available, the time reduces to 1 week, whereas if only one man were available, the time increases to 4 weeks.

Activity	Week 1	Week 2	Week 3	Week 4
Excavate foundation	—2—	—2—		
Prepare driveway	—2—	—2—		
Concrete foundation			—4—	
Erect fencing			—2—	—2—
Labour total	4	4	6	2

Figure 16. *A bar chart showing activities and resources.*

The total labour required for the activities shown on the bar chart may be displayed on the bottom line as indicated and leads to the introduction of another important concept — the labour histogram — used for planning purposes. This concept is examined later. For the moment, the display of resources for planning consideration and analysis is further explained.

Labour is but one resource which may be usefully called up on a bar chart. Since all plans represent a process whereby resources are to be converted for project objectives, it follows that useful information can be obtained by showing the expected results of the conversion on the activity line. For example, extending the consideration of the activity 'excavate foundation', the following points can be shown:

- The use of money in achieving the activity objective. For example, if the two men are each using an excavator, the quantities of work done and costs involved are very different from hand-digging.
- If a surveyor is engaged for the first week or the previous week in setting out the lines and levels, his knowledge-work and resource costs can be extracted for the total cost of the activity.
- If other indirect overhead costs, such as supervision, are involved, these can also be displayed.

At the strategic level, the information thus conveyed may form a framework for decision, for example, on whether or not to use a subcontractor for this particular activity or group of activities. The bar chart may then be extended as in Fig. 17. This example shows the necessity of activity management, because important interrelationships between activities, physical resources and finance/cash-flows may be more real than is apparent from the simple bar chart.

Management considerations of this group of activities may result in delaying driveway preparation and concentrating on foundation work so that concreting can start earlier – or the finish-to-start relationship implied between 'foundation excavation' and 'concrete foundation' may be changed by commencing concreting operations as soon as practical after commencing foundations, as shown in Fig. 18(a) and (b). Thus manipulation of bar-chart activities may be necessary depending upon other project considerations.

Comment on these proposed situations:

- Fig. 18(a) is the initial draft and mainly considers times.
- Fig. 18(b) is the revised version offering:
  (a) An earlier start on concreting (possibly higher revenues or earlier completion of other activities).
  (b) A constant labour-force requirement – this process is known as 'resource smoothing' and must be actively considered when resources are limited, even in the smallest project.

Histograms (resource profiles)

In a real project situation, it could be very difficult to manage large fluctuations in demand for resources. The bar chart in this case would

Activity	Week 1	Week 2	Week 3	Week 4
Excavate foundation	—2—	—2—		
Prepare driveway	—2—	—2—		
Concrete foundation			—4—	
Erect fencing			—2—	—2—
Labour total	4	4	6	2
Supervision	1	1	1	1
Equipment	3 x JCB	3 x JCB	1 x dumper 2 x augers	2 x augers
Gross value				
Excavations	£1 000	£1 000		
Driveway	£ 750	£ 750		
Concrete			£20 000	
Fencing			£ 3 000	£ 3 000
Total			£23 000	£ 3 000
Costs				
Labour	£ 800	£ 800	£ 1200	£ 400
Indirect	£ 300	£ 300	£ 300	£ 300
Materials			£15 000	£4 000
Hire of equipment	£ 500	£ 500	£15 000	£ 500
Total	£1 600	£1 600	£18 300	£12 000

Figure 17. *Bar chart extended to show activities, resources, values and costs.*

Activity	Week 1	Week 2	Week 3	Week 4
Excavate foundation	—— 2 ——	— 2—		
Prepare driveway	——2——	—2—		
Concrete foundation			—4—	
Erect fencing			— 2 ——	—2—
Labour total	4	4	6	2

(a)

Activity	Week 1	Week 2	Week 3	Week 4
Excavate foundation	— 3 ——	— 1—		
Prepare driveway	— 1 ——	— 1—	—1—	—1—
Concrete foundation		—2—	—2—	
Erect fencing			—1—	—3—
Labour total	4	4	4	4

(b)

Figure 18. *Bar charts from (a) Fig. 16 and (b) from Fig. 18 (a) with different activities/labour.*

normally be reviewed by rearranging activities or groups of activities which have the greatest impact on the resource requirements.

Histograms or resource profiles may be used for further analysis of the peak requirements and resource smoothing or levelling, where:

● Smoothing means altering activity durations or start times to reduce fluctuations in demand.
● Levelling means imposing a limit on available resources even if the total time for the project has to increase.

Consider a bar chart which has been analysed over all activities for labour requirements with the results shown in Table 2. The resulting bar graph is known as the labour histogram or labour-resource profile and may be shown as in Fig. 19. This may be extended to show a cumulative effect as shown in Fig. 20.

Table 2 Proposed labour requirements

	Week									
	1	*2*	*3*	*4*	*5*	*6*	*7*	*8*	*9*	*10*
Total	6	10	14	14	18	26	22	22	12	12
Cumulative	6	16	30	44	62	88	110	132	144	156

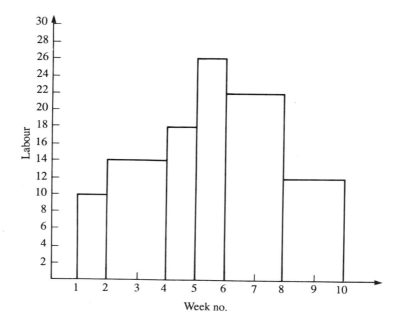

Figure 19. *Labour histograms plotted from Table 2.*

After reviewing the implications of the labour histogram shown in Fig. 21, revised bar charts and corresponding histograms were derived as shown in Figs. 22 and 23. These changes were made by reorganizing both the resources and the activities and were intended to affect only the total resources required at any one time. These examples show the endless planning possibilities which are available prior to the start of even a simple project.

In practice, resources are generally limited or not available exactly as and when required – or may be more or less productive than planned

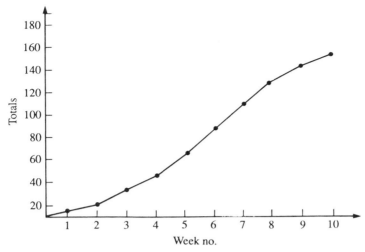

Figure 20. *Cumulative labour-weeks plotted from Table 2.*

for any number of reasons. The chart will therefore need to be revised and updated regularly on the basis of the actual results achieved in the project.

The use of the bar chart to display resources and subsequent development of a histogram to be read in conjunction with the bar chart is the first real example of an attempt to integrate project planning data. In addition to the direct-labour histogram and its use in strategic considerations of labour resources, the financial picture can be readily displayed in the same way.

This leads to a consideration of the time-related budget or revenue picture, useful for forecasting project cost expenditures or incomes and this is shown later in a chapter on cost control (Chapter 8).

Activity	Week 1	Week 2	Week 3	Week 4	Week 5	Week 6	Week 7	Week 8	Week 9	Week 10
Fabricate steam pipe	4	4	4							
Erect steam pipe				8	8	8	8			
Install electrics				8	8	8				
Install equipment					6	6	6	6		
Insulate pipe								6	6	
Insulate equipment									3	
Install instruments							6	6		
Check-out									4	
Test run										4
Total	4	4	4	16	22	22	20	18	13	4

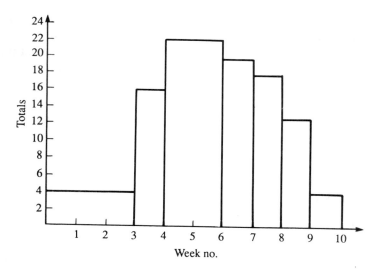

Figure 21. *Bar chart and labour histogram for installing an industrial machine (initial proposal).*

Activity	Week 1	Week 2	Week 3	Week 4	Week 5	Week 6	Week 7	Week 8	Week 9	Week 10
Fabricate steam pipe	4	4	4							
Erect steam pipe		4	8	8	8	4				
Install electrics		4	6	6	4	4				
Install equipment			2	4	6	6	4			
Insulate pipe						3	3	3	3	
Insulate equipment								3		
Install instruments						3	3	3	3	
Check-out									4	
Test run										4
Total	4	12	20	18	18	20	10	9	10	4

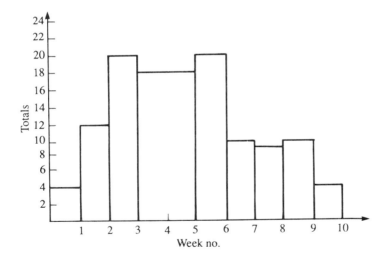

Figure 22. *Bar chart and labour histogram for installing an industrial machine (revised proposal).*

Activity	Week 1	Week 2	Week 3	Week 4	Week 5	Week 6	Week 7	Week 8	Week 9	Week 10
Fabricate steam pipe	4	4	4							
Erect steam pipe		4	6	6	6	6	4			
Install electrics	4	4	4	4	4	4				
Install equipment				4	5	5	5	5		
Insulate pipe							6	6		
Insulate equipment									3	
Install instruments					3	3	3	3		
Check-out									4	
Test run										4
Total	8	12	14	14	18	18	18	14	7	4

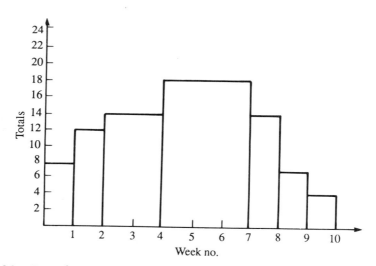

Figure 23. *Bar chart and labour histogram for installing an industrial machine (final proposal).*

3

Planning projects – networks

Summary

A plan is 'a detailed table indicating time-periods, dates, places, etc., of intended proceedings – a scheme of arrangement'. The important word in this definition is 'intended', i.e. has not yet happened.

Project management, concerned with the ordering of current and future events, requires plans for:

- Communicating ideas or requirements relevant to the project.
- Focusing attention on the importance of managing relevant activities to maintain a desired sequence.

The plan based on realistic assumptions, a practical level of detail and realistic activity time-periods can be endorsed as the basis of authority and accountability for results. As such, it can fulfil its main function as a control document. The bar-chart method of displaying planned activities is very useful but limited in some ways which are better handled by using networks.

Types of networks

Network development and analysis is based upon logic. Two independent methods have been developed:

1 The arrow diagram which shows activities as arrows going to node points which represent events (Fig. 24).
2 The precedence diagram which shows activities as nodes while the arrows are used to show the logic between activities (Fig. 25).

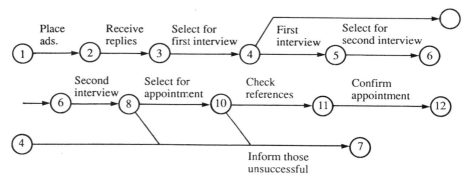

Figure 24. *An arrow network for recruiting staff.*

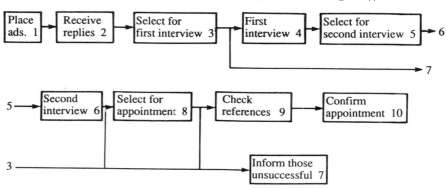

Figure 25. *A precedence diagram for recruiting staff.*

Arrow networks

The basic procedures for considering arrow networks are relatively simple and easily appreciated. Thus:

- Activities are uniquely described by their preceding and succeeding events' numbers (Fig. 26).

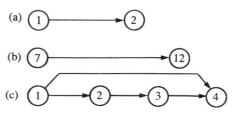

Figure 26. *Activity numbering. (a) Represents activity 1–2, (b) represents activity 7–12 and (c) represents activities 1–2, 2–3, 3–4 and 1–4.*

● The length of the arrows is irrelevant (Fig. 27).

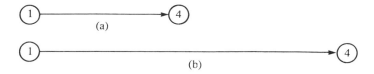

Figure 27. *Arrow lengths: (a) means the same as (b).*

● All activities to an event must be finished before any activity from the event can be started (Fig. 28).

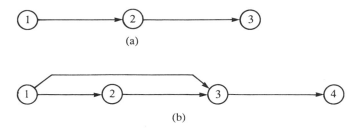

Figure 28. *Activities and events. (a) Activity 1–2 must be finished before 2–3 starts. (b) Activity 1–2 must be finished before 2–3 starts. Activities 2–3 and 1–3 must be finished before 3–4 starts.*

● Activities may be real or token (dummy). Dummy activities (Figs 29–31) are necessary for computer input to avoid having two activities with the same preceding/succeeding event numbers. They are used to show relationships such as:
   (a) Two parallel activities from event 1 to event 3.
   (b) Events depending on other events.

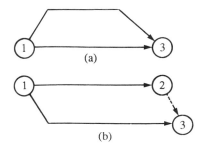

Figure 29. *Dummy activities. (a) becomes (b). Activities 1–2 and 1–3 are* real. *Activity 2–3 is a* dummy.

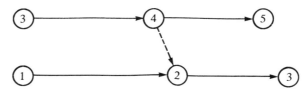

Figure 30. *Dummy activities. Activity 4–5 can start when 3–4 is complete but 2–3 cannot start until both 3–4 and 1–2 are complete.*

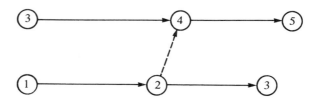

Figure 31. *Dummy activities. If the dummy relationship is reversed, then activity 2–3 can start when 1–2 is complete but 4–5 cannot start until both 1–2 and 3–4 are complete.*

● All sequences and relationships must be logical (Fig. 32)

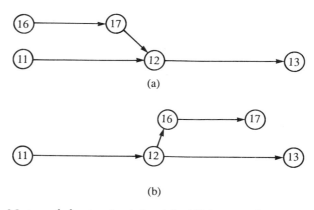

Figure 32. *Network logic. Activity 16–17 (e.g. order equipment) must be positioned to show completion before activity 12–13 (e.g. install equipment); thus (a) is acceptable but (b) is not.*

Constructing an arrow network

Networks can be established to show an overall project or a particular section (as in Fig. 33). This example illustrates a number of points:

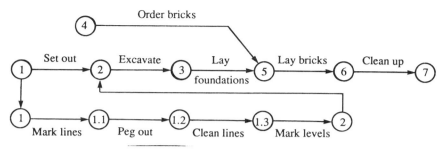

Figure 33. *A network for building a brick wall.*

- Activities on the overall project network are at an appropriate level.
- Activities may be concurrent, e.g. 4–5 may be concurrent with 1–2, 2–3 and 3–5.
- Activities may be expanded into subactivities.
- Time-periods can be estimated and shown on the diagram (as in Fig. 34.

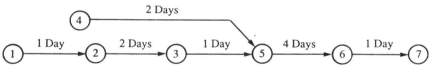

Figure 34. *Putting time periods on network activities.*

Assuming that activity 4–5 is completed on time, inspection will show that the total time to finish the wall depends on the duration of each activity on the sequence 1–2–3–5–6–7.

Activities and their corresponding durations may be summarized in a table (as in Table 3). The total is both the minimum and maximum time

Table 3. Activities and durations.

Activity	Time (days)
1–2	1
2–3	2
3–5	1
5–6	4
6–7	1
Total	9

necessary to finish the overall project and the activities required are said to be on the *critical path*. Activity 4–5 is not on the critical path provided the bricks are ordered within 2 days of the start of the project.

If the wall builder in this case had given an estimated time of completion of 3 weeks, with 5 working days per week, he will be able to organize the work sequences with more flexibility and may transfer the network to a calendar for time scheduling on:

- A bar-chart form showing the float available for each activity.
- A bar-chart form showing earliest/latest starts and finishes for each activity.
- A time-scaled network logic diagram showing the duration of each activity together with the earliest/latest starts and finishes.

These are shown in Fig. 35. This network can be analysed by inspection, as shown in Table 4, and extended to the sequence of events, as shown in Table 5.

Table 4. Activities on a network.

Activity	Duration	Earliest start day	Earliest finish day	Latest start day	Latest finish day
1–2	1	1	1	7	7
2–3	2	2	3	8	9
3–5	1	4	4	10	10
5–6	4	5	8	11	14
6–7	1	9	9	15	15
4–5	2	1	2	9	10

This type of analysis, where activities, events and times can be stated as numbers, is extremely useful for computer handling. It forms the basis of all computer-based network analysis programmes and illustrates the simple and practical logic behind them. The analysis can now be extended to include several other concepts concerning 'float'.

Float

Positive float is spare-time and is known as:

- Total float – the time which can be used up on an activity or group of activities without affecting the overall duration of a project. It is

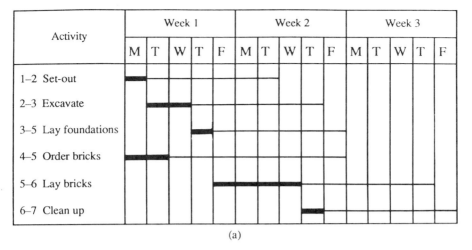

(a)

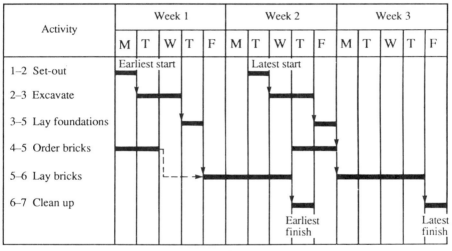

(b)

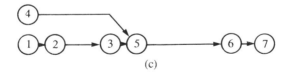

(c)

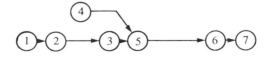

(d)

Figure 35. *Bar charts showing (a) float available and (b) earliest/latest start/finish times and logic diagrams showing (c) early start and (d) late start.*

Table 5. Events on a network.

Event	Earliest time	Latest time
1	1	7
2	2	8
3	4	10
5	5	11
6	9	15
7	9	15
4	1	9

represented by the duration of an activity subtracted from the difference between its latest finish time (LF) and earliest start (ES) time (Fig. 36). It is only available:

(a) Prior to the ES time.

(b) Where the duration is less than the difference between LF and ES.

Figure 36. *Total float.*

- Free float – the time available between the early finish time of an activity and the early start time of *succeeding* activities (Fig. 37). It is independent of activity duration times. It is only available:

(a) Where ES1 − ES2 is greater than ES1 − EF.

(b) Where a constraint prevents the succeeding activity from commencing before ES2.

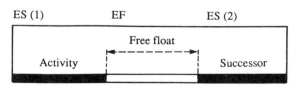

Figure 37. *Free float.*

- Shared float – the total float time shared over more than one activity on a common path (Fig. 38). It is only available where a successor

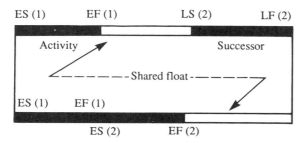

Figure 38. *Shared float.*

activity cannot start prior to the latest finish time of the last in the pair or group of considered activities.

- Independent float: the time available where the difference between the latest start of an activity and the latest finish is greater than the expected duration (Fig. 39).

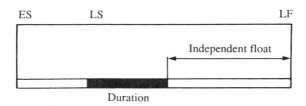

Figure 39. *Independent float.*

- Negative float occurs where the anticipated finish time of an activity is later than the latest start time of its successor (to achieve the required end date) (Fig. 40).

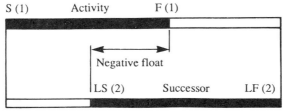

Figure 40. *Negative float.*

Network shapes

Many shapes and layouts have been used to display networks. The common intention to each, however, is to configure the arrangements so that the logic is clear. Fig. 41 show some possibe layouts. Note that these networks are all confined to one page. However, it is very easy to continue network development on a multipage basis by using a consistent reference system so that node points and relationships can be picked up. For example, if graph paper is used prior to numbering, an arrow on page 6 continuing to a node on page 7 might be referenced '07CJ' meaning that it joins the node at coordinates C–J on page 7.

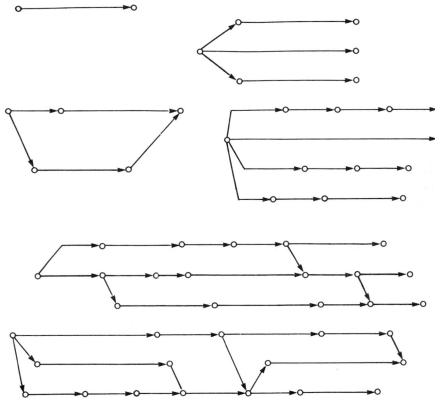

Figure 41. *Different network shapes.*

The network critical path

A critical path in a network is that continuous sequence of activities which produces *both* the maximum and the minimum duration time for the whole network. Since the activities are based on events, a critical path is identified by critical events, where the event earliest time = the event latest time.

By definition:

1 The critical path must pass through critical events.
2 The duration of the activity between two critical events must equal the difference between the latest calculated time of the preceding event and the earliest calculated time of the succeeding event.

The numbers shown above each event in Fig. 42 are obtained by working *forwards* through the network, adding duration times for each activity; those shown below the events are obtained by working *backwards* through the network, subtracting the activity duration times from the previous total.

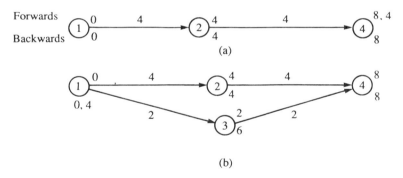

Figure 42. *The forward and backward pass through a network.*

In Fig. 42(a), path 1–2–4 shows a total duration of 8. According to the logic shown, this is both the minimum and the maximum total duration. Activities 1–2 and 2–4 are therefore critical activities on the critical path 1–2–4. In Fig. 42(b), path 1–2–4 is again the critical path. Activities 1–3 and 3–4 on path 1–3–4 are not critical because the total of their durations on this path is less than the minimum total time through path 1–2–4.

The network in Fig. 43 has *two* critical paths through events 1–2–5 and 1–3–4–5. Therefore, all the activities are critical. If the duration of

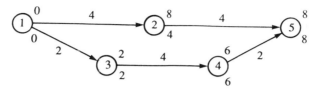

Figure 43. *A network with two critical paths.*

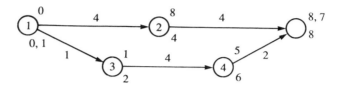

Figure 44. *Activity durations affect the critical path.*

any of the activities is altered, e.g. activity 1–3 in Fig. 44, then only one critical path is identified, i.e. through events 1–2–5. The path through events 1–3–4–5 has a minimum duration of 7 and a maximum duration of 8. Since the critical path represents the minimum duration for the whole network, this sequence is not critical.

Finding the critical path

If a triangle shows the earliest event time and a square shows the latest event time, then the network in Fig. 45 has earliest event times,

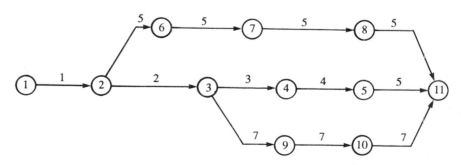

Figure 45. *Network for analysis.*

calculated by working forwards, as in Fig. 46. Working backwards through the network, using 24 as the maximum network duration, the latest event times are as in Fig. 47. The critical events will have the same

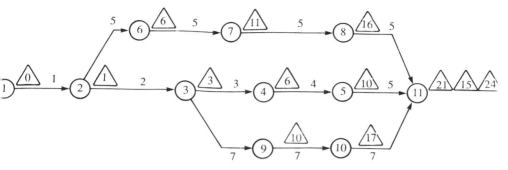

Figure 46. *The forward pass through the network. The maximum time to event 11 is 24 through events 1–2–3–9–10–11.*

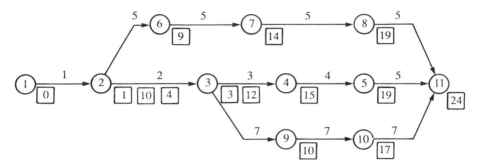

Figure 47. *The backward pass through the network.*

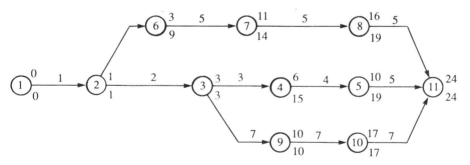

Figure 48. *Identifying the critical events.*

figure above and below the event numbers. Fig. 48 shows the forward pass and backward pass together.

Thus, from Fig. 48.

- Events 1–2–3–9–10–11 are critical.
- Activities 1–2, 2–3, 3–9, 9–10, 10–11 are critical.

- The total float for each of the other paths is the difference between the critical-path duration for the network and the earliest total time through the other path to its latest event.
- The path through events 1–2–6–7–8–11 has a minimum duration of 21 and therefore a total float of 24 − 21 = 3.
- The path through events 1–2–3–4–5–11 has a minimum duration of 15 and therefore a total float of 24 − 15 = 9.
- If any of the activities on either of these alternate paths is affected during the network progress, such that the total float is used up or exceeded, then a new critical path will be determined.

The precedence diagram

The basic rules for constructing and using precedence diagrams are very similar to those for arrow diagrams. The major difference is that activities are drawn as rectangles which are connected by arrow lines showing relationships.

The network logic is constructed using start/finish relationships for each activity (Fig. 49). The possible relationships are shown in Fig. 50.

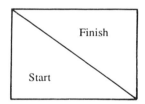

Figure 49. *An activity on a precedence diagram. The upper triangle has two finish sides. The lower triangle has two start sides.*

The logical restraints governing the precedence of an activity may:

1 Come from the preceding activities (Fig. 51).
2 Go to succeeding activities (Fig. 52).
3 Show lag times (replacing dummy activities on arrow networks) (Fig. 53).

Using these conventions, typical elements from a main project network may be constructed as shown in Fig. 54.

Comments on Fig. 54:

- A must finish before B can start.
- B must start before D or F can start.

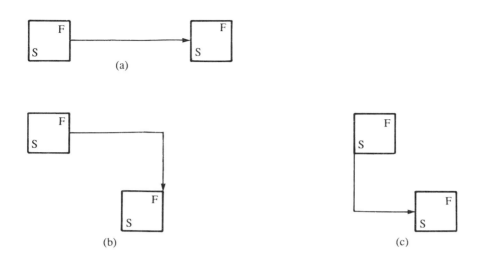

Figure 50. *Relationships on a precedence diagram: (a) finish to start, (b) finish to finish and (c) start to start.*

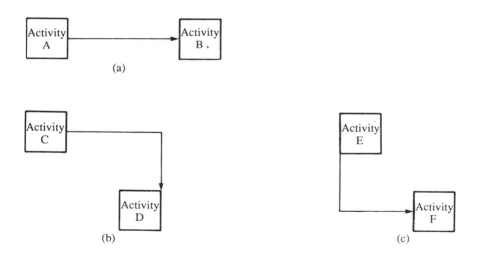

Figure 51. *Restraints from preceding activities. (a) Finish to start. Activity B can start when A is finished, but not before then. (b) Finish to finish. Activity D can finish when C is finished, but not before then. (c) Start to start. Activity F can start when E starts, but not before then.*

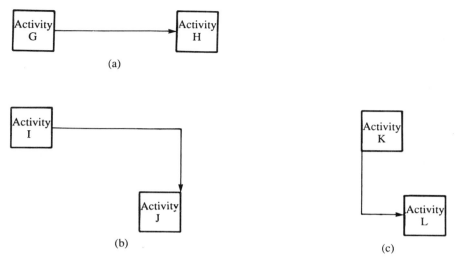

(a)

(b)   (c)

Figure 52. *Restraints to succeeding activities. (a) Finish to start. When activity G is finished, H can start, but not before then. (b) Finish to finish. When activity I is finished, then J can finish, but not before then. (c) Start to start. When activity K starts, L can start, but not before then.*

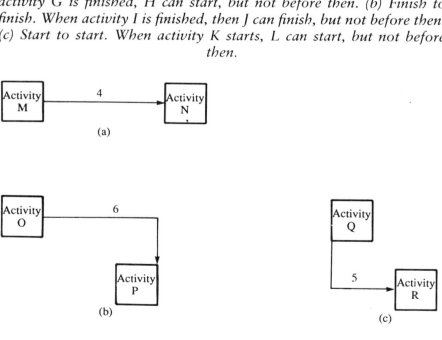

(a)

(b)   (c)

Figure 53. *Restraints with lag times. (a) Finish to start. Activity N can start 4 weeks after M is finished, but not before then. (b) Finish to finish. Activity P can finish 6 weeks after O is finished, but not before then. (c) Start to start. Activity R can start 5 weeks after Q starts, but not before then.*

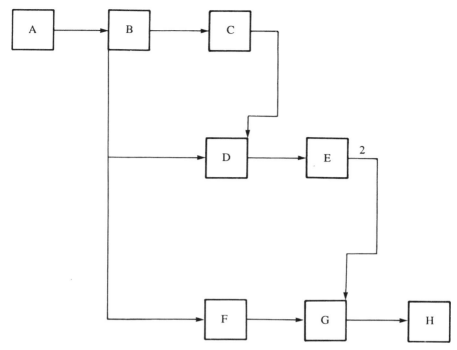

Figure 54. *A precedence network.*

- B must finish before C can start.
- C must finish before D can finish.
- D must finish before E can start.
- F must finish before G can start but
- G cannot finish until 2 weeks after E is finished.
- G must finish before H can start.

If the duration of each activity is taken as 2 weeks, then the network may be as shown in Fig. 55. Working *forwards* through the network and showing the earliest start of the earliest finish times gives Fig. 56. Working *backwards*, showing the latest finish and latest start times

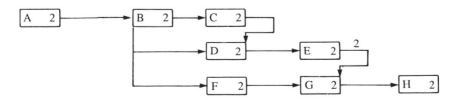

Figure 55. *Network showing activities/durations.*

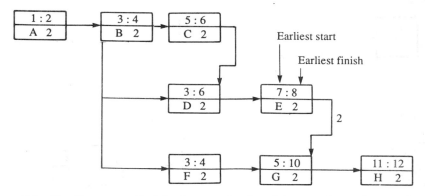

Figure 56. *Earliest start/finish times calculated by working forwards.*

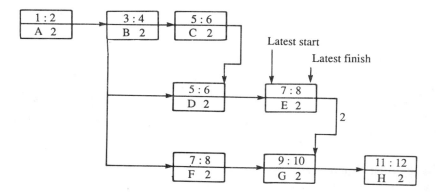

Figure 57. *Latest start/finish times calculated by working backwards.*

gives Fig. 57. By inspecting Figs 56 and 57, it can be seen that activities A, B, C, E and H have early start times equal to late start times and early finish times equal to late finish times. This indicates that these activities are on the network critical path.

The data calculated from both the forward and backward passes may be shown as in Fig. 58. Using this convention and the data from Figs 56

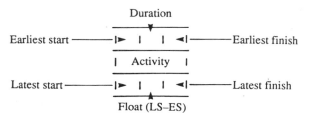

Figure 58. *A convention for showing activity data.*

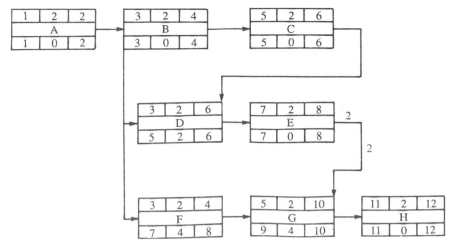

Figure 59. *The precedence diagram analysed.*

and 57 the precedence diagram can be shown as in Fig. 59. This diagram can readily be translated into a bar-chart representation, or a time-scaled logic network, showing earliest start dates and total float (Fig. 60) or showing latest start dates and total float (Fig. 61).

Comment: The longest and shortest duration for this network is through activities A, B, C, E and H. These are critical-path activities

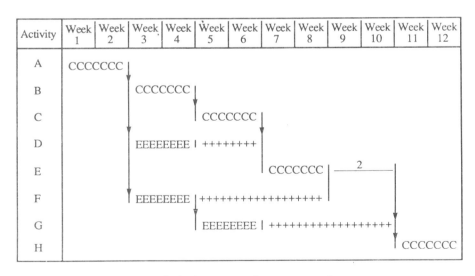

Figure 60. *A time-scaled diagram showing early starts and activity float. CCCC indicates a critical activity, EEEE indicates the early start on an activity and ++++ indicates available float.*

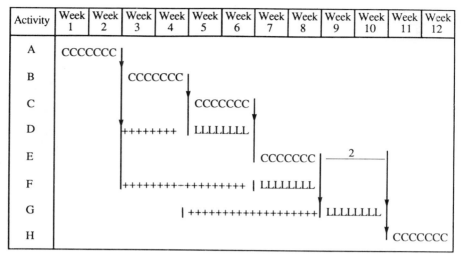

Figure 61. *A time-scaled diagram showing late starts and activity float.*
LLLL represents the late start on an activity.

with no float available. Activity D has 2 weeks of total float. Activities F
and G have 4 weeks of shared float.

Significance of the critical path

Critical-path analysis of a network will offer the following:

1 Determination of the overall project duration.
2 Identification of the series of key dates which must be met during the
  life of the project.
3 Identification of those activities which must be managed on the basis
  of no float availability.
4 Indication of those activities which have float available and which
  may have their durations extended.
5 Indication of better use of resources, e.g. by using float.
6 A basis for updating and monitoring progress.

Note that the initial network construction is normally carried out
assuming that unlimited resources are available. This allows concentration on:

- The logic which forms the relationships between relevant activities.
- The estimated times for activity durations *after* the logic is drawn.

Estimating activity durations

The estimated and actual duration of any activity on a plan depends on a number of elements such as:

- The volume or scope of work involved.
- The resources allocated.
- The productivity of the resources.
- The combination of other dependencies which affect the activity. For example, different materials deliveries may be involved, quality standards may not be achieved, and so on.
- Actual time available.
- The method of management of the activity.
- The nature of the activity – e.g. if the activity involves innovative or R&D (research and development) type work, the time required may be much more difficult to estimate than if it involved repetitive work for which established factors are available.

Initial project planning starts with the selection of activities and the level of detail. Estimation of the activities' durations may be based on judgement and practical experience, productivity factors/volume of work and the PERT duration-estimate method.

Judgement and practical experience

This is the most common method of initial duration estimate. It is as reliable as the information available and the experience of the planner or activity-duration estimator.

Productivity factors and volume of work

This method may be used where the volume of work, the resources available and the historic productivity factors are all known. For example:

- A shipbuilder may offer an overall construction time of 24 months for a 25 000 t vessel or 30 months for one of 40 000 t.
- A roofing contractor may have resources available to produce 200 m^2 of finished roof per week and a planner may reliably take the duration of the roofing activity as 10 weeks for an area of 2000 m^2.

The PERT duration-estimate method

This method relies on a formula for combining the estimate for three cases for an activity, namely:

- An optimistic time, which is considered to be the 'best' time given that all associated factors fall into place.
- A pessimistic time, which is the 'worst-case' scenario, with everything going wrong which could go wrong.
- A most likely duration, which is the 'normal' time for the activity, based upon judgement, experience or other factors.

(The PERT method was originally developed by the Special Projects Office of the US Navy in collaboration with the management consulting firm of Booz, Allen & Hamilton. At the same time, the Du Pont company was developing critical-path methods (CPM). PERT is essentially the same as CPM on arrow networks and differs only in the loading given to the *probability* of meeting the time estimates for activities.)

The PERT method was designed to calculate the normal probability of meeting scheduled dates and uses statistical analysis, which, when applied to the three time estimates above, indicates

$$\text{expected duration} = \frac{\text{optimistic} + 4(\text{normal}) + \text{pessimistic}}{6}$$

Thus if an activity duration estimate is

10 days for the best case,
60 days for the worst case,
20 days for the normal case,

then the expected duration is

$$\text{expected duration} = \frac{10 + 4(20) + 60}{6} = 25 \text{ days.}$$

Resource allocation, smoothing and levelling

The time-only consideration of the network will satisfy the time-sequence logic. However, project-management considerations must extend to the identification and use of the resources required. This requires knowledge of the work content of the identified activities and the resources required or available to achieve the expected durations. From earlier considerations on labour/resource histograms (see Chapter 2), it is necessary to relate network activities to a time-scale to summarize the various resource requirements and construct the relevant histograms.

Development of the resource histogram will lead to further consideration of how the sequences can be realized in practice, and, for a project of any size or value, how the resources can be smoothly introduced and phased-out on completion. Examples of networks and resource histograms applied on this basis appear in the following chapter.

4

Computer applications

It is not always possible to obtain ideal plans or histograms even in the planning-development phase. However, examination of network logic for both time sequence and use of resources is absolutely essential for any structured approach to the compromises which may be necessary.

The calculations involved in analysing resources and manipulating the float/activity durations require the use of a computer for all but the smallest networks. This also applies to the updating of networks showing progress on activities during a time-unit and revising the critical path(s) if necessary.

Software programs currently available for such project analysis can handle networks containing thousands of activities, with multiple resources for each activity. These programs can be used to generate many useful forms of project status report, for example:

- critical path(s),
- resource histograms,
- bar charts by activity, early start and late start,
- cumulative resource usage,
- cash flow,
- activities with float remaining.

Developing a network – the planning hierarchy

While the basic principles behind network analysis are easily understood, in practice the development of large or complex networks can be both time-consuming and costly. In addition, complicated-looking diagrams and computer print-outs tend to daunt all except the specialists. Therefore, prior to undertaking this particular activity, it is necessary to question the benefits which are to be expected and to ensure that the project environment exists to realize the potential of the benefits.

The fundamental consideration is in the essence of the planning exercise and its presentation to those parties who will execute the plans. Broadly speaking, the planning hierarchy will be as previously described in Chapter 1, i.e.:

1 The broad plan based upon major activities or groups of activities (not exceeding say twenty or thirty) with key dates or milestone events clearly marked. This plan level is suitable for use by top management and must be capable of constructive updating, review and monitoring at that level.
2 The working plan or network developed for use by senior project-management staff and in sufficient detail to be used as the working document for the whole project. The project reporting systems must be able to sustain the data collection necessary for, say, monthly updating and monitoring of the network and the network must be designed with this in mind. The major feature of the network development is that it is ongoing over the life of the project. For example, on a typical construction project, the concept-to-completion cycles are as shown in Fig. 62. This diagram shows that, in general, a network is not definitive at the start of a project – it progresses with the project on the basis of the available information about the activities, current/expected productivity ratios and so on.

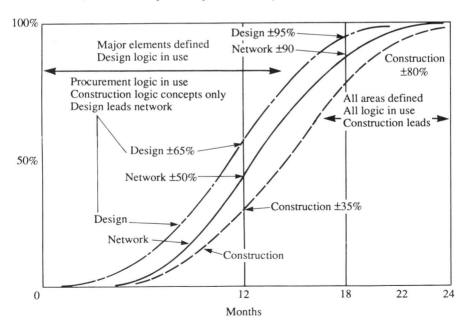

Figure 62. *Network development at various project stages.*

3 Detailed plans which may consist of subnetworks and are generally presented in the form of bar charts for use in day-to-day management activities.

This approach to planning and scheduling is known as the planning hierarchy and is the basis for the majority of network developments. The hierarchy may be based on a suitable work-breakdown structure and numbering system which permits analysis at various levels and with parameters such as resources or costs. (The concept of a work-breakdown structure is further enlarged in this chapter and in Chapter 7.)

Description of a project-management program

Aside from the main-frame computer systems used in major projects, a number of software suppliers have developed packages for integrated project management on personal computers. Such packages are essential for exploiting the potential of networking methods and one such package, Primavera, like several others, provides the following comprehensive capabilities:

Tutorial

It is essential to complete a tutorial and fully understand the elements of any system – like learning the multiplication tables – before being able to use the facilities available. Hands-on experience, based on a practical project scenario, is provided in this package and introduces the main features.

Network development

It is not easy to lay out a large, complex network by hand. However, many elements of subnetworks are based on repetitive activities common to disciplines such as procurement or design. Therefore, one of the most useful features available is the merge capability. This means that networks can be developed on a modular or library basis where the main work elements can be subdivided into various sections and individually modelled. These may then be automatically combined whilst retaining the logic of the networks.

Relationships

Primavera accepts either precedence or arrow networks. Within these, the range of possible relationships is covered for successor activities with conventional (i.e. finish to start), start-to-start or start-to-finish logic lines. Lag-times or lead-times are called up simply in the activity/ relationship specification for precedence networks; arrow networks are entered simply an *i-j* basis, where *i* defines a preceding event and *j* defines the succeeding event.

Calendar and start-date

Assuming that a basic network has been developed by hand, the process of entering the network begins with describing the project calendar, i.e. specifying years, holiday periods, etc. A project must be entered with a definite start date.

Specifying activities

Activities are specified by entering the activity parameters into various databases designed for manipulation by the software, e.g.:

- Number – each activity on a precedence network must have a unique number and, on an arrow diagram, unique event numbers to avoid activity duplication.
- Description – this may use letters, words and numbers, e.g. Stage 1– Recruitment or Set Process Mech Eqpt.
- Relationships – as described above, may include successors and predecessors for each activity.
- Duration – an essential element of the activity parameters.
- Resources – these are initially set-up on a separate Resources Code Directory, which may be very comprehensive. Resources allocated to an activity may be called up from the directory as required, together with unit costings. For example, various craft labour such as carpenters, electricians, etc., may be described in the directory with daily or weekly costings. These may be later shown on resource histograms to examine the overall network in terms of the resources.

Constraints

On many networks, certain activities may be constrained by events, not necessarily included in the networks, which determine expected start/ finish dates or mandatory start/finish dates. Use of these constraints may affect the defined logic of the network but may contribute to a more practical use of the network analysis as shown later in this chapter.

Scheduling and error detection

The program schedules the network, i.e. calculates activity calendar data such as early/late start/finish dates, by making forward and backward passes as described for the simple networks in Chapter 3. Before the scheduling process, the software will identify and report on the following:

1 'Loops', where the network logic has been defeated by a later scheduled activity having a logical constraint on an earlier activity. An example is shown in Fig. 63, where activity 4–7 has been wrongly entered as 7–4. Detection of loops will prevent execution of the forward and backward passes until the loop errors have been corrected.

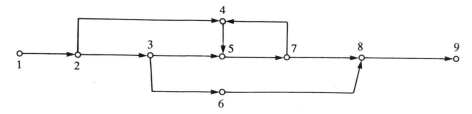

Figure 63. *Loop detection.*

2 Activities with no predecessors or successors. These may be intentional or the result of an entry error. For example, in the network in Fig. 64, the activity 7–10 will be identified by a report indicating that activity 10–11 has no predecessor. If this is accidental, then activity 7–10 may be entered. Otherwise, the early start of activity 10–11 will be calculated, on the backward pass, as equal to that for the start date of event 1 for the network unless it has been constrained, e.g. by the constraint 'start no earlier than . . .'

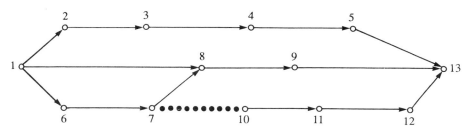

Figure 64. *Detecting activities with no predecessors/ successors.*

Editing and updating activities

An activity is simply called up in the 'activity-data' mode on the computer by pressing 'N' for 'next' and entering the activity number or *i-j* events. For rapid updating of a group of activities, two modes are available, namely:

1 Batch processing, in which a file of activity data is created and exported to a separate editing program for later re-entry into Primavera.
2 'Autosorting', where activities may be selectively sorted by using parameters such as:
   (a) select by activity number = (a value),
   (b) select activities having a particular resource, e.g. 'bricklayers',
   (c) select activities which are the responsibility of 'x' (company or person, etc.).

Viewing

Using Autosort it is possible to view the results of a scheduling run as bar charts, tables or resource profiles for further consideration prior to printing reports or graphic output. In this mode, critical activities are highlighted in a different colour for easy identification.

Printed reports

The program can generate reports in an extensive range of ways and contains more than twenty standard report formats which may be customized for particular requirements by combining dates, percentage completions, float, duration, resource usage and so on.

Graphic output

Primavera works with another program, Primavision, to produce graphic reports such as bar charts or time-scaled network logic diagrams. Output of this nature can be displayed on the screen and drawn on a printer or plotter-driver which may be either electrostatic or precision pen-type. Pens used in pen-type plotters can use different coloured inks for showing, e.g. green for progress or red for critical activities.

Basic applications

The arrow network analysed manually in Chapter 2 has been entered on Primavera. The results are shown in Figs. 65–68.

Figure 65 is the basic arrow network time-scaled by early dates. The network was entered as an *i-j* network with a start date of 1 January 1988. The activities are named activity *i-j* where, e.g. activity 5–11 has *i*-node 5 and *j*-node 11. The output in Fig. 70 is shown with activities described on activity bars as in a precedence diagram. This format is most useful in the time-scaled logic diagram for clearly displaying the activities and events relative to the time-scale. The numbers above the activity bars refer to:

1 The *i-j* nodes on the left-hand side, identifying the preceding and succeeding events.
2 The float available on the right-hand side, showing 0 for the critical activities 1–2, 3–2, 3–9, 9–10 and 10–11 and 3 days or 9 days for the other activities.

The bottom right-hand corner of the diagram shows the legend for the activity bars (with the critical activities and progress bars coloured red and green, respectively, on the actual plot for easy identifications), while the data date and plot dates are shown at the bottom right. The vertical data date bar passes through the date line on 1 January 1988.

Fig. 66 is the basic arrow network bar chart plotted by early start dates. Critical activities are identified as on Fig. 65 and the summary on the left-hand side of the diagram shows:

1 The activity description, e.g. activity 3–4.
2 The *i-j* nodes, e.g. 3   4.
3 OD – the original duration for the activity.

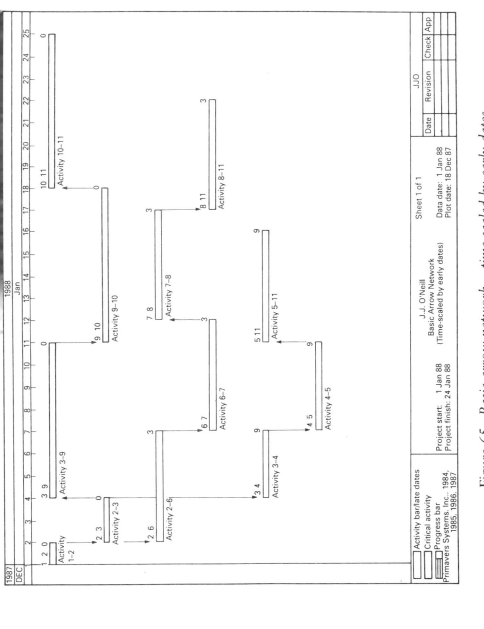

Figure 65. *Basic arrow network – time-scaled by early dates.*

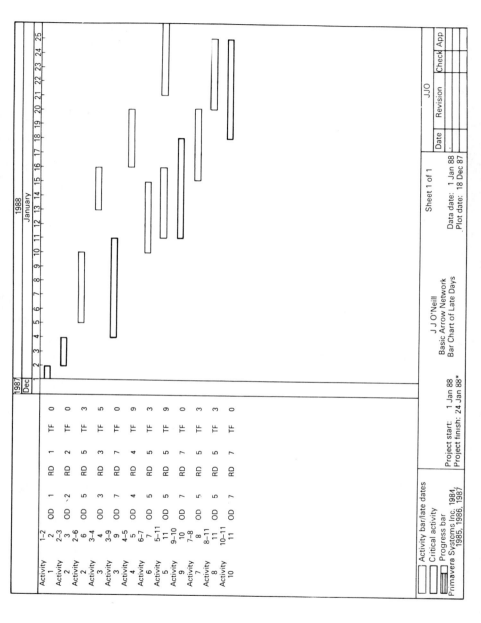

Figure 66. *Basic arrow network – bar chart of early dates.*

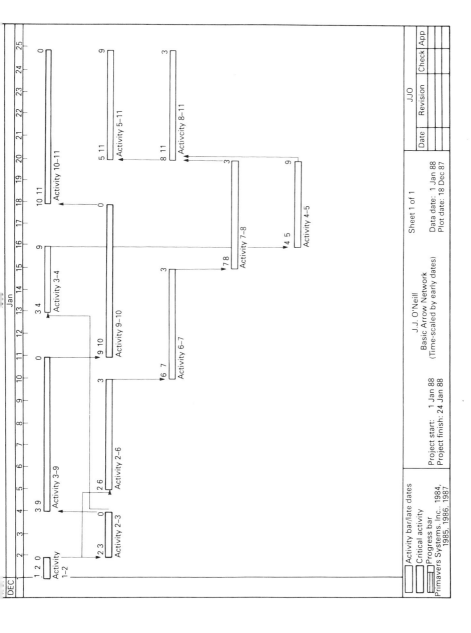

Figure 67. *Basic arrow network – time-scaled by late dates.*

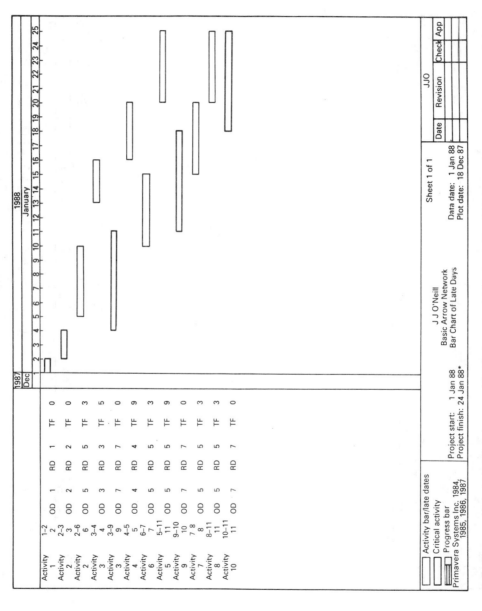

Figure 68. *Basic arrow network – bar chart of late dates.*

4 RD – the remaining duration (= OD since no progress has been reported).

5 TF – total float.

Figs. 67 and 68 are the plots obtained using the exact same network data but, in these figures, plotting by *late dates*.

It is very important to realize that the same data can be used to give results which, at first sight, appear to be so very different – Figs 65 and 67 seem, in fact, to be different networks while Figs 66 and 68 seem to be different bar charts. In practical use and analysis of plotted output, it is *vital* to note whether the results represent an early or late start.

Practical applications – a case study

The Du Pont company, in common with other large organizations, uses many different application programs for project control and reporting. No one 'best' method is favoured and different sites and different project directors and managers have discretion in the choice of programs, although certain integrated packages must be used as they apply on a world-wide basis. These include proprietary Du Pont systems such as:

- FLCS – or 'Field Labour Control System'. This is used by Du Pont for estimating, trend analysis and cost control of field labour elements on a common coding system.
- WMMS – or 'Wilmington Materials Management System', used for global procurement management of materials purchased through Du Pont's central procurement department in Wilmington (USA)
- FMCS – or 'Field Material Control System', which is used to track and allocate materials required for project use whether purchased through local sites or through Wilmington.

However, because of the initial extra expenses involved in using network methods for project control, a project has to satisfy certain parameters, including value and complexity, before network-analysis programs are used in design, procurement or construction control in the main design office.

The use of Primavera for schedule control is described for one particular project with a capital value of £45 million in this multiproject environment, where hundreds of projects or potential projects are in various stages of analysis, progress or finalization.

Initial network development

The design contractor, in consultation with client representatives, set up a work breakdown and numbering system, generally as shown in Fig. 69. A network was used for main design and procurement control until each work package was released for construction. Construction activities were dependent upon these package release dates and initial construction activities were controlled at that level.

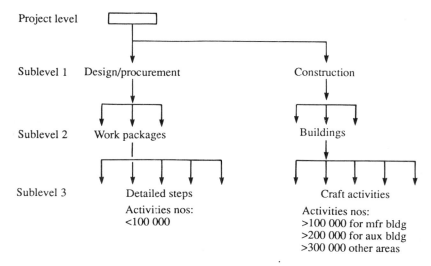

Figure 69. *Work breakdown and numbering system for case study.*

Network development for construction control

As the construction proceeded to about 50 per cent completion, the network was 'rolled-over' to a more detailed expansion of craft activities. At that stage in construction, it was possible to define the project in terms of 'systems' and to agree the 'turn-over' dates for each system to the client operating company. Each system was by then fully described in terms of scope of work, including all equipment, pipework, electrical/instrumentation and insulation.

This analysis work was carried-out in June 1987, and the project work remaining was set up as a series of about forty mini-networks,

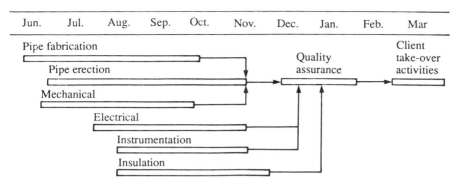

Figure 70. *Simple system network for case study.*

based on the simple network shown in Fig. 70. These networks are easily defined for resource allocation by using the work units as indicators of the work-load on a histogram print-out. For example, the pipe fabrication and erection elements are based on SFUs (shop fabrication units computed from pipe isometric sketches on a company-wide standard) and SEUs (site erection units on the same basis).

These can be individually determined for each system and entered as a 'resource' − although they are actually not resources but represent work-units required. The histogram print-out, however, is an *exact* reflection of manpower requirements as these units are factored on a target productivity basis.

The 'rolled-over' network developed in this way is ideal for communication of requirements to craft supervisory level because the individual crafts can receive weekly updates in the form of easily read bar charts and histograms. Examples of these are included in Figs 71–75.

Fig. 71 is the output on 9 November 1987 for a system known as 'Chilled Water'. Note from the figure:

- The data-date vertical line is 9 November 1987.
- Activity numbers 2606, 2607, 2601 and 2602 are all shown as complete.
- Activity number 2605 is shown as critical, with a negative float of − 31. (In fact, the activity description is Chilled H_2O Mech-0 and the '0' indicates that this sytem had no Mech components. The activity is shown as critical because it had not been updated.)
- The other activity descriptions are explained as follows:
  2606 Chilled H_2O Inst-5 means that the system has five instrumentation 'loops'.

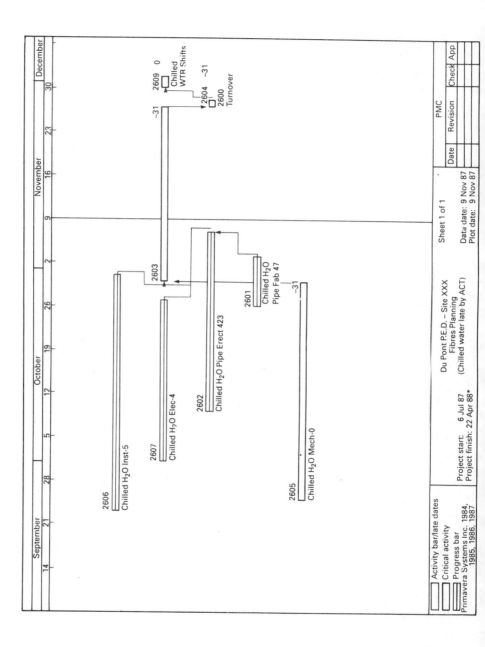

Figure 71. *Time-scaled network logic diagram for 'chilled water' system on a fibres project.*

2607 Chilled H_2O Elec-4 means that the system has four electrical cables tied into the instrumentation (all completed).

2606 Chilled H_2O Pipe Erect 432 means the system has 432 SEUs.

2601 Chilled H_2O Pipe Fab 47 means the system has 47 SFUs.

2603 2600 QA represents the quality assurance activities carried out by the construction and client representatives, based on a period of 4 weeks from initial construction completion to client acceptance. (This item also shows a negative float of $(-)31$ days because of the effect of activity 2605 and because no progress has been reported although the activity start is on the left-hand side of the data-date line.

2604 2600 Turnover represents the 1-day 'turnover' activity where the 2600 system is formally accepted. This activity is constrained by an entry 'finish no later than 27 November 1987', which represents the network end date for this system.

2609 Chilled WTR Shifts represents the start of the client take-over activities, with a constraint 'mandatory start on 1 December 1987'. Use of this mandatory start date means that the constraint will override the basic network logic even if the calculated end date for the turnover activity is later than the constrained date.

Figure 72 is the resource profile for the electrical craft, plotted by 'early dates'. Note from the figure:

- The report date is 27 November 1987, data date 26 November 1987.
- The time-scale is daily.
- The resource is 'terms' – the electrical unit of measurement representing a number of man-hours.
- The resource is profiled based on the scheduled early completion of activities and indicates that about 60 terms per week are required now for early completion, compared with 40 (8×5) achieved in the previous week.

This figure should be read with Fig. 73 which is the resource profile as in Fig. 72 but based on 'late dates'. The 'A's in this case represent what has been achieved plus what should have been achieved and indicate that between 40 and 50 'terms' a week (8–10 terms per day) are now required to achieve 'late-date' completion. The interpretation is best made in conjunction with the bar chart of Fig. 74.

Fig. 74 is the bar-chart output on 4 December 1987 for presentation

Du Pont F.E.D. Sire XXX	Primavera Project Planner	Fibre planning – duplicate of DUVL
Report date 27 Nov 87 Run no. 44	Resource Profile	Start date 6 July 87 Fin date 22 Apr 88
EVUL electrical terms by early dates		Data date 26 Nov 87 Page no.

Resource terms – elect unit   Time-scale – daily

```
  20......./...............*..........................................................................
    ,,    ,    ,    *    ,    ,    ,    ,    ,    ,    ,    ,    ,    ,    ,  ,,  ,    ,
    ,,    ,    ,    *    ,    ,    ,    ,    ,    ,    ,    ,    ,    ,    ,    ,    ,
    ,,    ,    ,    *    ,    ,    ,    ,    ,    ,    ,    ,    ,    ,    ,    ,    ,
    ,,    ,    ,    *    ,    ,    ,    ,    ,    ,    ,    ,    ,    ,    ,    ,    ,
  18...............*.............................................................................
    ,,    ,    ,    *    ,    ,    ,    ,    ,    ,    ,    ,    ,    ,    ,  ,,  ,    ,
    ,,    ,    ,    *,   ,    ,    ,    ,    ,    ,    ,    ,    ,    ,    ,    ,    ,
    ,,    ,    ,    *    ,    ,    ,    ,    ,    ,    ,    ,    ,    ,    ,    ,    ,
    ,,    ,    ,    ?,   ,    ,    ,    ,    ,    ,    ,    ,    ,    ,    ,    ,    ,
  16............,..*,..............................................................................
    ,,    ,    ,    .EE,    ,    ,    ,    ,    ,    ,    ,    ,    ,    ,    ,    ,
    ,,    ,    ,    .EEE    ,    ,    ,    ,    ,    ,    ,    ,    ,    ,    ,    ,
    ,,    ,    ,    .EEE    ,    ,    ,    ,    ,    ,    ,    ,    ,    ,    ,    ,
    ,,    ,    ,    .EEE    ,    ,    ,  EE  ,    ,    ,    ,    ,    ,    ,    ,
  14.................EEEEE.................EEEEEE...............................................
    ,,    ,    ,    .EEEEEE ,    ,    ,  EEEEEE    ,    ,    ,    ,    ,    ,    ,
    ,,    ,    ,    .EEEEEEE    ,    ,  EEEEEE    ,    ,    ,    ,    ,    ,    ,
    ,,    ,    ,    .EEEEEEEE   ,    ,  EEEEEE    ,    ,    ,    ,    ,    ,    ,
    ,,    ,    ,    .EEEEEEEE   ,    ,  EEEEEE    ,    ,    ,    ,    ,    ,    ,
  12.................EEEEEEEEE,,EE..........EEEEEEEEEEEEEEE........................................
    ,,    ,    ,    .EEEEEEEE  EE.   ,    ,  EEEEEEEEEEEEEEE  ,    ,    ,    ,    ,
    ,,    ,    ,    .EEEEEEEEEEEE.   ,    ,  EEEEEEEEEEEEEEE  ,    ,    ,    ,    ,
    ,,    ,    ,    .EEEEEEEEEEEEEEE ,    ,  EEEEEEEEEEEEEEE  ,    ,    ,    ,    ,
    ,,    ,    ,    .EEEEEEEEEEEEEEE ,    ,  EEEEEEEEEEEEEEE  ,    ,    ,    ,    ,
  10.................EEEEEEEEEEEEEEEEE........EEEEEEEEEEEEEEEEEE...................................
    ,,    ,    ,    .EEEEEEEEEEEEEEEEE   ,  EEEEEEEEEEEEEEEEEEEE.  ,    ,    ,    ,
    ,,    ,    ,    .EEEEEEEEEEEEEEEEEE  ,  EEEEEEEEEEEEEEEEEEEE.  ,    ,    ,    ,
    ,,    ,    ,    .EEEEEEEEEEEEEEEEEE  ,  EEEEEEEEEEEEEEEEEEEE.  ,    ,    ,    ,
    ,,    ,    ,    .EEEEEEEEEEEEEEEEEE  ,  EEEEEEEEEEEEEEEEEEEEEE ,    ,    ,    ,
   8.........,AAAAA,.EEEEEEEEEEEEEEEEEE.......EEEEEEEEEEEEEEEEEEEEEE...............................
    ,,    ,  ,AAAAAA EEEEEEEEEEEEEEEEEE   ,  EEEEEEEEEEEEEEEEEEEEEE  ,    ,    ,
    ,,    ,  ,AAAAAA EEEEEEEEEEEEEEEEEE   ,  EEEEEEEEEEEEEEEEEEEEEE  ,    ,    ,
    ,,    ,  ,AAAAAA EEEEEEEEEEEEEEEEEE   ,  EEEEEEEEEEEEEEEEEEEEEE  ,    ,    ,
    ,,    ,  ,AAAAAA EEEEEEEEEEEEEEEEEE   ,  EEEEEEEEEEEEEEEEEEEEEEE ,    ,    ,
   6.........,AAAAAA,.EEEEEEEEEEEEEEEEEE......EEEEEEEEEEEEEEEEEEEEEEEE.............................
    ,,    ,   AAAAAA EEEEEEEEEEEEEEEEEE   ,  EEEEEEEEEEEEEEEEEEEEEEEE  ,    ,    ,
    ,,    ,   AAAAAA EEEEEEEEEEEEEEEEEE   ,  EEEEEEEEEEEEEEEEEEEEEEEE  ,    ,    ,
    ,HA-HAP-HAAAAAAAAAAAAEEEEEEEEEEEEEEEEEE  ,  EEEEEEEEEEEEEEEEEEEEEEEEEE  ,    ,
    ,-HHAAHAAAAAAAAAAAAEEEEEEEEEEEEEEEEEE  ,  EEEEEEEEEEEEEEEEEEEEEEEEEEEE  ,    ,
   4.,-H-HH-AHAP-AH-HFAAAAEEEEEEEEEEEEEEEEEE.......EEEEEEEEEEEEEEEEEEEEEEEEEEEE...................
    ,HAP-HHHH-HH-HP-HAHAAAEEEEEEEEEEEEEEEEEE  ,  EEEEEEEEEEEEEEEEEEEEEEEEEEEE  ,
    ,-HHHH-HHH-HH-HHAAAAEEEEEEEEEEEEEEEEEE  ,  EEEEEEEEEEEEEEEEEEEEEEEEEEEEE.  ,
    -H-HHHHH-H-AHAHAAAAAEEEEEEEEEEEEEEEEEE  ,  EEEEEEEEEEEEEEEEEEEEEEEEEEEEEE.  ,
    -HHHH-HHHHH-HHAAAAAEEEEEEEEEEEEEEEEEE  ,  EEEEEEEEEEEEEEEEEEEEEEEEEEEEEE.  ,
   2.,-HH-HHH-HH-HHHHH-HAAAAEEEEEEEEEEEEEEEEEE.....EEEEEEEEEEEEEEEEEEEEEEEEEEEEEEE...............
    ,-HHHH-HHH-HH-HHHHH-HHAAEEEEEEEEEEEEEEEEEE  ,  EEEEEEEEEEEEEEEEEEEEEEEEEEEEEEEEE.
    ,-HHH-HHHHH-HHHHH-HHHHAAEEEEEEEEEEEEEEEEEE  ,  EEEEEEEEEEEEEEEEEEEEEEEEEEEEEEEEEEE.
    ,-HHH-HHHHHH-HHHHAAAAAAEEEEEEEEEEEEEEEEEE  ,  EEEEEEEEEEEEEEEEEEEEEEEEEEEEEEEEEEEE.
    ,-H-HH-HH-AHH-HHHHAAAAAEEEEEEEEEEEEEEEEEE  ,  EEEEEEEEEEEEEEEEEEEEEEEEEEEEEEEEEEEE.
   0.,H-HHH-HH-HH-HHAAAEEEEEEEEEEEEEEEEEEHHHHHHHHEEEEEEEEEEEEEEEEEEEEEEEEEEEEEEEEEEEEEEEE......HHH...
     02   09   16   23   30   07   14   21   28   04   11   18   25   01   08   15   22   29   O7   14   21   04   11
    NOV  NOV  NOV  NOV  NOV  DEC  DEC  DEC  DEC  JAN  JAN  JAN  JAN  FEB  FEB  FEB  FEB  FEB  MAR MAR MAR APR APR
     87   87   87   87   87   87   87   87   87   88   88   88   88   88   88   88   88   88   88   88   88   88   88
```

Figure 72. *Resource profile for electrical craft on fibre project – plotted for early dates.*

Pont P.E.D. – SITE XX   Primavera Project Planner   Planning – Duplicate of DUVL

Report date 27 Nov 87 Run no. 45   Resource Profile   Start date 6 Jul 87 Fin date 22 Apr 88

EVUL (electrical terms by late dates)   Data date 26 Nov 87 Page no.

Resource terms – elect unit   Time-scale – daily

```
 20 . . . . . . . . . . . . . . . . . . . . . *. . . . . . . . . . . . . . . . . . . . . . . . . . . . . . . . . . . . . . . . . . . . . . . . . . . . . . . . . . . . . . . . . . . . . . . . . . . . . . . . .
    . .    .     .     .    *  .   .   .   .   .   .   .   .   .   .   .   .   .   .   .   .   .   .   .
    . .    .     .     .    *  .   .   .   .   .   .   .   .   .   .   .   .   .   .   .   .   .   .   .
    . .    .     .     .    *  .   .   .   .   .   .   .   .   .   .   .   .   .   .   .   .   .   .   .
 18 . . . . . . . . . . . . . . . *. . . . . . . . . . . . . . . . . . . . . . . . . . . . . . . . . .
    . .    .     .     .    *  .   .   .   .   .   .   .   .   .   .   .   .   .   .   .   .   .   .   .
    . .    .     .     .    *  .   .   .   .   .   .   .   .   .   .   .   .   .   .   .   .   .   .   .
    . .    .     .     .    *  .   .   .   .   .   .   .   .   .   .   .   .   .   .   .   .   .   .   .
    . .    .     .     .    *  .   .   .   .   .   .   .   .   .   .   .   .   .   .   .   .   .   .   .
 16 . . . . . . . . . . . . . . *. . . . . . . . . . . . . . . . . . . . . . . . . . . . . . . . . . .
    . .    .     .     .    *  .   .   .   .   .   .   .   .   .   .   .   .   .   .   .   .   .   .   .
    . .    .     .     .    *  .   .   .   .   .   .   .   .   .   .   .   .   .   .   .   .   .   .   .
    . .    .     .     .    *  .   .   .   .   .   .   .   .   .   .   .   .   .   .   .   .   .   .   .
    . .    .     .     .    *  .   .   .   .   .   .   .   .   .   .   .   .   .   .   .   .   .   .   .
 14 . . . . . . . . . . . . . . *. . . . . . . . . . . . . . . . . . . . . . . . . . . . . . . . . . .
    . .    .   ÄÄ–ÄÄ    *  .   .   .   .   .   .   .   .   .   .   .   .   .   .   .   .   .   .   .   .
    . .    .   –ÄÄ–ÄÄ   *  .   .   .   .   .   .   .   .   .   .   .   .   .   .   .   .   .   .   .   .
    . .    .   –ÄÄÄÄ    *  .   .   .   .   .   .   .   .   .   .   .   .   .   .   .   .   .   .   .   .
 12 . . . . . . . . . ÄÄÄÄÄ. .*. . . . . . . . . . . . . . . . . . . . . . . . . . . . . . . . . . . .
    . .    .   ÄÄÄÄÄ   *  .   .   .   .   .   .   .   .   .   .   .   .   .   .   .   .   .   .   .   .
    . .    .   ÄÄ–ÄÄ–  *  .   .   .   .   .   .   .   .   .   .   .   .   .   .   .   .   .   .   .   .
    . .    .   ÄÄ–ÄÄÄ  *  .   .   .   .   .   .   .   .   .   .   .   .   .   .   .   .   .   .   .   .
    . .    . ÄÄÄÄ–ÄÄÄÄ *  .   .   .   .   .   .  LLLL   .   .   .   .   .   .   .   .   .   .   .   .   .
 10 . . . . . . . .ÄÄÄÄÄÄÄÄÄÄ*. . . . . . . . .LLL. . . . . . .LLLL. . . . . . . . . . . . . . . . . .
    . .    ÄÄÄÄÄÄ–Ä–ÄÄÄÄ*  .   .    LLL.   .  LLLLLLL  .   .   .   .   .   .   .   .   .   .   .   .   .
    . .    ÄÄÄÄÄÄÄÄÄÄÄÄ* .   .  LLLLLLLL   .  LLLLLLL  .   .   .   .   .   .   .   .   .   .   .   .   .
    . .    ÄÄÄÄÄÄÄÄÄÄ–ÄÄ* .   .  LLLLLLLL   .  LLLLLLL  .   .   .   .   .   .   .   .   .   .   .   .   .
    . .    Ä–ÄÄÄÄÄÄÄÄÄÄ* .   .  LLLLLLLL .  LLLLLLL  . LLLL .   .   .   .   .   .   .   .   .   .   .   .
  8 . . . ÄÄ. ÄÄÄÄÄÄÄÄÄÄÄ*. . . . . . .LLLLLLLLLL . . . .L-LLLLL . . .LLLLL . . . . . . . . . . . . .
    . .   –ÄÄÄÄÄÄÄÄÄÄÄÄÄÄ* .  LLLLLLLLLLL  .  LLLLLLL  .  LLLL . .   .   .   .   .   .   .   .   .   .
    . Ä–ÄÄÄÄÄÄÄÄÄÄÄÄÄÄ–* .  LLLLLLLLLLL  .  LLLLLLLL.  .LLLLLLLLLLLL  .   .   .   .   .   .   .   .   .
    . ÄÄ–ÄÄÄÄÄÄÄÄÄÄÄÄÄÄ* .  LLLLLLLLLLL  .  LLLLLLLL.  LLLLLLLLLLL  .   .   .   .   .   .   .   .   .
    . Ä–ÄÄÄÄÄÄÄÄÄÄÄÄÄÄÄ* .  LLLLLLLLLLL  .  LLLLLLLLLLLLLLLLLLLLLLL  .   .   .   .   .   .   .   .   .
  6 . ÄÄÄÄÄÄÄÄÄÄÄÄÄÄÄÄÄ*. . . . . .LLLLLLLLLL. . . .L-LLLLLLLLLLLLLLLLLL. . . . . . . . . . . . . . . .
    . –ÄÄÄÄÄÄÄÄÄÄÄÄÄÄÄÄ* . LLLLLLLLLLLLLL    .  LLLLLLLLLLLLLLLLLLLLLL . . LLLLLLL. . . . . . . . .
    . –Ä–ÄÄÄÄÄÄÄÄÄÄÄÄLL.LLLLLLLLLLLLLL    .  LLLLLLLLLLLLLLLLLLLLLLL . LLLLLLLL. . . . . . . . .
    . ––ÄÄÄÄÄÄÄÄÄÄÄÄÄÄÄLL.LLLLLLLLLLLLLL    .  LLLLLLLLLLLLLLLLLLLLLLLLL. . . . . . . . . . . . . . .
    . Ä–ÄÄÄÄÄÄÄÄÄÄÄÄÄÄÄÄLLLLLLLLLLLLLL    .  LLLLLLLLLLLLLLLLLLLLLLLLLLLL. . . . . . . . . . . . . . .
  4 . –Ä–Ä–ÄÄÄÄÄÄÄÄÄÄÄÄÄLLLLLLLLLLLLLLLL. . . . .LLLLLLLLLLLLLLLLLLLLLLLLLLLLLL. . . . . . . . . . .L. . .
    . –Ä–ÄÄÄ––Ä–ÄÄÄÄÄÄÄÄÄLLLLLLLLLLLLLL    .  LLLLLLLLLLLLLLLLLLLLLLLLLLLLLL. . . . . . . . . . . . .
    . –Ä–ÄÄÄÄÄÄÄ–ÄÄÄÄÄ–LLLLLLLLLLLLLL    .  LLLLLLLLLLLLLLLLLLLLLLLLLLLLLLLLLL. . . . . . . . . . . . .
    . –Ä–ÄÄÄÄ–ÄÄÄÄÄÄ–LLLLLLLLLLLLLL    .  LLLLLLLLLLLLLLLLLLLLLLLLLLLLLLLLLL. . . . . . . . . . . . . .
    . –ÄÄÄÄ–ÄÄÄÄÄÄ––ÄÄLLLLLLLLLLLLLLL    .  LLLLLLLLLLLLLLLLLLLLLLLLLLLLLLLLLLLL. . . . . . . . . . .
  2 . Ä–ÄÄÄÄ–ÄÄÄ–ÄÄÄÄÄLLLLLLLLLLLLLLL. . . . .LLLLLLLLLLLLLLLLLLLLLLLLLLLLLLLLLLLLLLLLLLL. . . . . . .
    . –Ä–ÄÄÄÄÄ–ÄÄÄÄÄ–ÄÄÄLLLLLLLLLLLL    ,  LLLLLLLLLLLLLLLLLLLLLLLLLLLLLLLLLLLLLLLLLLLLL. . . . . .
    . ––Ä––ÄÄÄÄ–ÄÄÄÄ–ÄÄLLLLLLLLLLL    .  LLLLLLLLLLLLLLLLLLLLLLLLLLLLLLLLLLLLLLLLLLLLLLLL. . . . .
    . ––––ÄÄÄ–ÄÄÄÄÄ–ÄÄÄLLLLLLLLLLL    .  LLLLLLLLLLLLLLLLLLLLLLLLLLLLLLLLLLLLLLLLLLLLLLLLLLL. . . .
  0 . –––––ÄÄÄ–ÄÄ–ÄÄÄLLLLLLLLLLLLLLL TÄÄÄÄÄÄÄÄLLLLLLLLLLLLLLLLLLLLLLLLLLLLLLLLLLLLLLLLLLLLLLLLLLL---. . .
    02   09   16   23   30   07   14   21   28   04   11   18   25   01   08   15   22   29   07   14   21   04   11
   NOV  NOV  NOV  NOV  NOV  DEC  DEC  DEC  DEC  JAN  JAN  JAN  JAN  FEB  FEB  FEB  FEB  FEB  MAR MAR MAR APR  APR
    87   87   87   87   87   87   87   87   87   88   88   88   88   88   88   88   88   88   88   88   88   88   88
```

Figure 73. *Resource profile for electrical craft on fibres project –*
plotted for late dates.

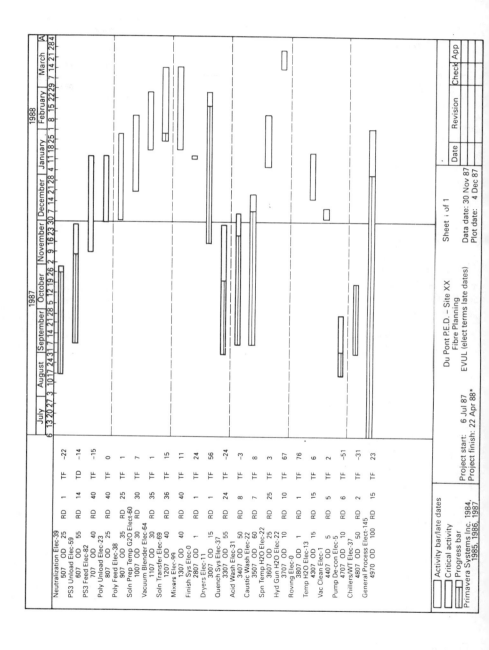

Figure 74. *Bar chart for electrical craft on fibres project.*

presentation to the electrical crafts personnel – on items with progress less than 100 per cent complete. Note from the figure:

- The data-date vertical line is 30 November 1987.
- The bar-chart only shows activities with either no progress or partial progress, i.e. completed activities are not shown.
- The left-hand column contains the relevant information as follows:
  (a) Activity description, e.g. 'Caustic Wash Elec-53' where 53 is the number of 'terminations' required on the system.
  (b) 3507 is the activity number.
  (c) OD means original duration, in this case 60 working days.
  (d) RD means remaining duration, in this case 7 working days.
  (e) TF means total float, in this case 8 working days.
- The graphic display draws immediate attention to areas which are critical and targets action areas for the following reporting period.

Fig. 75 is the Resource Control Report which provides a tabular summary with total figures and overall percentage progress, etc., at the bottom. This is useful for comparing progress with estimated costs, etc., although these were not included in these simple networks and resources analyses.

This type of weekly status updating shows that otherwise complex planning can be reduced to a practical level for everyday use. The key factors are:

- The whole project is broken down into a series of discrete systems.
- Each system can be fully described in terms of its scope of work together with resources required.
- The end date for each system is taken as the 'absolute', i.e. not to be changed except by agreement with all parties and only when the overall completion date is not affected.
- Weekly reporting of progress is essential. At this stage in a project, monthly reporting is too 'coarse' for day-to-day control.

The weekly bar charts are based on items which are less than 100 per cent complete and should show progress where indicated by the date line. This means that completed activities are dropped from the bar-chart report, while incomplete items are brought into focus. This demands attention from the relevant craft department (or other responsible party) to the items identified as most critical. For example, in Fig. 74, these would be activity numbers 507, 607, 3307, 3407, 4707 and 4807. The primary advantage of this approach is that weekly updating becomes very simple and forces attention on weekly performance at the craft/output level.

Du Pont P.E.D. – SITE XX   Primavera Project Planner   Planning

Report date 13 Nov 87 Run no. 26   Resource Control Report   Start date 6 Jul 87 Fin date 22 Apr 88

EUVL elect terms by activity no.   Data date 12 Nov 87 Page no. 1

Activity ID	Resource	Cost account	Account category	Unit meas	Budget	PCT CMP	Actual to date	Actual this peirod	Estimate to complete	Forecast	Variance
			Terms – elect unit								
107	terms				14	100	14	0	0	14	0
207	terms				24	63	15	0	9	24	0
307	terms				15	100	15	0	0	15	0
407	terms				18	28	5	0	13	18	0
507	terms				39	100	39	0	0	39	0
607	terms				59	27	16	0	43	59	0
707	terms				85	0	0	0	85	85	0
808	terms				23	0	0	0	23	23	0
909	terms				38	0	0	0	38	38	0
1007	terms				60	0	0	0	60	60	0
1107	terms				64	0	0	0	64	64	0
1207	terms				69	6	4	0	65	69	0
1307	terms				99	0	0	0	99	99	0
1607	terms				0	100	0	0	0	0	0
2007	terms				16	100	16	0	0	16	0
2107	terms				3	100	3	0	0	3	0
2207	terms				8	100	8	0	0	8	0
2307	terms				28	100	28	0	0	28	0
2407	terms				4	100	4	0	0	4	0
2507	terms				87	67	58	0	29	87	0
2607	terms				4	100	4	0	0	4	0
2707	terms				15	0	0	0	15	15	0
2807	terms				0	0	0	0	0	0	0
2907	terms				10	100	10	0	0	10	0
3007	terms				11	0	0	0	11	11	0
3307	terms				53	32	17	0	36	53	0
3407	terms				38	21	8	0	30	38	0
3507	terms				73	58	42	0	31	73	0
3607	terms				22	0	0	0	22	22	0
3707	terms				8	0	0	0	8	8	0
3807	terms				0	0	0	0	0	0	0
4307	terms				13	0	0	0	13	13	0
4407	terms				1	0	0	0	1	1	0
4507	terms				27	96	26	0	1	27	0
4607	terms				7	100	7	0	0	7	0
4707	terms				5	40	2	0	3	5	0
4807	terms				37	97	36	0	1	37	0
4907	terms				129	88	114	0	15	129	0
Total terms					1206	41	491	0	715	1206	0
Report totals					1206	41	491	0	715	1206	0

Figure 75. *Resource control report.*

5

Project cost estimating

Project management means the control of all project resources. Cost estimating and control methods focus on the specific management of the money resources.

In the project, estimates are needed to predict the *total costs* involved. Budgeting and cost control, which deal with the logistics of controlling the money flow and cost performance, must be based on an estimate in the first instance. The preparation and use of the estimate must be considered at the strategic level because achieving the financial objectives is always a key factor in project success. Consequently, it is a major area for allocating effort or resources for effective project control.

The project manager needs skill and knowledge to produce the desired estimating and control results because he may be held accountable as a matter of project policy. He must, therefore, have the authority to select and use the necessary resources.

An estimate, by definition, is not an *exact* measurement. Its quality crucially depends both on the quality of the information currently available and how it is processed. It is not, therefore, always possible to produce a definitive, single cost estimate at the start of a project. In this case, the estimate, like a network, must be regarded as developing with the project and, therefore, subject to regular review and adjustment as a process.

The characteristics of all reliable estimating techniques are embodied in the steps of the process, namely:

1 Define the requirements.
2 Focus on the relevant issues.
3 Find the information available.
4 Highlight the main assumptions.
5 Present the information in a suitable format.

6 Record deviations.
7 Review the total estimate regularly.

These are described as follows:

Define the requirements

(i) Preparing and reviewing cost estimates uses up resources. It is, therefore, essential that the requirements which the estimate must fulfil are defined for each step of the process. Only then can the estimator or estimating department be judged on results and the estimate confidently applied in the overall project process.

The requirements for cost estimates vary from project to project. Similarly, the degree of accuracy required or obtainable will be inherent in the project and will vary from stage to stage.

Preliminary estimates are normally based on inaccurate or incomplete information and must be used accordingly, especially where they form the basis of 'go, do not go' decisions. These estimates are frequently prepared for investment considerations and may be assessed from statistics or data available from previous, similar projects or work of a similar nature. At this stage, relatively small expenditures in refining information can vastly improve the quality of an estimate. For example, where only preliminary designs are available, a balance must be struck between the information available and the importance of the decision. The lack of information calls upon the *judgement* of the estimator rather than scientific accuracy.

Estimates of a higher order of accuracy may be prepared for tender purposes, based on a client's detailed requirements, or for cost-control purposes. The costs of preparing an estimate of this nature could be 1 or 2 per cent of the total project costs.

(ii) 'Define the requirements' also means to define the scope of the work to be estimated. This is particularly relevant where a project is broken down into various stages or subsections and perhaps a number of estimators are working independently on the various sections. In this case, they must have clearly defined limits on the work involved. Similarly, an estimate prepared in response to a tender inquiry must have a clearly defined scope of what is included or omitted. However, this is often easier said than done and adequate definition/control of scope very much depends on the pressure to get the project moving. Nevertheless, the estimator can only allow for the items included in the scope – the defined requirements – or make assumptions about scope growth.

(iii) Cost estimates or reviews intended for later stages in the project are able to take account of those factors which up to then might have influenced the project costs; they should be directed mainly at refining the cost estimates for work still to be completed. Thus if estimates are to be valid within a range of ± 20 per cent, the range of accuracy of the total project costs can be narrowed with each successive stage. The estimate *range*, though, may still be ± 20 per cent of the *total balance* of costs, as shown in Table 6.

Table 6. The range of accuracy of an estimate through the project stages.

Stage (%)	Value of work done	Estimated total cost	Estimate range (%)	
			Total	Balance
0	0	$0.80x$ to $1.20x$	± 20	± 20
50	$0.5y$	$0.90y$ to $1.10y$	± 10	± 20
90	$0.9z$	$0.98z$ to $1.02z$	± 2	± 20

The relevant issues

The requirements for an estimate should be based on examination and selection of *significant* items for cost-control and result-control purposes. Every proposed project can be broken down into components, sections or stages for cost estimating. It can then be further subdivided into the elements of people and things, represented by any category of cost headings such as those shown in Table 7.

Table 7. Elements and categories of cost headings.

People	Things
Design fees	Cost of capital
Lawyer fees	Materials
Labour	Equipment including computers
Secretarial	Plant or plant hire
Management	Consumables

For example, consider an estimate for an earth dam, whose detailed bill of quantities may run to several volumes. However, 80 per cent of the actual work may be represented by excavation (say $500\,000\,\text{m}^3$) and fill (say $2\,000\,000\,\text{m}^3$). Cost estimates for this project will be most appropriate if these two units' costs can be predicted accurately. It is a waste of resources to spend time or money accurately costing the brickwork in ten manholes which represent a tiny fraction of the total costs. However, this does happen because of insufficient awareness of the relevant factors involved.

The 80/20 rule, which states that 80 per cent of the total costs result from 20 per cent of the sources of the costs, applies almost universally. This, in itself, is a powerful indicator of where cost-consciousness should concentrate. It emphasizes that, in most projects, the largest percentage of costs is spent on a small proportion of the work items.

This important statement is based on the work of an Italian economist, Wilfredo Pareto. In the late nineteenth century, he discovered that 80–90 per cent of the income in a country was earned by about 10–20 per cent of the population. This work has been developed by many others, particularly in industrial and economic applications. It has proved to be very useful in drawing attention to the significance of that small percentage of all activities or costs accounting for the greatest percentage of total costs, as shown in Fig. 76.

For estimating purposes the difficulty lies in identifying the most relevant cost sources. These will be discussed in more detail in

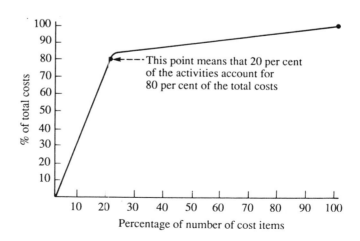

Figure 76. *A Pareto diagram.*

succeeding chapters. However, it is useful at this stage to appreciate the implications of the statement.

Estimates of total or constituent project costs may be prepared by:

- A client/promoter, who needs to know:
  (a) the order of costs involved before proceeding in the initial stages,
  (b) more accurate/detailed estimated costs for final project or investment approval.
- A contractor or vendor, either by pricing the client/promoter's detailed inquiry documents or pricing from a promoter's description of the work to be done, goods to be supplied or service to be rendered.

As few as two major items may account for the bulk of the costs involved, as shown in the example of the earth dam. Therefore, whether in pricing an estimate for a client or for a contractor, the estimator should firstly identify those cost-significant items in *groups*, rather than as individual items. For example, preliminary analysis of the capital cost estimate for a £10 million industrial project may give the results shown in Table 8. The range of values to be extracted for each area can then be assigned by considering the potential for impact on the total and the figures in Table 9 might emerge. This table contains a number of significant points for comment:

- The whole project is described in six main areas.
- Although there is a very wide (± 60 per cent) variation on a particular area, the entire estimate ranges from £8.8 million to £11.2 million (average of £10 million), i.e. a range of ± 12 per cent.
- The costs in each area can be assessed on the basis of people and things.
- The 80/20 rule can be applied in each cost area. For example, if the average number of costed items in each is 100 then 20 out of that 100

Table 8. Percentages of costs from preliminary analysis.

Description	Percentage of total cost
Civil/structural/architectural work	8
Electrical and instrumentation work	10
Mechanical work including equipment	28
Piping work including boiler plant, etc.	17
Design and project management	20
Land and buildings to be acquired	17

Table 9 Costs from preliminary analysis.

	(£)			Percentage (approx.)	
	Minimum	Most likely	Maximum	Min	Max
Civil/struct./arch.	500 000	800 000	1 300 000	−60	+60
Elect. and Instr.	900 000	1 000 000	1 200 000	−10	+20
Mech.	2 500 000	2 800 000	3 000 000	−11	+7
Pipe	1 500 000	1 700 000	1 800 000	−12	+6
Design/project managment	1 800 000	2 000 000	2 100 000	−10	+5
Land and buildings	1 600 000	1 700 000	1 800 000	−6	+6
Totals	8 800 000	10 000 000	11 200 000	−12	+12

will probably be the most cost significant. Out of the total of 600 costed items, therefore, probably 100–120 will represent 80 per cent of the total value.

- These are the items where the estimating effort should be concentrated.

In this case, although the civil/structural/architectural values cannot be accurately estimated for whatever reason, the total estimate may still be in the range − 12 per cent to + 12 per cent. Obviously, most effort in terms of verifying information and assumptions could be directed towards the mechanical and pipeworks sections, which together represent 45 per cent of the most likely total.

Find the information available

The estimator, under the authority and guidance of the project manager, must be in a position to make the most effective use of his skills by:

- Provoking those from whom he must extract the relevant information.
- Using previous or similar project data (an estimating database) in the most constructive format and manner.

At the preliminary stages, it must be clearly understood that the estimator's role is not that of a passive recipient and collator of data on materials and methods. On the contrary, he must be entitled to seek explanations and ensure that alternatives are properly considered. In fact, preliminary project plans and strategy for any project should be bound by the requirements of estimation as much as by any other discipline.

The flow of information can then be seen as a three-way exchange process channelled through and controlled by the project manager. The cost picture developing on the basis of the resources and methods approach can then effectively contribute to the project strategy conceptual development.

Two examples will help to illustrate this:

1 In the industrial project above, the wide variation in possible civil-work costs might be due to insufficient site-investigation data, which could mean the difference between conventional or piled foundations. If conducting a thorough site investigation indicates unforeseen drainage or flooding problems, this could finally result in a choice of an alternative site – a strategic decision.
2 In a computerization project, the cost differences and benefits between producing new software or adapting company procedures to suit off-the-shelf software packages may be enormous. More thorough examination and distinction between client wants and needs may result in considerable cost savings with little reduction in benefits – again a strategic decision.

In cases like these, the cost estimator through the project manager can, indeed must, play a crucial role in exploring and provoking the cost implications of the information available on resources and methods. The use of information in a database is discussed later.

Highlight the governing assumptions

Cost estimates should contain a *narrative* description for each section under consideration. The description might draw attention to the factual and assumed information on resources and methods and highlight those areas with potential for significant impact on cost increases or reductions. In this way, users of the estimate can readily understand or question the contents from the written description rather than just the numbers.

Too often, estimating information merely reflects design data or costings for equipment or labour/staff. This alternative approach demands that each significant cost factor must be able to be defended by whoever contributed the relevant information. For example, an overseas project could be strongly influenced by currency-exchange fluctuations or differing rates of inflation. The cost factors involved must be highlighted on the basis of the governing assumptions. 'What if?' questions should be the keynote on all major assumptions and alternatives must be considered and costed.

Frequently, the most significant area for consideration is time-related:

- What if a project scheduled for completion in 2 years actually required 2½ or 3 years?
- What are the cost implications?
- Are the time assumptions valid in the first instance?
- What if the project can be completed 3 months earlier?

These questions can be generated by or for the project manager or estimator and must be then built-in to the project-strategy concepts. Other significant areas for consideration might concern the scope of work, project staffing and so on. Any assumptions made in these factors which could significantly influence the estimate need to be highlighted for the attention of those who will use the estimate.

Present the information in a suitable format

The reason for presenting any information on paper is to communicate, i.e. to make it understood. The quality standard of the presentation, therefore, is not so dependent on the presentation format as on the effectiveness of the communication. This means that the end-user should be able to extract and apply information from the cost estimate easily. Accordingly, the needs of the various end-users must be considered and the presentation(s) tailored to suit.

Many industries have their own basis for communicating cost data, either in estimate or tender forms. For example:

1 An inquiry document may simply request a vendor to submit his price for an individual item – or it may be used for the purchase of a hundred items, with appropriate headings, as shown in Fig. 77.

Item no.	Description	Quantity	Unit	Price	Total
1	xxxxxxxxxxxxx	10	Metre	£12	£120
43	zzzzzzzzzzzzzzz	6	Each	£3.10	£18.60

Figure 77. *Headings on an inquiry form.*

2 A jeweller's estimate for a repair job may state the basic costs as shown in Table 10.

Table 10. A jeweller's estimate.

Labour	£60
Materials	£50
Total	£110

3 A builder's estimate to a private householder for the construction of a garage may list all materials separately and quote one item for labour (Table 11).

Table 11. A builder's estimate.

Bricks	£400
Cement	£150
Windows	£200
Doors	£100
Guttering	£120
Roofing Tiles	£300
Labour	£1000
Total	£2270

4 A tender to a local authority for the construction of 200 houses may be prepared by professional quantity surveyors, working to standardized rules and procedures. This means that, if ten different firms submit tenders, they can all be evaluated on a comparatively equal basis. The main cost areas may be divided into groups of work by trade, etc., and presented in a standard format as shown in Fig. 78.
5 A estimate prepared by an in-house estimating section for a large industrial contracting company may have standard cost code headings as shown in Table 12.

Trade: Plasterer					
Item no.	Description	Quantity	Unit	Price	Total
800					
801					
802 etc.					
Trade: Electrician					
Item no.	Description	Quantity	Unit	Price	Total
900					
901					
902 etc.					

Figure 78. *Use of standard cost headings.*

Record deviations

The flow of cost and estimating information as a project develops must be effectively channelled to the estimator. He can then analyse and report the effects, particularly where the estimate is used as the basis of the project cost control system.

Except for the smallest projects, review of all deviations and their effects on project final costs must be made regularly. Ideally, good internal communication between members of the project team will allow deviations to be identified as early as possible; the timing of a report issue, say monthly, will then depend on the project schedule. This is a necessary discipline for management information and control, but is surprisingly often lacking, even in large organizations. Frequently, the cost estimate is regarded as 'frozen' at an early approval stage and may be ignored until too late, when extras have mounted-up and the project is financially insecure.

Table 12. Cost headings for a contracting company.

Design	Categories for civil, mechanical, electrical, etc.
Field construction	Categories for direct, indirect, supervision, etc.
Procurement	Categories for each material class
Overheads	Categories for head office, field, etc.

The estimate by nature is a look into the future. As each project month goes by, work is done, value is earned, commitments are undertaken, contracts are completed, etc. All of these factors have an influence on project cost information and, consequently, the estimator must know of their occurrence.

The project manager's attitude to this discipline of collating, analysing and feeding back the information to the relevant parties for corrective action, where necessary, is very important. It has a fundamental bearing on the overall cost-consciousness of everyone involved in the project. Therefore, he must be seen to believe in the value of the exercise and must be able to insist on its requirements both to and from the estimator.

Review the estimate

As a project progresses and generates hard cost data, so the estimate must progress in parallel. If the costs are going right, it is an excellent indicator of all areas of performance. Unfortunately, the converse is also true. Thus the estimate which is reviewed regularly and accounts for all known information and changes to assumptions performs as a project signpost.

In addition to the monthly update, it is essential that the fundamentals of the estimate be subject to regular review. For a typical 2-year project, this is best carried out, say, every 4 months or at predetermined stages of completion. A review of the fundamentals should account for all expenditures and commitments to date and strategically examine the balance of work yet to be done. It must, therefore, not be considered as an update but as an in-depth evaluation of the financial status of the project. For this reason, all parties whose activities influence or have influenced the project costs should be able to account for their contribution and must be involved in the evaluation.

6

Data and information for estimating and tendering

Data required for preparing estimates has to be generated by investigation if it is not already held in a database. A database is simply an organized collection of relevant data indexed for easy reference. It could be computerized or operated manually, e.g. a card-indexing system. 'Information' in this context could be inferred from the data; or it might mean knowledge of relevant factors which affect the prices, e.g. cost of capital, scarcity of labour, delivery times compared to schedule needs, etc.

In either case, the build-up of any estimate requires access to data and information on the current prices of materials and labour, together with factors for productivity, etc. For example, a small builder offering a price to a householder for the construction of an extension requires the following:

1 A breakdown of all the materials involved (perhaps known as 'a materials take-off') where the items needed are detailed both in quantity and specification.
2 A breakdown of the work units involved, e.g. the square metres of brickwork or the cubic metres of concrete.
3 His own estimates of productivity, e.g. the rate at which bricklayers can lay rough blockwork. This might be four times faster than they could lay facing bricks to form an exposed wall surface and will affect his pricing accordingly.

Even in this simple example, the small builder is actually using a database of information which is:

- Factual – the materials and labour prices are relevant and current, as he uses them on a daily basis.

- Retrievable – the information could be in his head or easily obtained by phoning his local builder's supplier/hardware merchant or consulting a price-list.
- Based on experience – in pricing for the labour content, he will draw on his knowledge of similar jobs and the main variables which affect his outputs. For example, outdoor operations in winter might only be 75 per cent as productive as the same operations in summer. Or local shortages of a particular skill/trade could mean that he has to pay premium rates to attract the necessary labour.

On the other hand, an estimator working for a large multidisciplinary industrial contractor, following the same basic steps, will use a much more sophisticated system and database. Such organizations hold vast quantities of data and information on the factors involved in pricing every conceivable work operation. These range from conceptual design to final hand-over of a complete unit, such as a factory, a hospital or an office-block.

The data and information could be used to prepare preliminary estimates at the start of a project or to submit tenders for work where the contractor will be bound by his submitted prices – whether he makes a profit or loss. The approach in these two cases will be different:

1 For preliminary estimates for a promoter, an acceptable margin may be ± 30–50 per cent, generated simply by looking at the main elements of the project as shown in Table 13.

Table 13. Preliminary estimates based on main elements.

Project type	Unit	Order of cost (£)	Main variables
Hospital	Bed	100 000	Design, location
Hotel	Bed	40 000	Grade A, B, etc.
Road	Kilometre	700 000	Standard, urban/rural
Ship	Tonne	1 500	Function (passenger/ container/tanker, etc.)
House	Square metre	400	Design/location/ standard
Power station	Megawatts	500 000	Location, fuel, design

2 Detailed estimates must be built up on much more data and information about the actual scope of work, including designs and specifications. Such estimates could be used as the basis for 'go/do

not go' decisions or for committing an organization to a particular project path. The guidelines in Chapter 5 can apply equally to any type of project. However, the organization and extraction of relevant database information varies according to the nature and scope of a project as indicated above. Most industries have their own combination of traditional and modern methods of estimating costs.

3 An estimate prepared by a contractor for a fixed-price tender needs to be based on all the information relevant to the project. The project documents must provide a complete, accurate picture of what the price covers, particularly where the contractor is competing with others. In this case, a distinction needs to be made regarding price and cost. Generally, the 'cost' refers to the direct cost associated with an activity; the 'price', however, could be higher or lower than the cost depending on the contractor's tender intentions.

As examples, the approaches of different client and contracting organizations are shown in the following four case studies. The cases are chosen from selected project categories which are not 'hard and fast' categories – indeed, there are many more similarities than dissimilarities.

The project types are outlined as follows:

- Rule-book projects, where the projects are mainly guided by bureaucratic rules and procedures. The example chosen, tendering for an aerial survey in Thailand, illustrates this category because:
  (a) The project was a government-type job.
  (b) The process of surveying means following the rules to obtain the required results, i.e. one cannot creatively construct aerial photographs – they must be produced to a certain clarity, at a certain speed, certain height, etc.

- Creative projects, where the success of a finished project may be judged on its creative content as a main criterion. The example given consists of the outline approach to preparing a cost estimate for the production of a documentary film.

- Team-work projects, which are characterized by a diversity of disciplines organized to achieve a common objective. While all projects require a team-work approach to some extent or other, the task of specifying, designing and building the new chemical plant, in the example, well illustrates the range of skills which are required for many complex industrial projects. Preparing cost estimates for such work requires a highly skilled and disciplined methodology.

- Task-work projects, which are characterized by having a high degree of physical skilled or unskilled labour input. Such an environment exists in site construction work and the cost estimates for this type of work rely on accurate scopes of work and productivity factors, adjusted for the actual job.

Case study 1: Tendering for a rule-book project

The Government of Thailand intended to review and update some of its ordnance survey maps for the north-western provinces, covering an area of 2000 square miles. For this purpose, it required an aerial survey to produce 5000 high-definition photographs suitable for photo-grammetric analysis. An Australian-based company was prepared to submit a tender although it had never worked before in Thailand.

In preparing a tender for the project a visit to Thailand was required and the following outline questions considered:

1 Special conditions of contract:
   (a) Currency – method of payment.
   (b) Air/sea/land rescue arrangements
   (c) Air-traffic control regulations/liaison with the Royal Thai Airforce.
   (d) Taxes and duties payable/recoverable for temporary importation of aircraft and equipment.
   (e) Special licences required.
   (f) The plan and schedule for the work including air-time, developing, printing and submitting results.
2 General conditions of contract:
   (a) Time of year/meteorological data (e.g. cloud cover, suitable lighting only available seasonally and at certain times of day).
   (b) Living expenses and conditions for staff including two pilots, mechanics, local drivers, etc.
   (c) Cost of insurances and local representation, e.g., agent's fees, legal fees, etc.
   (d) Operating expenses, e.g. hire/purchase of local transportation, cost/availability of aviation fuel in the region, petrol/diesel and other 'consumables'.
   (e) Communications and administration costs.

The answer to each of these questions affected the price-level of the tender submission and the company concerned had to look for both hard data and risk factors in its assessment.

The hard-data items, such as cost of living or operating expenses, could be readily priced. However, it was a more difficult exercise to provide cost data on risk items such as:

1 Arrangements for paying and recovering monies for taxes and duties.
2 Assessing the relevant flying times/ground times which depended on weather conditions and time of year.

On the other hand, the government department involved had made its own estimate of the project costs. This estimate could have been based on entirely different premises than those of the Australian company. For example, it may have taken into account:

1 Recent experience of similar works carried out by a local company or a company based in a neighbouring country such as Malaysia.
2 Use of a locally based aircraft temporarily fitted with hired equipment and local film processing.
3 Use of a locally based aircraft fitted with newly purchased equipment and local film processing.

Comment: Consider these two perspectives of the job estimate from both the client and supplier's viewpoints concerning motives:

• The supplier may have believed that he could command a high price because of his expertise.
• The supplier may have been prepared to take on the work at subeconomic rates to enter this particular market.
• The Thai Government may have been willing to accept a higher price on the understanding that high-grade results would be forthcoming
• The Government may have had a maximum budget price which forced it to use a lower grade but cheaper alternative.
• The Government may have wished to encourage a local organization to undertake this type of work with a view to developing local expertise.

Case study 2: Estimating for a creative project

Assume a National Broadcasting Corporation intends to produce a series of hour-long documentaries. These will deal with the typical cooking and eating habits and values of peoples from different cultural backgrounds, such as India, China, Russia, North and South America and Europe.

The value to the corporation of such a series is about £500 000. The corporation needs to estimate the costs of producing the series and the project may undergo the following development phases:

1 A 'project manager' (e.g. a producer) is appointed to investigate

feasibility. He considers general cost implications for items such as:

(a) scriptwriting,
(b) salaries and travel/living expenses for camera crews and production/direction staff,
(c) local technical support/casting,
(d) videofilm and editing costs.

2 Based on initially favourable estimates, a more detailed estimate is required for the basis of a go/do not go decision. The refinements necessary include:

(a) Estimating location times for different countries with a number of options
(b) More detailed costings for crews, including current costs of air-travel, hotels/accommodation, local transport rental, etc.
(c) Estimating costs for script writing with options.

3 This estimate is now presented for programme-board approval and, ideally, should have the following format:

(a) A summary and narrative outlining the project and the estimated total costs for different options, suitable for budgetary approvals.
(b) An explanation of the main assumptions and any other relevant factors such as estimated range of accuracy.
(c) A detailed, priced layout describing the items which have been analysed for each option.
(d) Supporting factual data such as quotations (written, where possible), costs for recent similar exercises in the various locations, etc.

Comment: This type of estimate is most frequently guided by the 'top-down' approach, where an imposed budget figure conditions and sets the attitude of the estimator. It is simple enough to imagine the estimator's job-approach if he is given budget figures of (a) £50 000, (b) £500 000 or (c) £5 000 000.

Artists, film-makers, chefs, research and development people, etc., can always expand their activities to suit the available cash, even though there is not generally a straight-line relationship between budget and quality of results.

Case study 3: Estimating for a team-work project

Assume the Du Pont organization, one of the largest producers of chemicals in the world intends to construct a textile fibre plant on its operations site in Northern Ireland. The fibre is already produced in a plant in the USA and Du Pont have decided, for strategic investment purposes, to construct and operate the new plant to serve the European market.

The local subsidiary, Du Pont (UK) Ltd, maintains a complete construction organization on this site, capable of undertaking relatively large-scale projects.

The estimate for the whole project will cover all cost elements, such as feasibility studies, capital costs, pre-production/start-up costs and staff recruitment/training.

The capital-cost estimate, for design and construction work, is prepared in the organization's own project engineering division in line with the client company's defined requirements. The development of this vital part of the overall estimate is based on mature project management systems and follows the path outlined below:

- The project parameters are developed under the guidance of an investment manager, who determines available options for initial estimating.
- The estimating function of the project engineering department is involved at the earliest phase and receives preliminary briefings and data from the client and the investment manager.
- The estimator is appointed and prepares initial outline costings based on general breakdowns of each involved asset and design discipline such as:
  (a) Buildings: civil, structural, architectural work.
  (b) Process: mechanical equipment; piping and storage vessels; electrical and instrumentation.
  (c) Services: heating, ventilating and air-conditioning; fire protection; lighting and communications.

- The initial estimate, known as a 'venture guidance appraisal' is based on judgement with minimum information and is open to a wide range of accuracy. It is subject to review by a project-management group and, after agreement with or without changes, is approved for the next stage.
- The estimate is now developed in detail, according to an agreed scope of work, project strategy and available design information. Major equipment items, for example, are costed by inquiry to manufacturers.

  Buildings are costed from databases of similar types, with factors for scope differences. Other elements are developed in outline and quantities of cables, cabletray, pipework, insulation and instrumentation are computed and costed from standard cost information relevant to the site.

Design fees for external design contractors, project engineering department fees, overheads (direct and indirect) are all considered and costed. The estimate is divided into *design areas* (perhaps up to fifty for this £40 million project) and *type of work categories* for costing of direct field labour. (These are also used later for tax/ accounting purposes.) Work suitable for contracting out is defined in packages where possible and cost-estimated accordingly.

- A standard coding system is used to identify each cost element of the estimate. This coding system is used for individual multiproject cost control and forms the basis of a computerized, integrated system.
- Currency implications and inflation rates are considered and summarized for projected movements over the expected life of the project. These costings are provided with descriptive comment on each item above and presented on a computerized print-out for distribution and comment from the main parties involved.
- Following client review and approval, the estimate is considered as 'frozen' with appropriate contingency factors, generally of the order of 3–9 per cent. This is then used as a basis for allocating capital funds.

Comment: As is typical in complex projects conducted by experienced groups, estimating is treated as a functional activity. The major project parameters are developed by others and the estimate relies for its quality both on the expertise of the estimators and the validity of the information provided. The general flow of information is illustrated in Fig. 79.

The main features of this type of estimate depend exclusively on whether or not an existing system is available. At either extreme the following comments are relevant:

- Project strategic considerations must take precedence, i.e. project-management performance objectives of time, cost and quality standards must be served by the estimating process; the purposes for which different estimates are required must therefore be clearly defined. (Although this particular estimate involves site construction work, the majority of the expenditures will be in professional services and materials. The direct-labour element on the actual construction site is perhaps 15–20 per cent of the total cost. Therefore, refinements in estimating accuracy will concentrate on those areas which account for 80 per cent of the costs.)

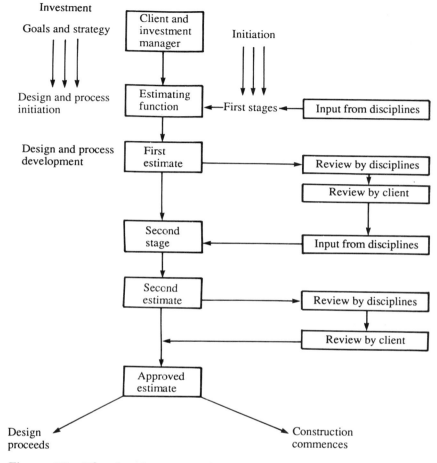

Figure 79. *The development of an estimate for a chemical plant.*

- The estimate must be reviewed regularly and critically examined on its main points with reference to expenditures already made, commitments in hand and the balance of works at that time. Erroneous assumptions must be highlighted and any course of action analysed and agreed by top management or the client whose money is at risk.
- If an existing, proven system is not already established, it is most important that the *basis* for an original estimate, and subsequent reviews, is sufficiently firm for overall project control (in relation to the total costs). It requires discipline to maintain, but this is preferable to unpleasant surprises at later stages. The attitude that 'it will cost

what it costs' is unnecessary and can be a recipe for disaster, as many promoters have discovered the hard way.

Case study 4: Tendering for a task-work project

An American corporation has built a $50 million medium-density fibre board plant in Ireland. At the heart of the process a 6400 t hydraulic press was to be constructed. The press was being manufactured in the USA (cost exceeding $1 million) and required extensive on-site mechanical assembly work. The press manufacturers had wide experience in this type of operation and estimated that around 20 000 man-hours were required for assembly over a period of 6 months. Five Irish companies were invited to submit fixed-price tenders for the work.

Apart from each company's managerial philosophy and political, market or strategic reasons for deciding on a price-level, the companies' estimators were required to visit the manufacturer. This was to gain knowledge of the machine, its components, methods of assembly and types of plant or equipment required for erection purposes.

Additionally, each estimator had to work with his knowledge about the levels of skill and productivity of his company's supervision and work-force. Their estimates for this job were thus conditioned by the knowledge of the organization and control of the physical efforts required as they envisaged them.

Tenders when submitted, ranged from £100 000 to £300 000. The contract was awarded to a company whose price was around £165 000 on the following basis:

- The company had a good reputation for work of this nature.
- The estimated total man-hours and breakdown into various subsections was in line with general expectations.
- Most importantly, the company stated without qualification that this was indeed a fixed-price and that all documentation had been sufficient. Their price included 10 per cent contingency factor for 'normal' unforeseen items not described or included (such as misfits, rework on site, damages, etc.). The other tenders were ambiguous on this point.

The client elected to award the contract at a fixed price of £150 000, removing several identified risk elements for his own expenses. These included costs of rework (his expenses to be recovered from the manufacturer) and costs of cranage which was estimated at £6000–£8000. The contract, in fact, was successfully completed.

Comment:

- Task-work projects involving physical labour depend largely on the attitude of management and commitment to the task in hand for success. When organizations like these Irish companies estimate the man-hours on such a project, they must do so with:
  (a) Experience of the general nature of the work tendered for.
  (b) An intimate knowledge of their own capabilities in organizing and achieving the output results required.

- Apart from standard rates on unit items (such as the labour times for fabricating and installing pipework on a per-metre basis), each site environment must be considered and given a factor or factors to be applied to standard rates. For example, a job on a small site based locally may have a man-hour factor of 0. 9, whilst a job carried out 100 miles from the home-base, on a large site with potential industrial relations or productivity problems, may have a factor of 1.8. These considerations can only be analysed on the basis of experience and judgement and should be subject to review at the tender stage by the site manager who eventually will be responsible for their achievement or control.

- From the client's point of view, it is always advisable that he carry out an analysis of the scope of work and estimates the man-hours involved before receiving tenders. This allows for a baseline comparison of all tenders and can validate other areas of his own control estimate (or cause them to be reviewed).

These examples have been chosen to show the wide range of conditions under which project cost estimates can be required and used. No estimate may be taken as infallible but nevertheless is an essential part of the project process. Certain industries use control estimates routinely, while others, particularly those new to the project management field, could greatly benefit from the contribution that effective estimating and estimate control/development offer to project success.

7

Cost-estimating terms and practices

The nature and general philosophy of estimating was described in Chapters 5 and 6. This chapter outlines the estimating process and the main terms used in practice.

Types and quality of estimates

The promoter's estimate

A client/promoter involved in a project uses estimates at different project phases and for different purposes. His estimates must cover the *total* project costs including, for example:

- development,
- design and construction,
- commissioning and preproduction/start up,
- operating and maintenance,
- finance,
- decommissioning,
- environmental protection.

It starts with an *indefinite* scope of work which is further refined as the project proceeds. There is not one 'best method' for such estimates – the methods chosen and used by various organizations are influenced by:

- Size – large organizations tend to have rules and procedures which lay down very definite methodologies.
- Industry – estimating methods vary considerably between industries, e.g. the construction industry has developed highly formalized methods of estimating for standard forms of construction. Other organizations, e.g. those associated with research and development

work, use a more open-ended approach. They tend to draw up a budget based on general assumptions rather than on an estimate for a defined scope of work.

- Stage of project and quality of estimate required. Since estimates depend upon the type of information available, the stage of the project life affects the nature and quality of the estimate. For example, in manufacturing or construction projects, the estimates for capital costs typically develop as shown in Fig. 80.

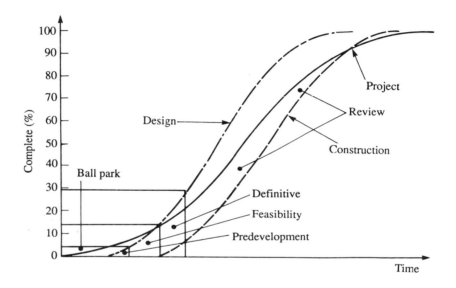

Figure 80. *Estimate quality at various stages.*

The estimate quality may be assessed as follows:

- Ball-park estimates are based on minimum information and indicate the *order of magnitude* of likely costs. They are used at the project committee level, where, for example, consideration may be given to various options on possible investments. If a client has funds available up to say £20 million, the ball-park estimate for a project of £15 million will receive much more thorough consideration than one of £50 million.

- Venture guidance or predevelopment cost estimates may be produced before design reaches 10 per cent (in some cases, where market pressures dictate an immediate decision, design work is not available).

Estimates at this stage will be prepared for economics comparisons with other projects and may be based on:
(a) Preliminary scope of work, design and study reports.
(b) An outline strategy, plan and schedule.
(c) Historical data available from similar projects.
(d) Current market prices for equipment.
(e) An assessment of real-estate or property costs if a new site is needed.

The range of accuracy may be ± 40 per cent and this may be sufficient for approval for funds to proceed to a further design stage only. ·

• Feasibility or budget estimates may be produced when design is about 5–15 per cent complete. They are generally prepared for full fund appropriation purposes or at least approval for further project action. Estimating will rely on:
(a) All major design elements defined.
(b) Strategy established
(c) Statistical data and current industry costs for similar work.
(d) Preliminary plant and building arrangements available.
(e) Site location and environmental studies completed.
(f) An industrial process flow-sheet, if there is to be one, developed sufficiently so that all major equipment, utilities and process services can be defined and costed.
(g) The level of grant-aid or capital contributions to/from public bodies or utility suppliers established.
(h) Sources, methods and costing of finance are known.

The range of accuracy may be ± 25 per cent.

• Definitive or control estimates are used both as the basis for full funding (if this was not granted at the feasibility stage) and for cost control. The range of accuracy is normally required to be in the area of ± 10 per cent; this means that the design process must be around 20–30 per cent complete with all main parameters identified and costed. For example, procurement needs to be at the stage where vendors' prices are firm with known delivery dates incorporated in the overall plan and schedule.
• Review estimates may be carried out at any time but will generally be related to 'estimates to complete' where the balance of work still to be done is critically examined in relation to the cost data generated in the project to date.

The vendor's or contractor's estimate

Whilst the project promoter may use an estimate based on indefinite information, at least in the initial stages, the vendor or contractor will require much more detailed information to prepare an estimate for tender or bid purposes. (The nature of contracts for fixed-price and other forms of offers is dealt with in Chapters 13 and 14.)

The vendor's estimate needs to be based on:

- A definite scope of work, described completely in drawings, specifications, etc.
- Defined conditions of contract which may be both general (for the industry) and particular (for the project).
- The owner's required delivery schedule.

The work-breakdown structure

The estimate is a collection of costs related to assessed quantities of work, materials and productivity ratios which will be agreeably generated in the project execution. It is essentially a static document, based on an overview which looks at a still picture of a project, as if it were completed in 1 day as in Fig. 81.

The estimate by nature is an expectation of what project activities will cost, even when regularly revised to reflect the latest project-

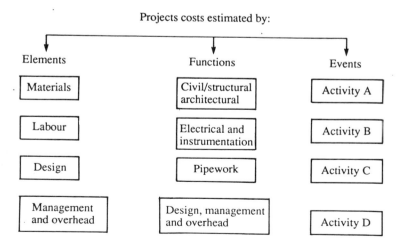

Figure 81. *Project cost estimating methods.*

generated data. Fig. 81 shows how estimates may be derived in different ways by using:

- Elements, where the whole project is broken down into its basic components, starting with people (labour, design, management) and things (materials, overheads). The individual items are then priced by whatever means are available to the estimator and are appropriate to the nature of the project.

- Functions, where the whole project is broken down into main categories of similar types of work. These categories, as shown in Fig. 81, are based upon project management by function and are particularly useful:

  (a) In a combined multidisciplinary and multiproject environment where individual managers are responsible for their own departments and as such provide a service to an individual project.

  (b) In a project allocated to a general or managing contractor who is responsible for the performance of individual specialist sub-contractors.

- Events, where the whole project is broken down into discrete 'work packages', representing individual project units. This type of estimating generally integrates the costing of functional elements and the two are frequently related according to a work-breakdown structure for control purposes. This may be activity-or event-oriented and can form a picture, for example, of the whole construction phase of a project as shown in Fig. 82. If, for example, the work was to be awarded to contractors with individual specialities, the project could

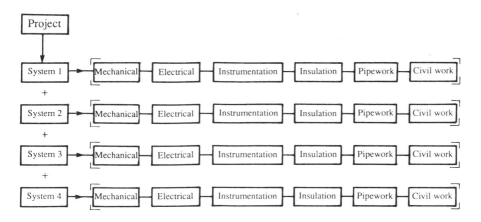

Figure 82. *Work breakdown by system.*

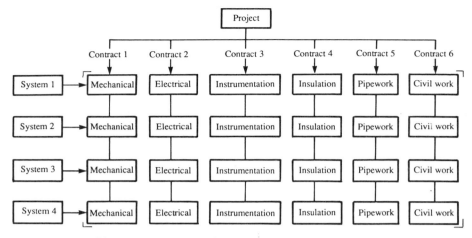

Figure 83. *Work breakdown by contracts.*

be represented as in Fig. 83. This type of work breakdown allows the whole project to be defined in 'work packages' which are subject to management control. The work packages can be chosen to fit into the overall project scheme for planning/execution and cost control. In this case, the work packages must be related to the coding of the various accounts used in the project.

The codes of accounts

The coding of constituent accounts in an estimate could be either uniquely derived for a one-off project or follow a standard convention in a multiproject environment. In either case, the accounts coding should relate to the work-breakdown structure so that consistency is maintained across the estimating and control systems. Consistent coding permits computer handling of all estimating and cost data. A typical coding system is shown in Fig. 84.

At the account level, the coding system may indicate:

Project	Area	Electrical work	Terminating cables
2487	5000	10	2330

Project	Pump station	Mechanical equipment	Air compressors
1321	70	5000	4018

This type of coding convention is most useful where different estimators are working on estimates for different areas in the same project. It is then possible to summarize all the related accounts for

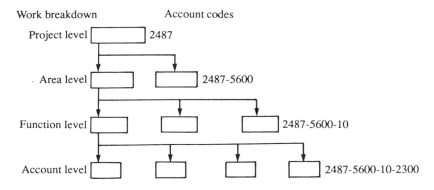

Figure 84. *Work breakdown and account codes.*

similar types of work as, for example, all the electrical-work codes will have the code -10- which may be used for indexing and computer sorting.

Fig. 85 is an estimate summary sheet based on a coding system; this system is owned by Du Pont and does not necessarily suit other companies. The accounts codes elements may be identified from this sheet as follows:

Site no.	8640	Identifies location
Project no.	3179	Identifies the project
Area	4051	Identifies the area
Unit	5	Identifies items related to the PS-3 storage tank
Item	1	Identifies items related to the units
TWC	1200	Type of work category for estimating labour elements
FUN	2	Identifies craft or function involved

A complete account code for an element of this project would then have the form:

8640-3179-4051-5-1 – for a purchased item

or

8640-3179-4051-1220 – for labour expenses.

The account coding standardized in this way can apply across all systems such as:

● estimating,
● cost control,
● cost accounting,

Proj: PPP   Part   Report 881   Date 01/23/8G   Time 08:9:14

Department – textile fibres   Title – Facility (CAC)   Site: International details   Site number – 8640   Estimated by

Pounds at 1.35 = $1.00

#	Design area	Unit	Item	elm	TWC	F U/N	Description	Amt UM	S R C	Labour	Field material	Wilm material	Total
1	4251				:DMF EQU:		Solution prep-common			Origin	Origin	Origin	Origin
3	4251	1	4		1200	2	Calibration pot, 340L S/S	1 EA	E			U 1590	1590
4	4251	1	4		1200	2	292 L, 2' dia, 2'TT, vert					U	
6	4251	2	1		1200	2	PS3 feed tank, 340L S/S	1 EA	E			134 10	134 10
7	4251	2	1		1200	2	23356 L, 8'dia, 15'TT, horiz					U	
9	4251	2	2		1200	2	PS3 sump pump alloy 20	1 EA	V	40		4620	4620
10	4251	2	3	60	1600	6	Motor & pump 2 hp	1 EA	V		30	200	200
12	4251	3	1		1200	2	PS3 feed pump, centrif.	1 EA	V			2230	2230
13	4251	3	1		1200	2	33.8 M HD, 16.3 M 3/H alloy 20						
14	4251	3	1	60	1600	6	Motor, 7.5 hp	1 EA	V	40	50	310	400
16	4251	3	2		1200	2	PS3 feed pmp, centrif.	1 EA	V			2230	2230
17	4251	3	2		1200	2	33.8 M HD, 16.3 M 3/H alloy 20						
18	4251	3	2	60	1600	6	Motor 7.5 hp	1 EA	V	40	50	310	400
20	4251	4	1		1200	2	PS3 filter, 3" S/S	1 EA	Q			109 80	109 80
21	4251	4	1		1200	2	Carridge w/legs						
22	4251	4	1	1	1200	2	Manual hoist, 2 ton 15' lift	1 EA	E			770	770
23	4251	4	1	2	1200	2	Manual hoist, 5 ton 10' lift	1 EA	E			1470	1470
25	4251	4	2		1200	2	PS3 filter, 3" S/S	1 EA	Q			109 80	109 80
26	4251	4	2		1200	2	Carridge w/legs						
28	4251	5	1		1200	2	PS3 cooler, SS/SS, 917 SF	1 EA	E			18 700	18 700
29	4251	5	1		1200	2	DBL tube sheet						
30	4251	5	1		1200	2	Monorail & man hoist			710	1780		2490
32	4251	5	2		1200	2	Chilled water heater, C/S	1 EA	V			2620	2620
33	4251	5	2		1200	2	78400K CAL/H 21SF 8'0 X 4' TL						
35	4251				1200	2	Equipment installation	1 EA	E	2750	420		3170
37	4251	500	1		1500	5	H & V unit #1	1 EA	V			106 830	106 830
38	4251	500	1	60	1600	6	Fan motor, 125 hp	1 EA	V	460	140	7280	7880
39	4251	500	1	61	1600	6	Fan motor, 20 hp	1 EA	V	120	60	730	910
40	4251	500	1		1582	5	Vendor start-up assistance	1 EA	E			2070	2070
42	42b1	500	2		1500	5	Sound attenuator @ H & V supply	1 EA	V			9420*	9420*
45							Page totals			4160	2530	196750	203440

Page 80

Figure 85. *Estimate summary sheet showing account codes.*

- permanent asset recording,
- procurement.

Estimating methods

Approximate estimating is based on the use of cost guides relevant to the nature of the work. Large client organizations and contractors maintain their own historical cost guides for categories of work which they normally encounter. In addition, a number of published cost guides are available for many industries.

The method is suitable up to feasibility-estimate level and is used where prices can be reasonably assessed on, e.g. a square metre basis for building elements or a per tonne basis for steelwork. Figure 86 is an example of an approximate cost estimating summary for electrical and mechanical installations, reproduced with kind permission of E. & F. N. Spon Limited (see acknowledgements and reading list).

Using factors is also suitable up to feasibility-estimate level and depends on the availability of cost data for a project(s) similar to that being estimated. Factors, from information based either on judgement or on general organization policies, are applied to scale-up or scale-down project costs relevant to a similar project in terms of:

- the scope of work or relative scale of the project,
- a cost index where inflation needs to be taken into account,
- location,
- currency,
- general project strategy.

A guide for the assessment of these factors and cost data may be applied to the previously outlined project categories as follows (see Table 14):

1 Hard data – items which can be quantified and costed accordingly on known or accurate estimated prices.
2 Soft data – items whose risk factor must be assessed or where accurate estimate costings cannot be obtained.
3 Ancillary data – relevant items peculiar to the operating environment of the project.

Detailed methods must be used for definitive or cost-control estimates. In these cases, it is necessary to have a detailed scope of work and complete specifications as well as a cost database.

ELEMENTAL COST PLAN

Element	Total cost of element	Cost of element per m² of floor area
ELECTRICAL SERVICES	£ £	£
Sub-mains installation		
Budget estimate for supply and installation of sub-station equipment @ approximately £46.64 per kVA. Floor area of 2400 m² at aproximately 0.777 kVA per m² . . .	8619.07	
12 way metal clad S.P. & N. sub-distribution board complete with M.C.B.s, 8 No # £118.70 (p. 333) . .	949.60	
100 amp T.P. & N. fuse switch, 1 No @ £171.95 (p. 331) .	171.95	
200 amp T.P. & N. fuse switch, 2 No @ £245.10 (p. 331)	490.20	
50 mm² four core PVC, S.W.A., PVC cable, 60 m @ £11.53 (p. 346)	691.80	
Terminations, 18 No @ £24.08 (p. 347)	433.44	
70 mm² four core PVC, S.W.A., PVC cable, 120 m @ £14.5 (p. 346)	1744.80	
Terminations, 4 No @ £25.23 (p. 347)	100.92 13,201.78	5.50
Power installation		
20 mm black enamelled conduit, 300 m @ £7.99 (p. 335) .	2397.00	
20 mm galvanized conduit, 40 m @ £9.27 (p. 335) . .	370.80	
2.5 mm² single core, PVC insulated cable,		
In conduit, 1500 m @ £0.54 (p. 355) . . .	810.00	
In trunking, 3000 m @ £0.44 (p. 355)	1320.00	
13 amp single switch socket outlet with plug, 40 No @ £9.8 £9.85 (p. 361)	394.00	
13 amp switch connection unit with neon indicator, 2 No @ £10.45 (p. 362)	20.92	
Budget estimate for conduit, cables and control gear for Kitchen equipment	4770.00 10,082.72	4.20
Connections to mechanical services		
2400 m² @ £5.30	12,720.00 12,720.00	5.30
Lighting installation		
2 mm black enamelled concealed conduit, 1150 m @ £7.99 (p. 335)	9188.50	
20 mm galvanized conduit, 100 m @ £9.27 (p. 335) . .	927.00	
100 × 75 mm steel cable trunking. 140 m @ £12.67 (p. 338)	1773.80	
Bends 12 No @ £10.87 (p. 339)	130.44	
Tees 12 No @ £13.60 (p. 339)	163.20	
Ends 30 No @ £2.67 (p. 339)	80.10	
1.5 mm² single core P.V.C. insulated cable,		
In conduit, 4000 m @ £0.48 (p. 355)	1920.00	
In trunking, 4000 m @ £0.38 (p. 355)	1520.00	
One gang, one way, 5 amp switch, 40 No @ £9.68 (p. 358)	387.20	
One gang, two way, 5 amp switch, 8 No @ £9.95 (p. 358)	79.60	
1200 mm single 40 watt fluorescent lighting fitting complete with tube, 75 No @ £29.50 (p. 364)	2212.50	
1800 mm twin 70 watt recessed fitting complete with tubes, 340 No @ £124.85 (p. 364)	42,449.00	
Emergency lighting circuits including fittings, 26 points (fluorescent) @ £159.00	4134.00 64,965.34	27.00
C/f	— 100.969.84	42.00

Figure 86. *Approximate estimate summary sheet (courtesy E. & F.N. Spon Limited).*

ELEMENTAL COST PLAN

		Total cost of element	Cost of element per m² of floor area
Element	*B/f*	£ £	£
		— 34357.71	14.32

MECHANICAL SERVICES *continued*

Heating installation
Low pressure hot water boiler plant having a total capacity of 275 kW comprising 2 No boilers with instruments and boiler mountings, burners for natural gas, 2 No heating circulating pumps, 2 No hot water service circulating pumps, 2 No calorifiers boiler control panel and thermostatic conrol for heating and hot water circuits, automatic controls, all interconecting pipework, fittings and valves with all necessary insulation, feed and expansion tank and cold feed and vent pipes, flues testing and commissioning 1 No £48,500.00 . . . . 48500.00
Black medium weight mild steel tube to B.S. 1387 with screwed joints and fittings,

	Total cost	
15 mm diameter tube and fittings, 120 m @ £24.00 .	2880.00	
20 mm diameter tube and fittings, 500 m @ £12.00 .	6000.00	
25 mm diameter tube and fittings, 140 m @ £14.00 .	1960.00	
32 mm diameter tube and fittings, 100 m @ £13.00 .	1300.00	
50 mm diameter tube and fittings, 240 m @ £30.00 .	7200.00	
80 mm diameter tube and fittings, 90 m @ £40.00 .	3600.00	
100 mm diameter tube and fittings, 100 m @ £36.00 .	3600.00	

Bronze globe valve with screwed joints,

15 mm, 70 No @ £15.94 (p. 248)	1115.80	
20 mm, 20 No @ £21.09 (p. 248)	421.80	
32 mm, 10 No @ £36.28 (p. 248)	362.80	
50 mm, 35 No @ £64.80 (p. 248)	2268.00	

Cast iron gate valve, flanged,

80 mm, 8 No @ £111.55 (p. 247)	829.40	
100 mm, 6 No @ £149.20 (p. 247)	895.20	

406 mm high continuous sill line natural convector front panel, 560 m @ £62.96 (p. 230) 35257.60
Corners, 30 No @ £45.93 (p. 230) 1377.90
Valve boxes, 72 No @ £38.33 (p. 230) 2759.76
35 mm single element finned copper tube, 230 m @ £33.01 (p. 230) 7592.30
25 mm thick foil faced pre-formed mineral fibre glass fibre rigid sectional insulation to:

	Total cost	Total	Per m²
15 mm diameter pipework and fittings, 120 m @ £5.90	708.00		
20 mm diameter pipework and fittings, 500 m @ £6.30	3150.00		
25 mm diameter pipework and fittings, 140 m @ £6.70	938.00		
32 mm diameter pipework and fittings, 100 m @ £7.10	710.00		
50 mm diameter pipework and fittings, 240 m @ £10.50	2520.00		
80 mm diameter pipework and fittings, 90 mm @ £16.3	1467.00		
100 mm diameter pipework and fittings, 100 m @ £18.25	1825.00	139301.56	58.04
		173659.27	72.36

Allow for marking of holes, testing and commissioning, protection of the the work, record drawings and identification equipment, add 1½% 2604.89 2604.89 1.09

		176264.16	73.45

Add for general contractors' discount, 1/39 . . . 4519.59 4559.59 1.88

Total cost of mechanical services 180783.75

Total cost per m² of floor area 75.33

Table 14. Assessing types of data.

	Data type		
Project type	*Hard*	*Soft*	*Ancillary*
Rule-book	Number of films Cost per film	Climate factors	Cultural factors
Creative	Size of crews Cost of travel	Cost of achieving acceptable scripts	Experience/success ratio of director
Team-work	Materials of construction	Design team productivity	Staffing levels/ availability for operating facility
Task-work	Number of components	Cost of cranage	Degree of cooperation from client representative

A computerized cost database for use in a multiproject environment should have records maintained and updated on the following basis:

- standard account codes,
- date of entry,
- description of costed item,
- labour factors,
- productivity factors,
- source of information,
- comparison between the use of the record for estimate purposes and actual costs recorded.

The use of the database will require:

- a detailed material take-off,
- an assessment of the methods to be used in the project execution.

For example, the project could involve a substantial proportion of standard work categories for which the database is entirely suited. Where it is not possible to use the database, for example, if the project contains a high proportion of innovative work or techniques, then the detailed estimate relies on the estimator's judgement. This relates to the basic elements of the people, materials, methods and quality standards involved.

The estimate in relation to the plan/schedule

The estimate results in a grand total as if all the money were spent in 1 day. However, it must account for the project time-scale in several areas such as:

- Base date, i.e. the date on which the estimate is actually based and the prices ruling at that date.
- Escalation, where provision is made for future expected inflation or other related cost increase. This may be allocated on a *pro rata* basis to work packages not completed when the escalation factor applies or may be added as a separate sum based on the balance of the work yet to be completed in the relevant escalation period.
- Currency fluctuation, where provision is made for future expected foreign-currency movements either for projects in another country or for goods, equipment or services with a foreign-currency element. This could be allocated on the same basis as the provision for escalation.
- Cash flow, where the timing of future payments affects the working capital requirements and the associated financing costs. (Working capital is the difference between cash inflow/outflow and is explained more fully in Chapter 9 (Cost Control Terms and Practices)).

The estimate in relation to project strategy

The estimate is an essential part of the project strategy and could be affected in areas such as:

- Management methods, e.g. if the project will be executed using direct labour or contractors.
- Management policy, e.g. in instructions to the estimator, the management might prescribe various factors to be used in relation to currencies, escalation rates and so on.
- Contingency, i.e. where a lump sum or a percentage of the estimated costs may be added to the base costs to cover elements of cost within the scope of an estimate but not precisely defined in it. The use of contingency sums is at the discretion of the project manager/team, although the estimator would necessarily be involved in providing the cost information, particularly if a good team atmosphere exists.
- Estimate reviews, where the data generated in the project may be compared to the estimated figures and the balance of work remaining re-estimated on this basis.

8

Cost control

Introduction

The cost estimate represents the total expenditure of money required to achieve the project objectives. The project budget is:

- The planned allocation of resources for expenditure against the objectives.
- The basis for ensuring that money is exchanged (in the project process) by earning equivalent or better value than planned.

By definition, there are no profit centres in a project – only cost centres. These costs cannot be controlled as such – the control is only possible in the management of the exchange process and this is the fundamental difference between the *function of cost control* and overall project management. It precisely explains why cost-consciousness from inception to completion is essential for project success.

Strategic considerations

Resources are required to prepare and use a budget and their consumption must therefore be supported by equivalent benefits. These benefits must be directed by management effort in the exchange process and depend on objective information. The reasons for and procedures used in compiling a project's budget, therefore, should be understood and agreed by the project manager if he is to obtain maximum benefit.

Project budgeting and control methods vary as much as the scope and content of projects themselves. However, the main considerations lie in the following:

1 The reasons for a budget or control system.

2 Identifying relevant data.
3 Estimating actual progress.
4 Estimating the balance of work.
5 The time-response lag

The reasons for a budget or control system

Management of a particular project, even in a multiproject environment, is concerned with the ordering of events in a one-off situation – each project is unique and has its own characteristics. The criteria for success, though, are inevitably based on performance of the project objectives in the time–cost–quality framework.

Therefore, those conditions must be generated which maximize the opportunities for achieving project completion within the desired framework. For effective control of costs, the conditions must be examined for compliance with requirements at regular intervals and the following considerations apply:

The estimate

Whatever the estimating method used, an estimate is not, in itself, a control system. For this purpose, it must be related to:

- the time framework,
- the planned activities,
- the productivity of the project process both from the level of the individual activity and the overall project level.

Collectively, these may be known as

The control estimate or budget

This is where the budget relates the estimated sums to the time frame and attempts to provide a basis for projecting expenditures on, say, a monthly basis against progress (as shown in Fig. 87).

The control system

Neither the budget nor the estimate alone (or together) are sufficient for control. Control means taking action (or the ability to do so) and cost

Month	1	2	3	4	5	6	7	8	9
Expenditure	250,000	500,000	750,000	1m	1m	1m	750,000	500,000	250,000
Cumulative (M)	0.25	0.75	1.5	2.5	3.5	4.5	5.25	5.75	6.00

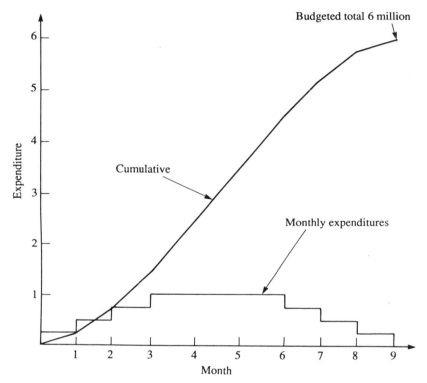

Figure 87. *Expenditure versus progress.*

control specifically means taking action on the basis of reports generated by analysing past and current activities together with the future projection indicated by the analysis.

Identifying relevant data

The budget is merely an indicator of what is planned; the only reliable data are facts of reality, not perception. This is the main issue in deciding which data/facts are relevant when a budgetary system is the basis of a control or decision-making tool in project management.

The strategic considerations in this regard, therefore, are not about the available computing power but in the directions and areas where that power should be best applied. The 80/20 rule (which states that 80 per cent of the costs arise from 20 per cent of the sources of costs) applies almost universally and is a powerful indicator of where the cost-consciousness should concentrate. For example, the productivity of construction workers on medium or large sites is often criticized. However, in examining the breakdowns of work/costs, the percentages shown in Table 15 may often be the case. Where are the greatest opportunities for cost control or cost incurrence? Or the greatest opportunities for cost savings?

Table 15. Sample breakdown of costs on a £50 million project.

	Percentage of total	Cost (£ millions)
Design, management, overheads	25	12.5
Materials	60	30.0
Labour on site	15	7.5

Precisely, they lie in the areas most effectively subjected to budgetary analysis and control – those areas where the most relevant cost-significant data are to be found. These may, of course, vary from project to project and the nature of what is relevant will vary accordingly.

These items, from a basic estimate, must be related to the project physical plans to extract the time-related budget. For example, if the total estimated or committed cost of a piece of equipment is £1 million the expenditures may be phased as shown in Table 16. The estimate for

Table 16. A capital expenditure budget

Month	Status	Percentage	Accumulated cost (£)
1	Deposit	20	200 000
2–11	Progress payment	5 each month	700 000
12–13	Delivery to site	10	800 000
14–17	Erection	5 each month	1 000 000

this project might show a total capital cost for this item of £1 million, whilst the *budget for expenditures* could be spread over nearly 2 years. This is very important where project cancellation must be considered. For example, if the project is stopped at month twelve, the committed expenditure at month ten could be either £700 000 or £800 000, depending on contract conditions. The committed expenditure (or commitment) is the money actually spent or committed to be spent and represents the *actual* exchange of budgeted resources as opposed to those estimated.

The primary differences between estimates and budgets can be detected in these simple examples and in the data and methods of measurements relevant to each.

Measuring progress

This is undoubtedly the most disputed area in any budgetary or cost-control system. The disputes happen because of the differences in personal assessments of progress compared with objective measurements. Physical quantities of hard-data items may be simple or complicated to measure; nevertheless, they can be measured. The difficulty arises in estimating the percentage of total progress against all the total effort which will actually be required. This can apply even where:

- Conditions of contract lay down the basis of measuring intermediate progress and how the payments are to be calculated and made.
- The client and the vendor have otherwise agreed, prior to the commencement of a contract, on these points.

For example, if progress payments are made to a manufacturer of a piece of equipment, it is quite feasible to pay 80 per cent of the total costs before he or the client discovers that a main shaft has been wrongly machined. Physical progress in that activity might then drop back from 80 per cent to 67 per cent complete if substantial rework is involved. (This is part of the 'cost of quality' – see Chapter 10.)

The considerations then are in regards to the actual situation, as opposed to the perceptions, and the total resources *exchanged* to have reached that actual situation. This is the area which really shows the comparative differences between a 'normal' operating business's yearly cost-budgeting system and the type of control system required in the project environment.

The project budget and control system simply must be tied in to the accurate assessment of progress and the resources exchanged to achieve that progress. Modern methods of cost control isolate units of the total work-load into discrete work packages. These are then related to scheduled events or activities on a network to examine the 'earned value' in relation to the progress made and resources exchanged.

These methods attempt to analyse the individual work packages, or cost accounts, to examine the effects of, for example, achieved productivity against estimated productivity and to use the results in a projection.

(The cost accounts in this context refer to the coding system used to identify uniquely the cost components in the estimate and control system. The codes used may relate to functions or disciplines. For example, design costs may be coded 1000xxxx, construction codes may be 2000xxx and operating codes may be 9000xxx. Coding like this assists cost allocation and computerized handling in a methodical way.)

Despite their individual merits, no single system has yet been devised to cover all eventualities in a unified manner reflecting the real-time project environment.

All major, experienced project-management organizations use more than one system and must be engaged continuously on upgrading their systems in the light of advancing technologies. The major aim of the advances is to tie-in the real situation with deduced facts, figures and projections which together form the project reality at any given time. For example, in practically every industrial project, a contract will be awarded to one or more companies to supply, fabricate and/or erect steel. Frequently, supply/fabrication and erection are separate contracts. Suppose the first contract is for 100 t, of which, at a particular time, 80 t have been delivered. The accountant or other financial person may accept that this represents 80 per cent of the value, i.e. progress jutifying 80 per cent payment. However, to the erection company or site project manager, the remaining 20 per cent may be the materials he needed first and, as far as he is concerned, progress is 0 per cent.

It is precisely in this type of subjective valuation that the real challenge in project budgeting and cost control lies. To take the example a little further, supposing the 80 t initially supplied has been erected, and the 100 t structure only requires another 20 t. In addition, of the 2000 man-hours estimated for erection, 1600 have been expended on the 80 t. Again, it would appear on straight facts to be permissible to pay both the fabricator/supplier and the erector 80 per cent on progress.

Maybe not so, however. Erection of steel commences with main members joined in a stable structural pattern. Thereafter comes smaller pieces of steel, known as in-fill steel. The whole must be plumbed, aligned, levelled and bolted to an acceptable specification. As much work may be required to fit the last 20 t as the previous 80 t. So the actual progress on the job may be closer to 50 per cent than 80 per cent.

The task of bridging the gap in this type of potential uncertainty belongs to the project manager. It is he, rather than the project accountant or accounting system, who must be trained to provoke the right questions because the truth is more readily exposed in this way than by accepting figures at face value. (In fact, systematic assembly/ erection sequences can be broken down into various elements; these elements may then be weighted by a proportional value for payment or progress reporting.)

Estimating the balance of work

This area of attention in the budgetary-control system follows on naturally from the previous consideration of estimating the progress. In simple notation:

Let A represent the original, total estimate.
Let B represent the expenditure at a later point in the project life.
Let C represent the balance of expenditure required to complete the project.

Then $A = B + C$ – doesn't it? The answer is, with the present state of knowledge, at best – perhaps. A better representation may be as follows:

1 The original, total estimate is based on the most accurate but incomplete knowledge. Therefore, it must be subject to a range, represented as $(A \pm \delta A)$, rather than a precise figure.
2 Similarly, the state of progress and resources exchanged at the point where B is measured may be represented as $(B \pm \delta B)$.
3 Finally, the estimated resources to be exchanged to complete the project may be represented as $(C \pm \delta C)$.

Then $(A \pm \delta A) = (B \pm \delta B) + (C \pm \delta C)$ is a more logical statement, and can be shown in graph form as in Fig. 88.

This simple straight-line form, showing progress versus costs, actually never occurs in practice. However, it is useful for showing that, at all times, some form of relationship must be defined for progress versus cost of that progress and cost of progress *yet to be made*. In essence, it states that, at point P, the future projection for the project

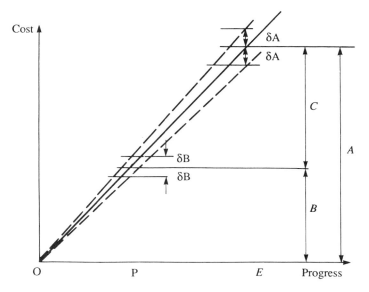

Figure 88. *The range of progress versus costs.*

must consider the balance of work to be done and the resources to be exchanged as a project in itself.

In the fundamental definition, a project has a definite start and end. Therefore, the project *OE* may be taken as two projects *OP* and *PE* where the point *P* represents the end of project *OP* and the start of project *PE*. This procedure demonstrates the argument for regular review of the total project in terms of the criteria established for project success. For example, 'Define the Requirements', page 80, Chapter 5 and subsequent sections of that chapter reinforce the view that the cost estimate must be regularly reviewed and revised in the light of changing project circumstances. The budget, equally, must be subject to review and revision at the same time.

The distinction is that, generally, the cost estimate lies within the functional territory of the estimator whilst the budget belongs to the accounting/cost-control sector which is more concerned with the logistics of the project cash flow rather than the detailed background to estimating data. The timing of and value earned by expenditures of cash are frequently as relevant to the project as the total cash resources to be exchanged.

The final point for examination is how increased *knowledge* of the project operating performance may contribute to the final project success. The initial approved project cost estimate and budget had to be

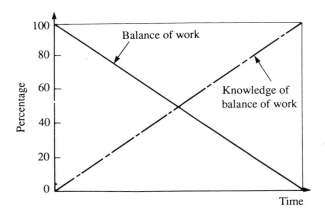

Figure 89. *Knowledge of the balance of work (1).*

based on the knowledge then available concerning the project objectives and the exchange of resources required to achieve the objectives. As the project progresses the balance of work decreases and the knowledge regarding that balance must increase. This is shown graphically in Fig. 89 which illustrates the extreme case over a project life-cycle, where, for demonstration purposes:

- At commencement, the balance of work is 100 per cent and the knowledge available is 0 per cent.
- The balance of work decreases uniformly whilst knowledge of the balance of work increases in direct proportion.
- The project is finally complete just as knowledge of the balance of work becomes complete.

Fig. 90 illustrates a more easily demonstrated case where:

- At commencement, the balance of work is at or near 100 per cent whilst knowledge of the balance of work is at or near 0 per cent.
- The balance of work progresses as an inversion of the typical project S-curve for completion.
- Knowledge of the balance of work follows its own S-curve, becoming asymptotic to the 100 per cent line and only finally reaching 100 per cent on project completion.

  These curves are hypothetical (how do you measure knowledge?) but serve to reinforce the argument for timely and regular review of all relevant project dimensions. Two final illustrations are provided to demonstrate the possible courses of a relatively unmanaged project (Fig. 91) compared with a relatively managed project (Fig. 92). These

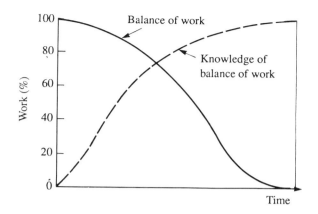

Figure 90. *Knowledge of the balance of work (2).*

figures show that knowledge of the work actually done and knowledge of the balance of work are intimately related in the context of project management and control.

Fig. 91 portrays the case where either adequate project-control systems are not available or are not properly used, while it can be seen from Fig. 92 that the regular review points could be used to:

- Assess the physical, financial and overall current project performance.
- Review the value of work done as earned value in relation to its effect on reducing the balance of work to be done.
- Take action to control deviations from plans.
- Determine and agree appropriate plans for future activities.

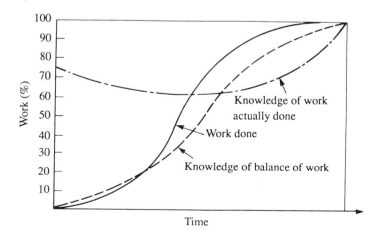

Figure 91. *Knowledge of the balance of work (3).*

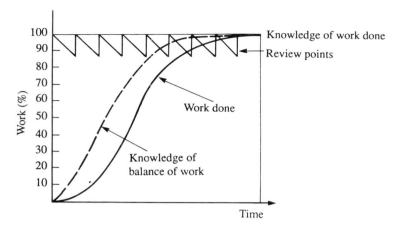

Figure 92. *Knowledge of the balance of work (4).*

These curves show that, whilst budget and cost-control considerations are important, the total project knowledge available and its use within the context of the budget are fundamentally more important.

Objective measurements

All estimates and budgets contain inaccuracies. These arise due to imprecision or uncertainties inherent in the particular project environment being considered as well as in the experience and range of knowledge or information available to the estimator.

The challenge, indeed requirement, in project budgeting and budget reviews is to keep identified risks within acceptable proportions by addressing both the uncertainties and hard data. It is the responsibility of those who operate the cost-recording and analysis capabilities to present the hard data on costs and physical progress. However, it is the responsibility of the project manager finally to endorse the budget or budget review.

Therefore, it is a definite requirement that the budget or budget review be treated with the greatest degree of objectivity possible. The decisions taken must be capable of defence on the grounds of good business practice alone, with all that that implies. For example, if uncertainty or risk in a particular area is so great as to alter the course of the project significantly, then all possible effort must be directed at the assessment and control of the identified risk. This is in keeping with the condition that knowing the balance of work to be done constitutes the basis of the estimates to achieve completion.

Similarly with knowledge of the work actually completed. Here the strongest temptation exists to report a higher percentage of physical completion than can be supported by later data. The balance between sufficient measurement and too little/much measurement depends upon the sensitivity of the items measured in relation to the project as a whole or to a particular element. These might lie within direct project control, like site activities, or be external, such as new government regulations or progress on externally supplied items. For example, if a new plant cannot be commissioned until high-voltage transformers are supplied and installed at site, then transformer manufacturing would be a critical factor if an indicated 3 month delay in delivery means late completion in any area or plant system. Similarly, delays in casting or script acceptance may fundamentally affect a film-making project even though other areas of the production are reported to be on budget time and costs.

Time-lag in information

Effective project management calls for decision-making in the light of the best available information. Consequently, project strategy should define levels of acceptability for the reporting of cost information in relation to the time-points of data collection and report presentation. This is the essential difference in approach required from the project-accounting and project-cost-control areas, as shown in Fig. 93 for an

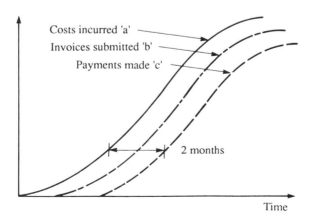

Figure 93. *Reporting cost information.*

assumed 12-month project period. In this figure it is assumed that the costs follow the line of physical completion. Line 'a' represents costs as incurred, 'b' represents costs as invoiced at the end of the month in which they occur and 'c' represents the payments made against certified invoices.

In relation to a 12-month project period, a reporting system which relies on payment disbursement only will have a 2-month lag between cost-occurrence and report. This is generally unacceptable, even for the smallest projects and indicates the scale of possible error.

Obviously, the closer one gets to a real-time total project-management system the better. However, in its absence, the system adopted needs to satisfy the best strategic compromise on the following factors:

- cost of measurement,
- cost of analysis,
- cost of reporting,
- anticipated productivity of resources versus actual,
- cost performance in terms of work done versus value earned (reduced balance of work to be done),
- schedule performance,
- projected expenditure commitments versus actual,
- trend analysis.

These factors are described in more detail in other chapters.

9

Cost-control terms and practices

The strategic considerations in cost control have been outlined in Chapter 8. This chapter describes the main terms and methods in cost-control practice.

The cost system

The cost system is the complete set of procedures established and used in a project for the express purpose of controlling the project costs. It includes the formal and informal relationships required with the estimating, planning/scheduling, monitoring and reporting functions, and, as such, provides the basis for:

1 Standardized methods of controlling individual project costs in the multiproject environment.
2 Cost control of individual projects by maintaining a current indicated total cost based on relevant, timely data and information from all sources.
3 Cost accountability by defining specific areas of responsibility within the system and by creating and maintaining the cost-consciousness of the responsible parties.
4 Performance monitoring by providing data and information on actual costs/quantities compared with those estimated.
5 Change control by recording deviations, e.g. in scopes of work and requiring relevant authorization(s).

The main terms used are defined as follows:

Authorizations are generally required for:

● Allocating funds to a particular project. Where an organization is operating in a multiproject environment, the limits of authorizations may follow the organization hierarchy and relate to general company policies (in this case, normally the higher you are in the organization, the more you can authorize).

- The spending of funds, again following the limits of the authorization. The distinction between allocating and spending funds is necessary because the spending must be controlled in line with the strategic reasons for which funding was allocated in the first place.

Contingency monies may be of different forms and intended for different uses, for example:

- Estimate contingency could vary with the quality of the estimate and at that level might provide for:
  (a) errors in estimating,
  (b) possible changes to design,
  (c) extra, undefined work which becomes necessary for the project execution,
  (d) management reserve funds.

- Budget contingency may or may not be approved in the same amount as estimate contingency; different elements of the budget might have different percentages for contingency.
- Forecast contingency may be based on factors which modify the contingency originally allowed in a budget on the basis of actual results generated in the project.

Net cash flow is the difference between income and expenditure for a specified period and could be:

- Positive if income exceeds expenditure.
- Zero if income equals expenditure.
- Negative if income is less than expenditure.

For example,

1 The promoter of a new manufacturing plant will have a negative project cash flow during the implementation and start-up phases. When the plant is producing, the net cash flow may be positive if the regular income is greater than the regular outgoings.
2 A contractor working on the construction phase will have an initially negative cash flow due to the costs of site establishment, work in progress and completed work for which payment has not been received. As the contract progresses, the contractor's invoices will produce income from the promoter and might lead to a net positive cash flow in a particular period. (Note that this will not necessarily

mean that the contractor will make a profit – this only happens if the total income exceeds the total expenditure).

Working capital represents all the money invested in expenditures like services, materials, work in progress and unsold finished goods. In accounting terms it is the difference between the current assets and current liabilities, where 'current' means payable or receivable within a year. Analysis of the working-capital requirement is necessary at the project funding level, where the financial arrangements are made:

1 For the promoter, at project appraisal, where external or self-financing may· be considered depending upon working-capital requirements.
2 For the contractor, in deciding whether or not to undertake a particular contract. In this case, particularly in a multiproject environment, the working-capital requirements for ongoing projects could exceed the contractor's capacity to borrow money and even a potentially lucrative contract might have to be declined on this basis (see Chapter 11) where 'Risk' is described as a project reality (pages 179–81).

Committed cost is the total value of the work and expenses which the promoter is, or will be, legally liable to pay at any particular stage in the project. It generally represents the value of all expenses incurred, whether or not they have been paid, together with the remaining value of any ongoing purchase orders or contracts, including possible cancellation costs.

Sunk cost at any stage is the total expenses which are irrecoverable in any event. For example, the sunk cost for a project cancelled at the half-way stage includes all committed costs, as defined above, less the value of any expenses recovered, for example, by resale.

Expenditure is the total value of expenses actually incurred and includes the value of invoices received or expected whether or not payments have been made.

Indicated total costs (or estimate to complete) may be compiled either by the estimating or cost-control function (or both) and is the best estimate currently available based on information from all relevant sources. A monthly financial or cost report, for example, could be in the form of an estimate to complete.

Trend analysis, as the name implies, seeks to confront variations in expected results with actual results for the purpose of extrapolating the perceived variance. A range of performance indices can be extracted from purely financial observations and these in turn could be used to provide insights into the behaviour of the project on a monthly basis. The method relies upon the use of a detailed budget projected from the start of the project to show the time/cost relationship between expected expenditures and the work done (or value earned) in the exchange. The relationship is generally in the form of an S-curve and requires the ability in the project system to identify various elements at a particular point as shown in Fig. 94. To forecast the final cost from the data at a point, the following procedure is used:

1 *Calculate the cost performance index* (CPI). This is the ratio between the budgeted cost of the work performed (BCWP) and actual cost of the work performed (ACWP) shown as CPI = BCWP/ACWP.

2 *Estimate the cost of the balance of work to completion.* The original estimate at completion (EAC) less the budgeted cost of work performed is divided by the CPI to yield the estimate to complete (ETC), i.e.

$$ETC = (EAC - BCWP)/CPI.$$

3 *Forecast the cost as the 'cost at completion'* (CAC). The figure calculated in 2 represents the anticipated cost of the balance of work to completion. When this estimate is added to the actual costs incurred so far, the total cost at completion is indicated, i.e.

$$CAC \text{ (forecast cost)} = ETC + ACWP.$$

Depending on how the project costs were originally allocated, trend analysis can be extended to examine unit elements of cost performance in areas such as:

- Craft labour or direct man-hour costs which have been estimated on the basis of target productivity. In these cases, where the cost codes for individual crafts cover a wide variety of work, both in quantity units and work-types, trend analysis will offer higher sensitivity to cost performance than a single, overall measurement because of an inherent 'smoothing' effect. Thus, if a particular activity was estimated to require 100 labour hours, but actually required 200 (i.e. a 100 per cent increase), then the reported CPI for that activity will be 0.5. However, because this performance is given a proportional weighted factor over the spread of total costs, the overall CPI will only be influenced in the same proportion. Nevertheless, attention will be drawn to all areas with a CPI of less than unity.

- Work packages, subcontracts, etc., where the accounts codes relate directly to individual work packages or subcontracts. The same argument applies as previously outlined for craft labour. However, it is difficult to match the sizes of individual work packages to a level

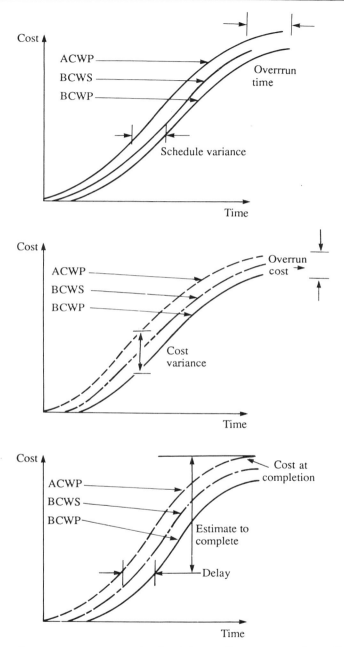

Figure 94. *Cost versus cost and schedule performance, where BCWS is the budgeted cost of the work scheduled, BCWP is the budgeted cost of the work performed and ACWP is the actual cost of the work performed.*

consistent with an idealized cost-reporting requirement. In this case, a compromise is necessary between the sensitivity of results required and a practical level of data collection/analysis suitable for the overall project-system capabilities. For example, if work packages are relatively small, it might be acceptable to report 50 per cent progress in the period when work actually starts on a particular package, with no further progress reported until 100 per cent completion of the package.

• Overall performance, where the benefits of trend analysis are applied to the objective of keeping costs within an authorized limit by using the indicators to direct management effort towards problem areas. The major benefit of this type of analysis is that it draws attention to potential cost overruns in stark money terms. This creates or maintains the environment where money-consciousness may be encouraged.

Change control methods provide for changes which may arise during the course of a project, such as:

1 Growth in the scope of work, related to either the schedule or quality/quantity of work in progress or required.
2 Costs associated with errors arising from design, estimating or methods of implementation.
3 Escalation or currency fluctuations.
4 Unforeseen conditions.

Whether or not provision has been made for these costs, their incurrence and effects must be recognized and controlled in the cost system. Particular types of changes are described in Chapters 12 and 14.

The cost system applied

Effective cost control must be directed by the person with cost performance accountability and depends more on result control than any other factor. Result control, in the context of cost control, means achieving planned value for money.

The reporting method needs to be tailored to the needs of individual projects and, like estimating, depends upon the size, type and nature of the organization's projects. Therefore, the effective project manager must look for those elements of the cost system which help, not hinder, this overall project result control. As in estimating, the effectiveness of the system will depend both on how the system is specifically applied and on the quality/quantity of the data and information available.

The data in this case will be relevant to the items of measured or assessed work, as discussed in Chapter 8. The relevant information, though, may be in regards to any internal or external factor which has a bearing on project costs, for example:

- Actual or possible future currency movements.
- Strikes or industrial-relations problems which affect the flow of equipment or materials.
- Legislation, e.g. new environmental requirements.
- Schedule deviations, due to productivity being higher or lower than expected or key items of plant not being available.
- Rises in the costs of fuels, materials or labour.
- Inflation.
- Extras or variations required which affect the scope and cost of works.

The use of a cost system cannot be treated in isolation from the general project environment – it must be an integral part of the total project-management effort and contain both formal and informal communications channels with all other functions. In this context it must be both efficient and effective where:

- Efficiency is derived from an adequate set of formal procedures and documentation.
- Effectiveness is derived from measuring, analysing and reporting upon relevant data and information *which is then acted upon* because it is relevant.

Examples of documentation used in the sophisticated project cost-control system of a promoter are:

1 Engineering department – work request (Fig. 95). This form is used to initiate or proceed with project engineering work such as studies. It is designed for use by the relevant engineer for submission to the business methods and investment department for authorization.
2 Engineering department change order. (Fig. 96). This form is used by design, plant or construction personnel for notifying project changes. The order is in a unique series for each project and form-type and contains fields for entering descriptions of changes, reasons, estimated costs, effect on project estimated cost, cumulative value of the services and authorization for the order.
3 ITC Report No. PCR-20-2 (Fig. 97). This form is referred to as a

EN-3278 Rev 8/88

ENGINEERING DEPARTMENT – REQUEST FOR FUNDS

TITLE_____

	PRIME	PART	SEC
ACCOUNT NUMBER			

PERSON REQUESTING
WORK_____

DEPARTMENT_____
SITE_____

REQUEST
RECD. BY_____

BUSINESS UNIT_____
FUNCTION_____

DESCRIPTION AND JUSTIFICATION OF WORK (Including Patent statement if applicable):

AMOUNT
REQUESTED_____

AMOUNT PREV.
AUTHORIZED_____

TOTAL INCL.
THIS REQUEST_____

RESPONSIBILITY
CODE NO._____

Work To
Begin:_____   Be Completed_____

ENGINEERING DEPARTMENT ONLY:
PROGRAM NUMBER_____

COMPLETE FOR SECONDARY

CLOSE TO_____

PREPARED
BY:_____

DATE:_____

APPROVED:_____

_____

_____

_____

_____

Authorizing Department
Must Complete:
1. Charge Code:

Gen. Ledger   Subaccount and Detail Codes [separated by (–)'s]

____ – _____

AUTH.:_____

DATE:_____

Figure 95. *Engineering department – work request.*

DESIGN DIVISION
HOW

PART 18
ITEM 202
PAGE 2
DATE 12/23/80

"D" CHANGE ORDER
EN-3915 REV 12/79

**ENGINEERING DEPARTMENT
A, C, OR D CHANGE ORDER**

CC: DPM _____(1)
PROJ. MGR _____(1)
CPM _____(2)
CONST. CONT. ENGR _____(1)
IN TURN:
MIE _____
PIM _____
IC 31 _____
INV. ENGG ___(Estimate Attached)___(1)
ENGG. DEPT IC-52 _____(1)

PROJECT NO ___1234___ ①

① D___ CHANGE ORDER NO ___2___ ①
(Separate Series for each type order for each Project)

FOLIO NO ___5___ ①

PLANT _____EDGE MOOR___ ①_____ PROJECT AUTHORIZATION S ___ ①

PROJECT TITLE ___FINISHED PRODUCT WAREHOUSE___ ①

TITLE OF CHANGE ORDER _____ADD 6" FIRE HYDRANT_____

DESCRIPTION OF CHANGE ②
Provide one 6" hydrant and
connecting piping (approx.
160 ft) adjacent to warehouse
truck dock.

┌─────────────────────────────────────┐
│ ① BY DESIGN ENGINEER OR DELEGATE   │
│ ② BY DESIGN ENGINEER   │
│ ③ CHECKED AND/OR INITIALED BY BM&I   │
│   INVESTMENT ENGINEERING   │
│ ④ BY DPM WHEN ABANDONMENTS ARE   │
│   SHOWN   │
└─────────────────────────────────────┘

NECESSITY FOR CHANGE AS PART OF THIS PROJECT

②

Per recommendation of Safety & Fire Protection Division.

1. Estimated cost – This change order at project level .... $ ② ③

2. Effect of this change order on estimated cost of this project .... $ ②

3. If line 2 is zero: Charge change order against ___②___ allowance

4. Total effect of _____ change orders (line 2) including this order .... $ ②

5. Abandoned design $_____ Abandoned related costs $ ② ③
(Not included in item 1, above)

Requested by _____ Date _____

Authorized by ___④___ Date _____

Figure 96. *Engineering department – change order.*

SITE NO 6550 NAME SPRUANCE VIRGINIA
REPORT NO. PCR20-2   DEPT-FIBERS
PROJECT NO. 4804   TITLE: DENIER/FOY CONTROL-PLANT 2

SUMMARY COST ANALYSIS FACE SHEET
(DOLLARS LISTED IN THOUSANDS)
AUTHORIZED 01-03-89   ENGR. MGR.   1100000   RANGE +10 -10   INV. MGR.
PAGE NO. 0120   DATE: 02-23-89   T B-REOC

DESCRIPTION (TITLE)	EXPENDITURES THIS MONTH	EXPENDITURES TO DATE	OPEN COMMITS	EXPENDS.-COMMITS TOT. DOLS	%AUTH KEY	AUTH 20. ESTIMATE DOLLARS	%AUTH	CONTROL EST.DOLS.	INDICATED TOTAL COST DOLLARS	%AUTH EST	NET EFFECT %AUTH +/-	KEY	PHYSICAL % COMPLETE
ENGINEERING & HOME OFFICE	12	199		199	99.5	200	18.2	228	210	105.0	+ .9	S	99S
FIELD INDIRECT	7	10		10	45.5	22	2.0	23	23	104.5	+ .1	S	
FIELD LABOR	83	206		206	93.6	220	20.0	231	231	105.0	+ 1.0	S	29C
FIELD MATERIAL	32	80	51	131	172.4	76	6.9	83	156	205.3	+ 7.3	S	
WILMINGTON MATERIAL	134	526	6	532	91.4	582	52.9	570	532	91.4	- 4.5	S	
PROJECT TOTAL	134	1021	57	1078	98.0	1100	100.0	1135	1152	104.7	+ 4.7	S	45S

SUMMARY PROJECT CHANGE ORDERS   AUTHORIZED DOLLARS %AUTH

DESCRIPTION	AUTHORIZED DOLLARS	%AUTH	KEY
C - CLIENT CHANGE ORDERS	35	3.2	S
TOTAL PROJECT CHANGE ORDERS	35	3.2	

COMMENTS
CAC. $800M AUTHORIZED 12/19/86.
CCE FOR PART II, TOTALING $1.100M AUTHORIZED 1/3/89.
PROJECT TEAM IS ACTIVELY REVIEWING SCOPE AND PLANS TO IDENTIFY
REMAINING TASKS AND COMPLETE THE PROJECT WITHIN
INDICATED CONTROL LIMITS.
AUTH P/C   9/89   M/C   7/89   ISSUED BY
FCST P/C   11/89   M/C   7/89

Figure 97. *ITC (Indicated total cost) Report No. PCR-20-2.*

'face sheet' and is used for the monthly cost reporting of a particular project on the basis of indicated total cost. This type of report is used for management appraisal of project cost performance and contains the essential comparative data on each item described on the basis of:

(a) Expenditure – this month and to date.
(b) Open commitments.
(c) Expenditures plus commitments – actual and its value as a percentage of the authorized estimate.
(d) Authorized estimate – actual and its value as a percentage of the total authorized estimate.
(e) Control estimate – which in this case is higher than the authorized estimate.
(f) Indicated total cost – actual, as a percentage of the authorized estimate and as a percentage net effect on the authorized estimate.
(g) The items in the 'Descriptions' column are self-explanatory except that 'Wilmington material' refers to the materials purchased through the Wilmington (USA) office.

4 Monthly reports by account (Fig. 98) and function summary (Fig. 99).
5 Management summary report (Fig. 100). This is a report prepared for use by a departmental project manager on the 'E & HO' (i.e. Engineering and Home Office expenditures).

The common feature of these reports is that they are using the same database but presenting selected information on specific report formats.

6 Engineering and Home Office 'Estimate to Complete' form (Fig. 101). This is a typical form used by the division for estimating the costs to completion of project-related work.

REPORT L~O13 FOR 89/05   PROJECT ENGINEERING DIVISION.   TIME 20:47:12   DATE 89/05/22   PAGE ~42

ACCOUNT SUMMARY - PROJECTS

21211   REOWILM   - MANAGER-RED-C&P WILM

ACCOUNT NUMBER PLANT / ACCOUNT TITLE	TOTAL AUTH $ / E&HO AUTH $	FUNCTION/ TWC	AUTHORIZED	CURRENT ESTIMATE	EXPENDITURES TO-DATE	EXPENDITURES THIS MONTH	BALANCE OF CURRENT ESTIMATE	% SPENT OF CURRENT ESTIMATE
6991-01 NIAGARA WORKS NY SODIUM-UPGRADE SALT CONVEYORS	1 750 000 265 000							
		2	132 450	132 450	125 396	10 801	7 054	94*
		3	4 000	4 000	1 752		2 248	43*
		4	27 000	37 000	23 985	3 055	13 015	64*
		5	6 600	6 600	3 278	980	3 322	49*
		13	68 500	68 500	53 872	5 717	14 628	78*
		15	10 100	10 100	8 663	1 908	1 437	85*
		22	8 500	8 500	8 716	1 063		102*
		23	1 350	1 350	1 142	590	208	84*
		24	4 500	4 500	3 711	684	789	82*
		25	2 000	2 000	1 620	160	380	81*
E&HO TOTAL		330	265 000	275 000	232 135	24 948	42 865	84**
					10 122	7 435		*

Figure 98. *Monthly report – account summary.*

REPORT L-5596 FOR 89/05 PROJECT ENGINEERING DIVISION TIME 20:52:12 DATE 89/05/22 PAGE 2817

271 EXPEDITING & PROCUREMENT - PROJECT DIVISION
28213 - MANAGER-REO-PETCHEM HSTN

FUNCTION SUMMARY - PROJECTS

ACCOUNT NUMBER / PLANT / ACCOUNT TITLE	TOTAL AUTH $ / E&HO AUTH $	FUNCTION/ TWC	AUTHORIZED	CURRENT ESTIMATE	EXPENDITURES TO-DATE	EXPENDITURES THIS MONTH	BALANCE OF CURRENT ESTIMATE	% SPENT OF CURRENT ESTIMATE
6402-01 SABINE RIVER TEXAS IMPROVED CATALYST DECANTATION	2 500 000 379 500							
28200 MANAGER-REO-HOUSTON		23	8 100	8 100	5 102	717	2 998	62*
TOTAL		23			5 102	717		
6403-01 SABINE RIVER TEXAS CENTRIFUGE IMPROVEMENTS	830 000 163 900							
28200 MANAGER-REO-HOUSTON		23	3 500	3 500	740		2 760	21*
TOTAL		23			740			
6565-01 VICTORIA TEXAS ADDITIONAL AQUEOUS WASTE INJECTIO	6 000 000 400 000							
28200 MANAGER-REO-HOUSTON		23	8 000	7 500	3 414	24	4 086	45*
TOTAL		23			3 414	24		
6780-01 SABINE RIVER TEXAS EAST AMMONIA STRIPPER CALANDRIA	550 000 96 400							
28200 MANAGER-REO-HOUSTON		23	1 900	1 900			1 900	´
TOTAL		23						
6869-01 SABINE RIVER TEXAS REPLACEMENT OF SUBSTATION NO. 9	440 000 100 000							
28200 MANAGER-REO-HOUSTON		23	2 000	2 000	72	72	1 928	3*
TOTAL		23			72	72		
6904-01 SABINE RIVER TEXAS PROPYLENE UPGRADE	5 600 000 793 000							
28200 MANAGER-REO-HOUSTON		23	16 400	16 400	766	537	15 634	4*
TOTAL		23			766	537		

Figure 99. Monthly report – function summary.

REPORT ...595   FOR 89/05   PROJECT ENGINEERING DIVISI...   TIME 20:53:36   DATE 89/05/22   PAGE 264

25230   B-REDC   MANAGEMENT SUMMARY - PROJECTS

    - MANAGER

ACCOUNT NUMBER / PLANT / ACCOUNT TITLE	TOTAL AUTH $ / E&HO AUTH $	FUNCTION/ TWC	AUTHORIZED	CURRENT ESTIMATE	EXPENDITURES TO-DATE	EXPENDITURES THIS MONTH	BALANCE OF CURRENT ESTIMATE	% SPENT OF CURRENT ESTIMATE
2838-01 SEAFORD DELAWARE IMPR QUENCH-EIGHT SPINNING MACHIN	1 800 000 226 000		226 000	227 000	173 709		53 291	76
4064-01 SEAFORD DELAWARE FREE DRAIN SALT HEADERS NYLON BCF	1 300 000 236 000		236 000	266 440	266 670			100
4449-01 SEAFORD DELAWARE UPGRADE FIVE T44 SM'S	3 500 000 380 000		380 000	599 000	689 874			115
4523-01 SEAFORD DELAWARE IMPROVED QUENCH T-44	1 100 000 120 000		120 000	212 000	197 421		14 579	93
4993-01 SEAFORD DELAWARE SPINNING COMPUTERIZATION-2 SPIN M	2 000 000 307 000		307 000	307 000	322 234	2 572		104
5641-01 SEAFORD DELAWARE IMPR QUENCH-SM 21/22/23/24	600 000 30 000		30 000	30 000	26 752		3 248	89
5823-01 SEAFORD DELAWARE SPLIT T-44 SM14	1 500 000 286 000		286 000	329 560	457 431	22 171		138
5992-01 SEAFORD DELAWARE BULK CHEST MODN-SM 27/28/29	1 000 000 250 000		250 000	250 000	152 128	10 062	97 872	60
5999-01 SEAFORD DELAWARE WATER TREATMENT UPGRADE	900 000 230 000		230 000	230 000	65 241	3 748	164 759	28
6220-01 SEAFORD DELAWARE SOL DYED ANTRON-SPIN MACHINE "M"	500 000 49 600		30 000	30 000	21 082	74	8 918	70
6347-01 SEAFORD DELAWARE DOW RECEIVER RELIEF VALVES	350 000 51 000		51 000	51 000	49 376		1 624	96
6362-01 SEAFORD DELAWARE DOWTHERM VAPORIZER FIRE PROTECTIO	600 000 149 000		149 000	149 000	25 288	3 391	123 712	16

Figure 100. *Management summary report.*

EN-1350A Rev. 6/85

ENGINEERING & HOME OFFICE ($M)
ESTIMATE-TO COMPLETE

DATE _____ REV. NO. _____

ACCT. NOS. _____ _____ _____
                WR   P&E   PROJECT

DEPT. _____

SITE _____

DM _____

TITLE _____

AUTHORIZED CONST. $ _____ % E & HO _____

ITC ___ / ___ / ___ $ _____ % E & HO _____

FUNCTION	CURRENT ESTIMATE	SPENT THRU _____	TOTAL	% OF E & HO TOTAL	APPROVAL
2 – PROCESS					
3 – MECHANICAL					
4 – ARCHITECTURAL & CIVIL					
5 – POWER-H&V					
8 – MECHANIZED SYSTEMS					
13 – ELECTRICAL & INSTR.					
14 – CONTROL SYSTEMS					
15 – COMPUTER SERVICES					
18 – DES. SEV. CONTRACTOR					
19 – PLANT CHARGES					
22 – INVESTMENT ENGG					
23 – ENGG SVCS-PROCUREMENT					
24 – ENGG SVCS-CONTRACTS					
25 – ENGG SVCS-PLAN & SCHED					
TOTAL					

● ABANDONED E & HO INCLUDED IN TOTAL

$M _____ % OF TOTAL E & HO _____

PREPARED BY _____

APPROVED BY _____
                        DM OR DESIGNATE

Figure 101. *Design estimate to complete form.*

10

Quality and quality assurance

Introduction

A customer buys/obtains products or services to satisfy his *own* needs – not those of the supplier. This simple concept indicates the starting point for *achieving* quality as '. . . the desire and capability to satisfy the customer's requirements'.

Managing a project is a service activity. The main issues, therefore, in the quality aspects of the service are in terms of:

- the requirements of the customer(s),
- the capability of the service to satisfy them.

These are expressed in the quality of service:

- available in the supplier,
- needed from the supplier,
- rendered by the supplier.

Quality in this type of consideration, though, is rather abstract for practical application. It essentially boils down to the 'I know it when I see it' definition – which might be fine for some customers but frustrating for the designer, contractor or vendor. These people need to know *exactly* what 'quality' means to the customer before they can deliver it.

For that reason, quality-related terminology has been built up on the basic definitions of quality, quality assurance and quality control. It is used to provide the distinctions needed in the concept of total quality, which is 'satisfying all the requirements of the customer'.

Terms and definitions

Quality terms are used in many international standards, including the British Standards:

BS 4778 Glossary of terms used in quality assurance (including reliability and maintainability terms) in two parts.

BS 5750 Quality systems (in seven parts), covering concept guides and specification for design, manufacture, installation, final inspections and test.

- Quality, according to one of the definitions in BS 4778 is 'The totality of features and characteristics of a product (or service) that bear on its ability to satisfy a given need.' This definition covers all general aspects of providing products and services. However, it may be extended to cover particular applications/topics by using 'determinants' and 'measures' as shown in Fig. 102. These describe the degree of 'fitness for purpose' of the product/service in terms of its ability to satisfy a given need; they also indicate how it 'conforms with its requirements' and these expressions are used in the general sense of quality.
- Quality assurance is to ensure that a project has been so designed and constructed that it performs as expected in service. It is the *result* of a planned system (covering all activities and functions) which *generates confidence* that services will be performed satisfactorily (or that products will perform satisfactorily when used for their intended purpose). Quality assurance, therefore, offers objective (i.e. independently verifiable) *evidence* of quality.
- Quality control, on the other hand, is the *implementation* of quality-assurance actions which *control* the processes or measure the characteristics of services/products to the specified requirements.
- A quality system (BS 4778) is the organization structure, responsibilities, activities, resources and events that together provide organized procedures and methods of implementation to ensure the capability of the organization to meet quality requirements.
- A quality programme (BS 4778) is the 'documented set of activities, resources and events serving to implement the quality systems of an organization'. This means that all aspects of a company's operations need to be written down so that:
  (a) Everybody involved internally in the organization has a reference baseline against which his activities can be measured.

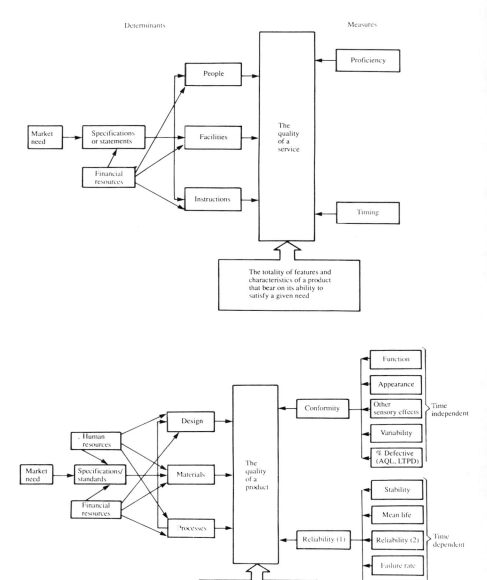

Figure 102. *Quality 'determinants and measures' from BS 4778.*

(b) External parties can come and inspect the documents and activities, e.g. to test/comment with reference to other standards.

The documents are shown in Fig. 103 and comprise the following:

- A quality manual (BS 4778) sets out the 'general quality policies, procedures and practices of an organization'; it represents the organization's quality 'philosophy' in conceptual terms.
- Quality procedures are descriptive narratives detailing specifics of:
  (a) What the procedure covers, e.g. procedure for testing concrete.
  (b) Who is reponsible, e.g. resident civil engineer.
  (c) How it is to be carried out, in detail, i.e. step-by-step instructions.

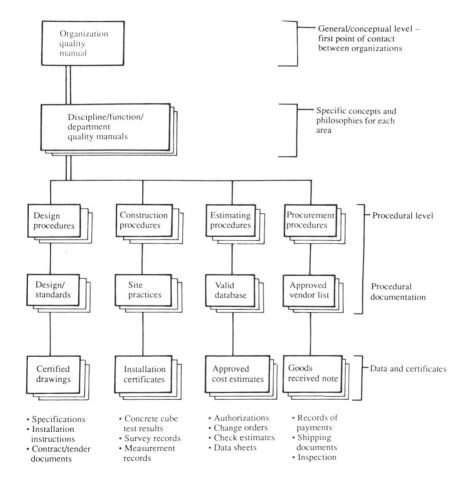

Figure 103. *Quality programme documents.*

(d) When, indicating the times in a process when tests are to be carried out, e.g. slump test to be performed on each batch of concrete before it is placed.

(e) Where, e.g. at the mixer or at the job-site.

- A quality plan (BS 4778) is a document derived from the quality programme (extended if necessary) setting out the specific quality practices, resources and activities relevant to a particular contract or project.
- Quality documentation records the result of tests or activities, e.g. cube test results/analysis sheets.
- Quality certification provides signed evidence, based on the quality documentation, that an item or service meets (conforms to) its requirements, i.e. it is fit for its intended purpose.
- A quality audit (BS 4778) is 'the independent examination of quality to provide information'. Quality audits may be carried out at different levels and for different reasons, e.g. products, processes or systems might be subject to internal or external audits.

Strategic considerations

Quality in its sense of 'fitness for purpose' is a key aspect of project management. As such, it needs to be considered at a high level – and executed at all levels. High-level consideration might lead to investment in a quality programme. This will define what is/is not acceptable quality for the organization – and will be the basis of the 'quality plan' for all phases of a project. The programme may or may not include the use of international standards or organizations certified to those standards. In any case, the main strategic considerations lie with the promoter of an industrial construction project and include, for example:

- Financial – the project must result in a facility/plant/installation which meets the cost objectives of the original investment decision.
- Reliability – (and integrity) of the construction in the long term.
- Safety – the owner could be legally responsible for the actions of all parties who work on his premises or property as his servants or agents. Consequently, he needs assurance that their actions do not leave him open for legal proceedings in the event of accidents during the construction; similarly, he needs assurance that the facility/plant will perform safely in production operations.
- Common understanding that the promoter/designers/contractors and

their representatives agree on the baseline standards required and the methods of measurements to be used. These could include, for example, relevant codes of practice for professionals (e.g. CP2001 'Structural Use of Reinforced Concrete') or self-developed organizational standards.

- Protection – against unfit design/workmanship/materials achieved by
- Implementing the agreed quality standards and quality control/ assurance actions during the course of the project through the quality management system.

In communicating his quality requirements to other involved parties, the promoter becomes a supplier – namely a supplier of information about the requirements. The quality of his input in this area is vital; the promoter's quality policy must therefore be developed through knowledge of his own needs and those of the *other* parties, for example:

Engineers/architects require	*Contractors believe/require*
Freedom to design creatively (but not to reinvent the wheel)	Time is money
To protect reputations	They may *legitimately* misinterpret specifications if wording is ambiguous
A clear brief or jointly agreed scope of work	To make a profit to stay in business
To understand where they carry responsibility for design adequacy especially if they could be sued later if faults occur	To minimize or avoid rework

These different interests need to be welded together. An approach based on early, clear, concise information to designers, contractors and vendors has a much greater chance of success than late developments of requirements. It is vitally important to avoid surprises when the project has gained momentum – changed requirements are likely to be very expensive.

The promoter's quality emphasis must then acknowledge that getting it right, first time throughout every project phase, will produce the cheapest, fastest and most acceptable results. On this basis, he must spend initial time planning for quality, thinking out direction and getting the strategy right – this is the basis for the quality plan defined before.

A quality plan is necessary in this key area because it:

- Forces people to be explicit – the terminology must have a common basis.
- Provides for understanding what is needed and how it is to be delivered.
- Can be declared 'up-front' and identified as to degree of importance.
- Encourages thoroughness.

The quality plan in industrial construction projects then needs to cover the areas of:

- organization,
- design,
- procurement,
- construction,
- start-up,
- documentation,
- inspection.

Organizing for quality

'Organization' is covered in Chapter 12. However, at this stage it is useful to examine the implications for quality. Firstly, quality upgrading in many companies is moving on the concepts of total quality. This covers *all* aspects of a company's activities, such as human resources, marketing, financial/operations/strategic management and so on.

While these activities affect projects, they are generally outside the scope of this book although some elements are covered in Chapter 12. 'Organizing for quality', therefore, refers here to the quality assurance/ control aspects of managing projects. These are sometimes known as 'little q' where 'big Q' is the total quality logo in the wider organizational sense.

BS 5750 requires that 'the supplier shall appoint a management representative, preferably independent of other functions, to be responsible for all inspection matters'. Inspection in this sense is not confined to physical inspections; it covers all inspection activities, including the quality programme and system.

The primary purpose of the quality programme is to ensure that verifiable evidence exists:

- In the completed article or item or delivered service.

- In all the activities involved in the production/completion including design, procurement, manufacture and installation.

Therefore, the 'inspector'/representative is responsible for ensuring that the system is not only capable of producing quality but is also enforced so that the evidence of quality is always available for external inspection. This means that he is obliged to act, in a sense, independently from company bias as if he were an outsider.

The challenge, then, is to maintain team performance by making sure that everyone involved understands that inspection activities, such as compliance auditing, are necessary and that quality/quality assurance is a top-level commitment. The quality organization for overall project control could then be established as shown in Fig. 104:

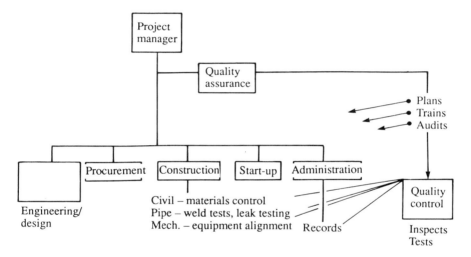

Figure 104. *Quality-assurance organization chart by function.*

Figure 104 shows an arrangement where the quality assurance (QA) department/manager reports to the top/project manager in a different relationship than other departments/managers. This allows the necessary degree of independence – but also shows that good relationships are needed with other departments as the quality-assurance/quality-control (QA/QC) activities affect all areas.

Quality in design

Design is a process which deals with the collection, analysis and synthesis of data and information. It generally divides into two main phases, namely:

- Conceptual design, which is the evolution and evaluation of possible solutions to generic requirements.
- Detailed design, which is the development of specific solutions based on data generated in the conceptual phase.

The client influences design quality (in its sense of fitness for purpose) by:

- Defining and effectively communciating his requirements, e.g. through scopes of work, detailed project objectives and so on.
- Systematically controlling design evolution/evaluation.
- Reviewing and approving acceptable solutions at every stage.

These are considered in the design phases as follows:

Conceptual design

This phase is used for endorsing the purpose of the project – studying/ testing/confirming for practicality, identifying constraints/obstacles, selecting project strategy/budget figures/time-scales and resource requirements. Designs at this stage are based on basic data (which is sometimes being assembled as design proceeds); studies are developed and options are proposed, analysed, evaluated and selected against relevant criteria.

Basic data is used to specify the functional requirements, e.g.:

- The raw materials used in a process; if the properties of raw materials vary locally it is vital to understand the variances and their influence on the process design. For example, tests for raw material character- istics are especially important in:
  (a) Timber processing, where the nature of local timbers may vary widely in different areas.
  (b) Petrochemical and chemical projects, where the nature and quality of the raw materials – 'feedstock' – can vary widely.
  (c) Cement plants, where clay quality is paramount.
  (d) Power stations, where choice of fuels may be decided by the economics and logistics of supply as well as the fuels' characteristics.

- The process design itself. Economies of scale might predetermine the nature and type of pressures, volumes, flow rates, equipment, materials of construction and so on. Innovation or technological advancement in process type or control could take the process design to the limits of, or beyond, existing knowledge.

- Plant location, e.g. based on economics or environmental considerations.
- Services requirements, such as electricity, industrial gases, processed waters.
- Design standards, e.g. standards/codes of practice must be acceptable in the country where the construction will take place – not the design. This fundamental item has been overlooked by organizations of international repute.
- Physical requirements, including land, buildings, infrastructure.
- Constructability.

These elements are all brought together for the first time at the concept design stage. It is clear that initial client actions and input at this stage set the tone for the quality of the result. Consequently, the system used for controlling the design development must be able to identify the critical issues for generation and use of the basic data – its type, quality and relative importance – in the design process.

The quality issues then revolve around:

1 The basic data, which is the input to the design process.
2 The conceptual design *process*, including its organization, control, phasing and costs.
3 The preliminary drawings, equipment arrangements, plans, schedules, specifications and cost estimates which represent the *products* of this phase.

These elements can be related to the basic definitions, namely:

- Design quality – is it fit for its purpose? Has it succeeded? Are the design philosophies consistent throughout? These might include, for example, 'minimum essential' design, safety, ecology, environment, use of vendor technology and so on. The design products will be used for procurement, construction, start-up and operations. The design quality, therefore, can be tested by how well it satisfies these requirements at each stage in terms of its functional purpose including timely delivery, cost effectiveness, practicality, meeting scope and overall accuracy.
- Design quality assurance – are there adequate procedures for using standard methods, checking layout drawings/calculations, specifications? Are the costs of using these procedures controlled? This is part of the cost of quality.
- Design quality control – is it being monitored/controlled against its

objectives as it is going along? Is there a system for quality control? For example, are all necessary data available before design starts on an area – are the design products subject to quality control against the agreed standards?

It is particularly important that calculations and deviations/changes to design are recorded. In this way, objective reviews/audits can be carried out by independent inspectors either internally or externally.

Client input at this stage, though, is *not* confined to 'reviews'. He should be actively involved, if possible, and ensure that all available resources are also involved. For example, concept designers can get out of touch with construction opportunities/constraints or the latest construction technology. There is no doubt that the input of experienced construction staff at this stage has a decided benefit to the overall design/construction process. (Construction staff in this context includes, e.g. quality assurance, procurement, general foremen/craft superintendents as well as field management. They do not have to be employed directly by the promoter – but clearly he needs to be convinced of the value of their input. They can contribute knowledge and experience of their specialisms by critically examining concept proposals for 'constructability' in the field. In addition, the involvement of construction staff at an early stage in the design development encourages a 'team' atmosphere which can only benefit the total quality effort.)

Detailed design

This phase builds on the option(s) selected from the conceptual design. For example, basic data may have been used for calculations on:

- The main forces involved for structural design (e.g. reinforced concrete or structural steel may have been selected depending on economics/suitability for design conditions). Detailed design will then concentrate on the selection of, e.g. section sizes, joint details and so on.
- The flow rates and pressures/temperatures in piping systems, in which case the detailed design will be concerned with the selection of pipe diameters/thicknesses, materials, jointing (e.g. welded or flanged), flexibility analysis and so on.

The architectural/process/engineering drawings, calculations and specifications are developed in line with the solutions generated in the concept phase. The important criteria in this phase include:

- Maintaining schedules for design stages and release for procurement and construction. This is a fundamental quality issue throughout the phase – unless the designers can meet their agreed schedules, they are not providing design fit for its purpose, i.e. on time.
- Controlling costs. Many design schemes are on the basis of 'reimbursable costs' which should provide value for money. Therefore, design costs must be monitored and controlled and the costs of quality assurance/control minimized, consistent with the quality results needed. Similarly, the *results* of design selections, which will be purchased, manufactured or constructed for the project, should be subject to cost reviews in terms of their effects on the overall budget. These might be part of wider constructability reviews, referred to above, which need to be carried out as detailed design proceeds, *not* on design completion, to minimize the costs of aborted design. It is still far cheaper to detect and correct possible errors or better detail solutions at this stage than under field construction conditions.
- Writing/preparing specifications, drawings and other construction documents for procurement and construction. These are the detailed products of this phase and some details of this activity are presented later under 'Quality in Documentation'.
- Obtaining planning/building permissions from the relevant authorities is a notable quality issue as even the most elegant design cannot be constructed in the field without planning/building permission!
- Safety/ecology/environmental considerations for all aspects of the proposed project.
- Interdependence between activities and design functions. Individual design disciplines depend on each other for accurate information:

    (a) Civil/structural designers are concerned with information on building loads, e.g. floor/wind/snow and equipment loads. Designs for rotating-equipment foundations use information on equipment weights, forces involved, torques developed (for holding-down bolt loads) and vibrations. Oversights or inaccuracies cause inadequate or overdesign leading either to wasted money or expensive field rework when (or if) the mistakes are later uncovered.
    (b) Piping designers need information on process/service conditions.
    (c) Heating and ventilating designers need information on heat gain/losses from equipment, structural elements and weather/operating conditions.
    (d) Noise control/acoustic designers need information on noise source amplitudes/frequencies.

(e) Mechanical designers need information on the process, materials required and operating conditions of service.
(f) Electrical designers need information on light/power requirements – motor sizes proposed, conditions of service (e.g. indoors/outdoors/explosion risks/environment classifications and so on.)

The room for error in these complex interrelationships is so great that a comprehensive system must be used. Liaison between functions is essential as the output from this phase (documents, specifications, drawings, detailed plans/schedules) is prolific. A typical £40 million project may have 3000–10 000 drawings, many with revisions, 200–300 procurement packages and over 100 separate contract packages. (Note that the percentage of revised drawings could reflect design quality.)

Therefore, the quality of the activities at this stage depends fundamentally on the quality of the interfaces between and within design/project management/construction disciplines. Many companies are now treating interface relationships' analysis and improvement (e.g. by team management training) as a vital part of their quality plans.

Controlling changes as design proceeds must be firm, because of the impact of change across all disciplines (see 'Systems for control of changes' in Chapter 12). This applies particularly to changes in scope or basic data which are likely to be very expensive at the detailed-design stage.

Quality considerations revolve around the areas of:

1 Quality assurance – are the right things being done? These include, e.g. coordination, liaison, organization, communication, the right standards for the various conditions, procedures which are known and understood by all.
2 Quality control – are things being done right? Standardized drawing controls are needed for uniformity; the numbering system must be consistent; the design standards must be appropriate for the construction and in-service conditions; drawings/calculations must be reviewed/checked both within disciplines and between them.

Quality in procurement

Procurement is an integral part of industrial projects and needs to be considered for quality issues in the following areas:

1 Planning/scheduling: procurement activities (including the provision

of current market prices for goods and services to cost estimators) start at project conception and run through all phases of a project including start-up. Overlap with design/construction is inevitable and planning/scheduling/control of procurement sequences is essential for maintaining progress.

2 Financial: typically, procured items and services form a very high percentage of project value – sometimes exceeding 90 per cent of the capital costs where the project is totally contracted out by the owner. Procurement activities, most of which affect project costs, require close control and liaison/exchange of information with estimating/cost-control functions.

3 Fitness for purpose of each procurement element including:

• Data and specifications (for issue to bidders) which may be prepared by others such as legal/commercial/technical staff. The procurement personnel are not necessarily required to be technically expert in all these areas; however, they must be familiar with the standards required of the documents.

The quality of the input to the procurement process at this stage is clearly of vital importance – it determines, to a large degree, all the downstream activities which go into the project. In this sense, all who contribute data/information for goods/services to be procured impinge on the quality effort in the project. For example, the quality of work packages forming contract documents is largely controlled by the engineers who prepare the designs, drawings, specifications and contract documentation. Control of bid package preparation might be in the hands of quality assurance engineers responsible for ensuring the adequacy of the package including references to inspection test plans, interdiscipline checking prior to issue and so on.

The procurement role by itself can influence the engineering quality of the 'bidders' packages' by checking that all the documents are included for each bidder and that they are properly delivered/collected. This activity, while seemingly small in itself, can contribute to the overall project quality, in addition to other input provided by procurement staff. This could be in areas such as contract preparation, where specialized knowledge of the flaws experienced in similar contracts could be invaluable.

• Procedures for developing bidders' lists, known as 'vendor appraisal' requires a documented review based on a survey of the potential supplier, including:

(a) Initial assessment which could be in a standard format or on a standard form completed by the supplier.

(b) Inspection of the suppliers' premises to ensure that any claims made on the forms are reasonable.

(c) Documentation recording, inter alia:

(i) Quality-system audit using standard procedures to ensure that required quality assurance and control are available. This includes a detailed examination of the supplier's quality-system documentation, if any, together with demonstration of work in progress, quality controls in use and samples of finished work.

When contractors are being assessed, in this way, a reference list of previous/current clients might be consulted and a site visit to a current operation is highly recommended. If the supplier normally uses subcontractors for any of the proposed work, it will be necessary to investigate to that level.

(ii) Mechanical/electrical capability including details of machines, tools and equipment used for manufacturing processes; non-destructive and destructive test facilities and qualified personnel.

(iii) Manufacturing/servicing capability, described by the organization structure and key management/skilled personnel; main items normally manufactured or services rendered; size and details of workshop/factory and facilities available such as cranage, electrical supply, transportation details such as limitations, access, low bridges, restricted headroom and so on.

- Dealing with interpretive inquiries from bidders in respect of issued documentation. Where items are not clear to any prospective bidder, the documentation will normally require him to contact the purchaser's representative in the first instance, e.g. the purchasing agent or member of the procurement staff. These inquiries need to be dealt with promptly, technical/commercial clarification, etc., confirmed with the originator and all bidders informed in good time. This activity is part of the cost of quality and reflects the total quality of the documents and all those activities which went into their preparation.

- Conducting site inspection/orientation visits might be a very important step in a particular order/contract/project. At these visits what is unsaid is equally important as what is said and the behaviour of the purchaser's representative must be exemplary. Queries raised by one supplier need to be brought to the attention of all and, in this respect, the purchaser's representative must be seen to be scrupulous.

- Receiving/analysing tenders will normally be coordinated by procurement and might involve:

  (a) Engineering review and comment, particularly where a supplier offers alternative materials, equipment or methods other than specified.

  (b) Quality-assurance review/comment.

  The tender analyses might follow a standard procedure; nevertheless, all tenders are unique, just as the projects are unique, and variations in price, delivery terms, supplier quality, market/ geographical conditions and so on require assessment (see Chapter 13 (negotiation is on page 242 *et seq*).). Even where the tender result appears obvious, e.g. because of clear superiority of tender, it is advisable to take a pre-award meeting to review all the supplier's proposals and to ensure that common understanding exists. At this stage, both the purchaser's and potential supplier's quality plans require particular attention and any grey areas need to be clarified.

- Contract documents, which are issued only to the successful bidder. These documents might be legally binding on both parties and need to be subjected to, e.g. interdiscipline checking/review to ensure that they are completely accurate and incorporate all agreed details of the supplier's offer and purchaser's requirements (see Chapters 13 and 14 on procurement and contract administration).

- Supplier evaluation, which is an assessment of a supplier's control of quality 'carried out *after* placing orders' (BS 4778), needs to be set in motion immediately (certainly within a week of contract award).

  For manufactured goods, this requires agreement with the supplier on an audit schedule, test programme, in-process or random inspection and documentation. In-process inspection details might require the supplier to 'hold' work in progress at various points pending inspection by the purchaser's quality-assurance personnel.

  Documentation control is particularly important where proof of source and materials' properties is required in the manufacture or construction. In this case *traceability* can be verified by working backwards from certified documents, although critical materials will always be subject to further properties' testing at the purchaser's discretion – no matter what the certification says. For example, in some chemical processes, corrosion evaluation is so important that, in essence, supplier's evidence is not trusted and the purchaser will verify the materials himself, even at extra expense.

Quality in construction

Construction quality is an essential link in the project quality effort. The perfect design, improperly constructed, might well be useless. Accidents, schedule overruns, inefficient/ineffective cost control, lack of security, rework, low morale on site are all factors which contribute to lack of quality in construction and add to the cost of quality. Conversely, a proper *system of control* for construction activities is the most significant precursor to achieving quality in the field.

The anonymous saying 'Contractors do not do what you expect – they do what you inspect' applies to many construction works. However, even with the most detailed and rigorous inspection systems, loop-holes exist which are open to exploitation. Therefore, the system must be set up in such a way that it is not only technically meritorious, but is also aimed at eliminating *temptation*. In this sense, *nothing* can be trusted unless it can be proven, by test, to match the specified requirements.

Two examples in construction materials control are:

- Expensive piping materials with false, fraudulent or misleading documentation or certifying stamps. Even legitimate/well-meaning manufacturers can produce substandard batches of material or finished goods. If these are not destroyed at source, they can find their way back into trade circulation – with potentially disastrous result in critical end-use conditions.
- Use of bolts in structural steel which do not comply with the specification.

Some examples of mistakes or abuse in construction practices are:

- Covering work, such as pipe joints in trenches, without inspection.
- Not compacting materials properly when back-filling.
- Using the wrong bolts in structural steel connections, not torqueing bolts properly.
- Incorrect surface preparation before applying paint systems.
- Improper storage and later use of materials which either have exceeded shelf-life or become affected by damp.
- Faulty welds in pipework.

The question of quality in construction, therefore, reverts to the quality policy, e.g.:

- Financial – proper controls are needed not only to highlight and correct over-expenditures, but also to prevent fraud, e.g. by false timekeeping or other record-keeping. For example, in earthworks, the same vehicle could be fraudulently weighed in/out of site several times – with the same materials on board.
- Reliability – (and integrity) of the construction in the long term can only be achieved by systematic control of the field-work, proper dimensional/tolerances checking or certification and so on. It has become increasingly accepted that the need for inspection can be minimized when each party involved in the production of any prefabricated or site-constructed/installed element handles his own quality-assurance programme. This is evident where, for example, each manufacturer, vendor and contractor is certified to a recognized quality standard such as BS 5750.
- Safety – accidents on construction works are not only avoidable/ preventable but also, in many cases, positively immoral; they generally result from neglect by construction staff, or contractors, of fundamental safety issues. Even health and safety legislation is not sufficient to deter unscrupulous operators. It is therefore up to the owner to take whatever steps are necessary to see that not only the letter of the law is enforced, but also that the spirit of safe working practice prevails. Every worker, in any corner of the globe, has a basic right to safe practices in construction operations. Safety, of course, is again part of the cost of quality by any standard. It is essentially 'good business' to make safety a top priority in construction practices.
- Protection – against poor workmanship and materials of construction can only be guaranteed by clear, accurate specification and field execution covered by a proper system for control and inspection.

Examples of specific discipline quality issues are in:

1 Building/civil/structural works:
   (a) Site investigations, e.g. adequacy of and correct interpretation by specialists in soil mechanics/foundations engineering or engineering geology.
   (b) Below-ground work, involving piling or other types of foundations, e.g. control of records for hammer blows in piling, fixing of steel reinforcing/placing of concrete.
   (c) Above-ground work, e.g. controlling reinforced-concrete con-

struction to specified requirements, including lines, levels and formwork/finishing details.

2 Piping systems:
   (a) Pipe materials, e.g. the grade of stainless steel, corrosion evaluation tests on samples of materials delivered to site.
   (b) Welding, e.g. carried out to relevant codes; welders qualified by procedural testing to those codes; correct weld preparation; use of welding rods/methods suitable for parent material; correct storage of weld rods; X-ray or ultrasonic or dye penetrant tests and interpretation by qualified inspectors.
   (c) Testing of systems or subsystems to specified test pressures/temperatures; inspection for leaks; proper venting; installation and testing of relief valves where required.

3 Electrical systems. These generally divide into classifications according to:
   (a) Voltages, e.g. high-tension transmission lines may be up to 275 kV (275 000 V) on National Grid distribution systems. Other recognized voltages are in the range from 110 kV (110 000 V) to 1.1 kV (1100 V); 440 V/three-phase systems; 220 and 110 V single phase systems; various lower voltage systems for use in batteries, alarm systems, computer operations, etc.
   (b) Environment classification which may call for the use of special protection or fittings, e.g. explosion-proof, flame-proof, water/temperature/chemical-resistant cables/cable protections.

Electrical installations require adequate quality control/inspection for, inter alia:
   (a) Insulation – rated according to the voltages and cable service conditions.
   (b) Cable installation – e.g. avoiding sharp/concentrated bending, penetration of insulation by nails or sharp objects, rubbing contact with moving parts, exposure to excessive temperatures and so on.
   (c) Terminations – e.g. for accuracy (the right cable/wire in the right location) and integrity.
   (d) Earthing/bonding – e.g. for adequacy of tests to ensure that earthing conditions are as required by the design.

4 Mechanical systems include:
   (a) Tanks – for storage, mixing, agitation.
   (b) Vessels – including pressure vessels, boilers, etc.
   (c) Equipment with rotating or moving parts such as refrigerators/chillers/compressors.

(d) Air-handling units/fans/turbines.
(e) Special materials including linings for tanks, e.g. plastics, fibreglass components and so on.

Quality mechanical field installations rely on proper reception, storage and handling, e.g.:

(a) Heavy loads need detailed attention to rigging/crane-handling procedures to avoid overstress or contact with other items which could cause damage.
(b) Certain equipment requires periodic lubrication in storage conditions and checks for adequacy of rust inhibition.
(c) Alignment checks during installation using appropriate methods to achieve required tolerances, e.g. on shafts, couplings, drives, fitted components. These installation/alignment/tolerance checks may need special equipment/instruments including sensitive optical equipment, optical gauges, callipers, etc. – all of which must be properly calibrated.

Quality in turnover/start-up

Construction/installation activities cannot be completed until the facility/plant has passed into the ownership/control of the client. This can be achieved in a number of ways, including:

- Turnover by area or section, determined perhaps by location, work package or building; this requires that each area is fully available in terms of services and process completion – otherwise temporary arrangements will be needed.
- Turnover by system, where the whole project is made available system by system. This can normally be broken down into sub-systems, components or supporting facilities such as:

Main system	Subsystem, components/supporting facilities
High-pressure steam headers	Insulation, safe access to valves
Process line	Services such as a steam or chilled-water supply to various parts of the process line, safe access, ability to control services
Mechanical equipment	Power supply to motors, instrumentation control through remote consoles, services, process connections, building/architectural finishes

Each turnover needs to be described in detail, with a clear statement of what is included, e.g.:

1 scope, extent or boundaries (with narrative description including supporting facilities/infrastructure, safety systems, statutory and other inspections required),
2 marked-up relevant drawings (by number and function/discipline)
3 mechanical/electrical equipment (each piece by number/description),
4 pipe systems (by each line number and service condition),
5 instrument (by each loop number/drawing/schematic),
6 power and instrument electrical supply (each identified on wiring diagrams).

A completely clear and unambiguous set of documents is mandatory; equally, all parties must be in agreement as to what is/is not included.

Two main options are then available for the turnover approach:

- Contractor resonsible for commissioning. In this case, the main contractor(s) reponsible for each area/system will complete commissioning before handing over to the client. While this might be known as 'turnkey' in theory, in practice the client's staff need to be involved where any substantial amount of equipment/services are included. Client takeover activities will require inspection and recording of performance tests under operating conditions; the client's staff must therefore have access to the complete scopes of work and become familiar with the performance requirements for comparison with the delivered installation.
- Client/operating division responsible for commissioning. In this case, the contractor will prepare the facilities for turnover, but will not actually commission. The client may either use his future operating staff or employ a commissioning/start-up team.

In either case, the future operating staff must be trained in the use of the equipment/process. The quality of this training is a fundamental factor in the quality of the start-up – because the start-up of a new facility/ plant (or any of its subsystems) might be the most hazardous situation in its planned working life. It is a time when nothing can be left to chance or risks taken on a 'push the button and see what happens' basis.

Therefore, *planning* for start-up should take place as early as possible in the project planning/scheduling so that:

- The philosophy is clear and responsibility is allocated accordingly.
- Start-up of each system is in a sequence which supports later systems.

For example, if instrument air is required for instrumentation on subsystems, then clearly an instrument air supply must be made available early in the turnover sequence.

Planning should include the production of a detailed start-up/commissioning *procedure* for each system describing:

- The nature of the system together with its operational characteristics, intended use, materials of construction and so on. 'Systems', in this context, can mean not only a service or process system but also any supporting facility such as infrastructure (roads, drainage, building) which needs to be included in a turnover/acceptance schedule.
- The certification required for examination before start-up, e.g. metallurgical test certificates for materials, alignment check records for equipment, setting and calibration details for relief valves, hydrostatic test certificates for pipe systems and so on. This can be extended to include joint inspections with the promoter/contractor/designer staff and the preparation of 'punch-lists' sufficiently in advance of commissioning for the punch-list items to be rectified. Frequently, these inspections are left until just before the scheduled commissioning/start-up date so that the contractor and commissioning staff are in each other's way. This can only be avoided by having completion inspections' dates included in the turnover schedule. These inspections might be called 'preliminary', 'physical or mechanical completion' and 'turnover' and staged so that the preliminary inspection takes place say 4 weeks before the turnover inspection.
- The commissioning/start-up sequences, responsibilities of personnel, communications safety requirements for anybody exposed to start-up conditions. This is the central planning activity which makes specific provision for:
  (a) What needs to be done, with a *complete* listing of all information relevant to the commissioning.
  (b) Who will do it, e.g. promoter/contractor/vendor staff, with what limit of authority.
  (c) Why it will be done, e.g. for personnel or equipment safety.
  (d) When it will be done, with timings, etc., clearly established in advance.
  (e) Where it will be done, taking communications into account.
  (f) How it will be done, e.g. stating requirements for individual testing of equipment, making sure that it is disconnected from piped services or that electrical motors are first turned before coupling to gearboxes.

- The dry-run conditions where harmless liquids or gases may be used in initial testing.
- The commissioning and start-up conditions where process liquids, gases, materials and energies/pressures are being introduced for the first time.

Turnover and start-up quality is extremely important for project success, representing the culmination of all the project effort to that point. Clearly, the key factor for a successful start-up is the experience and skills of the start-up team for drafting, reviewing and implementing the procedures – particularly if new or hazardous process technology is being introduced.

Quality in documentation

Documentation is needed for many activities from initial project scope memos (produced internally by the client) to close-out and acceptance letters. The quality issues are in the areas of preparation, checking, distribution and end-use as follows:

- Preparation – each party may have its own internal standards for documents such as drawings, specifications and so on. However, for effective use in the project, the client needs to agree the necessary standards with the other parties. For example, in engineering drawings, he may require all drawings to:
  (a) Be submitted on a particular paper or plastic film.
  (b) Be produced to drawing standards such as BS 308.
  (c) Display his own references, e.g. logos, copyright, quality or safety inscriptions.
  (d) Show the identity of, e.g. originator, draughtsman, checker.
  (e) Conform to grid references, preferred scales or units.
  (f) Show revision blocks and identifying marks, date(s) of preparation/ design review/issue(s)/revisions.
  Specifications may need to comply with his requirements for format, technical definitions, scope, company 'house-style' for language, e.g.:
  (a) Use of the word 'shall' rather than 'will, should, may' because shall applies regardless of circumstances.
  (b) Use of text instead of symbols, i.e. 32 m should be thirty-two metres, 20 kg should be twenty kilogrammes.
  Clearly, the personnel who prepare project documents must be qualified at an appropriate level and skilled in achieving the quality standards required.

- Checking – despite careful control in production, documents such as drawings and specifications need to be checked before issue. In particular, the responsible design engineer should be required to sign-off a drawing prepared by a draughtsman; the design review team needs to endorse all conceptual drawings; internal discipline/inter-discipline checks should be mandatory; external specialists might be legally required to check/verify certain design calculations for items such as pressure vessels. Explicit procedures are necessary for recording all the checked documents to ensure that all items for checking are covered.
- Distribution – distribution and transmittal requires a defined procedure to ensure that all relevant parties receive the correct documents in good time. This procedure generally comes into the area of project communications and must reflect the logistics of distribution. For example, ordinary postal distribution might be acceptable within a country but courier service or express postage could be needed to minimize time delay for overseas deliveries. A transmittal note or accompanying letter should accompany all drawing issues and instruct the recipient to destroy all superseded issues.
- End-use – the test of quality for a drawing is in the ease with which the drawing can be read and understood by the end-user, particularly in field conditions (assuming that the drawn information is correct in the first place). It can be difficult to find essential information even when drawings conform to standards and the designer has made sure that the information is present. The designer/draughtsman, intimately involved in the development of the drawing, knows exactly where everything is; on the other hand, the field craftsman working with the drawing is understandably frustrated when he cannot easily find information, particularly where revisions are not sufficiently high-lighted. Similarly, procurement/inquiry documents with errors or contradictions defeat the quality principle of fitness for purpose; this argument extends to all forms of documentation. Clear, concise language and layout is simple – but requires effort for quality.

Inspecting for quality

'Inspection' carries the connotation of policing – this cannot be avoided. A certain amount of policing/inspection is necessary in project/construction works and the inspection staff are the 'policemen'.

Several areas need to be considered in the overall inspection process, namely:

- Quality-system inspection or 'audit'. The quality system itself must be capable of standing up to internal or external inspection and an 'audit' means a regular, systematic independent examination. Normally, this requires trained people who are able to confirm/deny that the quality system is not only available but is actually being used.
- Design inspection which is likely to involve highly qualified design and construction staff capable of checking sophisticated design calculations or testing the fundamentals for constructability.
- Materials and fabricated products inspection which might include professionals who evolved the original designs and/or quality-assurance technicians/craftsmen skilled in carrying out dimensional/tolerance checks and materials tests.
- Field inspection which includes site engineers, quality-assurance staff or others with wider duties on small projects, e.g. clerks of works.

Inspection, therefore, is not a haphazard activity. It needs to be subject to procedures detailing the duties and the power of the inspector as well as the obligations of those whose work/products are to be inspected. Staff engaged on inspection work need certain attributes such as:

- Competence to inspect – many processes require qualified inspection staff, e.g. design, welding, X-ray/ultrasonic testing, materials control.
- Attitude:
  (a) Inspection duties carry authority which needs to be discharged properly. The inspector often meets situations which require careful handling and, sometimes, quick decisions. For example, stopping a job in progress is necessary if required quality or safety conditions are not going to be met.
  (b) The inspector needs a blend of personal and impersonal touch. If both cannot be handled simultaneously, then the impersonal should take precedence.
  (c) On field inspection, the inspector must not use statements such as 'That is no good for a start' about faulty workmanship. The approach should be to invite the constructor to comment and become increasingly firm until agreement is reached – not the other way around.

- Background – experience and training are essential in inspection duties. This does not mean that relatively young people cannot be involved in inspection – it does mean, however, that relatively more experience and training is required for complex situations where the

experienced eye can pick out future potential problems more readily.
- Ownership or stakeholding – transient inspection staff may be very competent. Nevertheless, the greatest sense of care in inspection duties will generally come from an element of future ownership or stakeholding. For example, the best inspectors in new equipment or systems installations are likely to be the mechanics or operators who will have to service/repair/operate the equipment in the future.
- Performance as team members – the Margerison–McCann team-roles concepts are described in Chapter 12. At this point, though, it is useful to relate a brief description of a 'controller–inspector'.

Controller–inspectors are reflective people with a high concern for establishing and enforcing rules and regulations. They are good at examining details and making sure that inaccuracies do not easily occur. They like to ensure that all the 'i's are dotted' and the 't's are crossed'. They will not always talk a great deal at meetings but when they do their contributions are usually well thought out. Very often they contribute to highlight an important item of detail. They are particularly good at ensuring the team knows exactly where it is with regard to facts and figures. As the name suggests, financial people often prefer to work in this way as do many quality-control people and quantity surveyors.

It is vital for all teams to have someone working with them who will take pride in checking facts and details and in bringing up key issues that could prevent the team from making mistakes. Often controller–inspectors will be seen as 'negative', always seeking to examine details rather than look at the whole picture. However, their contribution, if listened to, can have a major 'positive' effect upon problem solving.

Cost of quality

Systematic programmes for achieving quality are not free; their costs fall into two main areas, namely:

- Quality management system costs which are those costs associated with prevention and appraisal, i.e. the costs of activities such as inspecting, investigating, preventing or reducing defects and failure.
- Failure costs, which arise from:
    - (a) Internal failure/defects discovered by a quality management system before an item is passed on to a customer.
    - (b) External failure, where the failure/defect is found later, or in use, by the customer.

While some of these costs can be quantified (e.g. the costs of inspection, rework, work under warranty) and so on, other costs of quality arising from failures are not so easily figured. They include, for example, the loss of goodwill/custom, double-handling, wasted clerical work, production bottle-necks caused by rework, loss of morale among staff and work-force, and so on.

It is clear that there are two sides of the coin:

1 If you do not spend enough on prevention of defects, you have to pay for the defects, one way or another, if you are to stay in business.
2 If you spend too much, the customer will find another supplier who can produce the same quality at a lower price – assuming you do not have a monopoly situation.

Therefore, it is necessary to strike a balance between the productive and non-productive costs of achieving quality. BS 4778 defines economic quality as 'the economic level of quality at which the cost of securing higher quality would exceed the benefits of the improved quality'.

This is a generic definition which does not give specific guidance – because each organization, project/project situation has different requirements. However, as an approximation, those companies which try to measure their costs of quality are finding that perhaps 20–30 per cent of their total costs are related to quality costs.

Specific action can be taken to reduce these costs without lowering the quality/standards achieved. For example:

- *Estimate* the costs of quality. Even though the estimate may be inaccurate, it is better than having 'no idea'. Some obvious areas can be investigated, such as how much is spent on:
  (a) Inspection – direct/indirect inspection activities?
  (b) Appraisal – appraising/examining a product/service at various stages of its process, separating the 'good' (conforming with requirements) from the 'bad' (not conforming)? On destructive/non-destructive testing?
  (c) Failure – scrapping material/work such as aborted design or material subject to changed specification *after* purchase? Repair/replacement under guarantee due to faulty material/work delivered to a customer?
- *Use* the estimated costs to identify possible improvements. For example, if all the inspection/appraisal costs are less than failure costs, it might be better to spend more in these areas. This does not necessarily mean more inspectors. The same relative increase in quality/decrease in the costs of quality could possibly be achieved by

staff training in self-inspection/appraisal. In this way, faulty materials/ design/workmanship are detected early in the process – and habitual causes of quality problems eliminated. Pareto analysis (see Chapter 5) of the most frequent causes can lead to major improvements with reduced cost. For example, a site safety manual and procedures might run to several volumes. However, it is often the case that a single-figure number of *habitual* safety infringements can be isolated from data. These might include:

(a) Housekeeping not up to standard.
(b) Safe access/egress to/from places of work not always available.
(c) Barricades not set up for effective physical separation between construction/other work.
(d) Poor kinetic handling of work pieces leading to strained backs.
(e) Statutory certificates not in force at all times.

Data collection could be related to industry statistics or to site-specific records. In either case, analysis should be directed at finding relevant correlations or rankings for frequency in simple categories such as the top five in descending order or highest percentage/greatest effect and so on. The purpose of the ranking is to expose an area or areas for focus.

● *Make improvements* based on the data, for example, by eliminating the safety infringements described above. The costs of detecting/ inspecting/preventing these abuses are factors in the safety results, which are a definite cost of quality. Yet it could be found that a safety programme might be better directed if the standard of training in these specific areas were improved so that the work-force understood, e.g. *why* housekeeping is so important as well as *how* to achieve it. With that sort of understanding, people are more inclined to act in the spirit required. This leads to both improved standards and to less time spent enforcing them. Similarly with data on, e.g. the sorting of structural steel pieces on arrival at site. It is slightly more expensive initially to insist that the fabricator should stamp *every* piece accurately *and* identify it by a fabrication/erection drawing number. Nevertheless, it is eventually much cheaper and more effective than double-handling and field sorting if this is not done.

Quality, therefore, can be taken as satisfying the customer's requirements both in the functional and economic senses. And, further, the cost of quality is then the cost of all activities for preventing, appraising and correcting *departures from established customer requirements*.

This means that it is absolutely fundamental to correctly define the requirements. For example, a contract might miss some of the requirements even though it contains 1000 written pages and 500 drawings. Conversely, it may contain 'requirements' which are both onerous and unnecessary. The key issues, then, are in agreed interpretation of the requirements of the particular project or contract.

The quality emphasis can then be directed towards the concept that 'time is money' for all parties and that getting it right, first time, every time is the best route to economic quality. In this sense, where project management is a service activity largely performed through human resources, quality improvements must begin with the management approach to people and relationships, not only with 'systems'.

This means effort on the part of the promoter, not just the designers or contractors. The effort is better spent in cooperation in a partnership environment than through confrontation; in this way, you can imagine that team-work (or partnering) will contribute substantially to reducing the cost of quality. 'Attitudes' are discussed in the next section of this chapter while some details of team-work are given in Chapter 12.

A quality environment

The thrust of this chapter so far has been about quality in an industrial project, mainly from the promoter's viewpoint. However, some of these projects are so complex that their interrelated facets will be treated as separate project *types* by those directly involved in the particular area. For example, from the project types identified in Chapter 1:

- Specialist inspection engineers with the client's insurance company will act as if it were a rule-book type.
- An architect working on the design of the administration building entrance hall will maximize creativity within the limits of his brief.
- Various subcontractors will act as a coordinated team under the management of the main contractor.
- The crew of heavy-lift riggers/erectors will contribute their physical labour as if the project were the task type only.

The sum total of all their efforts may indeed produce a successful project by any standard. However, the quality standards do not legislate for human factors – those elements in the project environment by which people rise above the essential dryness of quality terminology and do their work so that it is *their result*, not the product of any standard.

These are the areas which distinguish successful organizations from the less successful ones; not only do they turn out a first-time quality job – they can do it again and again. Clearly, their approach acknowledges the standards by which their efforts are judged – yet some bond more pervasive than a 'standard' enables them to turn out their results. This is reflected in the *attitude* of the people involved, most of which is due to the people themselves. The rest is due to the enabling efforts of the project manager/staff who create the environment whereby people will develop the right attitude for the particular project type.

Some of the descriptive words for different project types/management styles (outlined in Chapter 1) and positive/negative key words for affecting attitudes are as follows:

Major grouping: rule-book projects.
Key management style: applying the rules effectively.
Examples: auditing, surveying, inspecting, conveyancing; refereeing, quality assurance; conducting a court case as a judge; implementing government policy through a civil service.

Key words for positive quality attitudes

Discipline, methodology, logic, systematic conclusion, organized, orderly, neat, trim, harmonized, deduction, by order, conformity, regulation, standard, by inference, constant, smooth, circular, square, inspection, customary, conventional, practice, orthodox, estimate, traditional, firm advice, tenets, lawful authority, investigation, evaluation, report, comment, criticize, censure, technocrat, bureaucracy, professional practice, codes.

Key words for negative quality attitudes

Exceptions, aberrations, oddity, nonconformity, contrast, eccentric, exemption, isolated case, specialty, dissent, misfit, arbitrary, law unto oneself, nonconformist, unidentifiable, unclassifiable, unfamiliar, unique, curious, unnatural, atypical, aberrant behaviour, incongruous, out of step, extraordinary, nomadic, nameless.

Major grouping: creative projects.
Key management style: encouraging.
Examples: research and development, design projects; writing, social projects; artistic projects, staff-recruitment projects; teaching/training projects; making motion pictures or videos; cooking a gourmet dinner.

Key words for positive quality attitudes

Invigorate, results desired, unpredictable, key ingredients, cause and effect, incubate, recipe, artistry, foundations, potency, promote, seeds, groundwork, beginning, fundamentals, influence, destiny, hot, cold, inspiration, back to the start, authorship, foster, nurture, minister, patronage, career, inducement, concern, care, discovery, vision, creative, sponsorship, auspices, mentor, expense account, invent, precipitate, of service, foment, nourish, dream, original, make or mar, subsidize, back-up, comfort, producer, tasteful, cheer, celebration, innovative, daring, self-reliance, contribute, provoke, endurance, animate, draw-out, educate, rally, masterpiece, instigator, arranger, founder, designer, modeller, excellence, possibilities, big picture, explore.

Key words for negative quality attitudes

Under a cloud, gloomy, glumness, disillusion, melancholy, poor opinion, censor, stern, strict, careless, wrong-fit, deject, unsatisfactory, hostile, disapprove, frighten, bore, destroy, erode, discredited, sarcastic, deface, erase, corrosive, wrecker, poor results, unpraiseworthy, impair, throttle, contempt, detraction, niggling, fault-finding, shortcomings, deficient, ineffective, off-putting, damning, blame, manipulation, rejection, criticism, poverty, fail to appreciate, ostracize, ban, boo, belittle, vilify, lecture, attack.

Major grouping: team projects.
Key management style: directing, team work leadership.
Examples: multidisciplinary engineering-design projects; information-technology projects; conducting an orchestra or ballet performance; winning the America's Cup; running a soccer team.

Key words for positive quality attitudes

Performing, executing, motivating, achieving, determination, application, concentration, enthusiastic, efficient, effective, experienced, navigating, regulating, brainwork, good atmosphere, cooperation, concord, managing conflict, selling ideas, common cause, solidarity, symbiotic, participating, making terms, rhythmic, leading, presiding, team spirit, harmony, going in the right direction, openness, sense of trust.

Key words for negative quality attitudes

Disharmony, laissez-faire, drifting, intrigue, bad feeling, off-schedule, off-course, indifference, out of tune, negligence, disarray, defeatism, dictatorial, rebellion, neglect, lack of planning, lack of trust, closed shop, destructive conflict.

Major grouping: task work projects.
Key management style: commanding, asserting authority.
Examples: direct-labour construction projects; building-contract projects; military operations in wartime; farming; producing a daily newspaper.

Key words for positive quality attitudes

Taskwork, battle, training, persevere, safe, a hand's turn, a day's work, man-hours, high productivity, rush job, urgent, immediate, every minute counts, craftsman, hard at it, industrious, hard-fought, tough, busy, muscle, bustle, winning, efficient, well-organized, progress, on the double, well-planned, good worker, early start, dedication, high morale.

Key words for negative quality attitudes

Leisurely, strike, bone-idle, sluggish, unproductive, inefficient, loafing, dodging work, no progress, standstill, uninterested, drone, non-worker, passenger, wishy-washy, uncertain, indecisive, putting-off, bad working conditions, lack of leadership, rework, start again, lack of materials, low morale, grey areas, demarcation, slavery, high turnover, unsafe.

Most projects/subprojects can be allocated a category within these groupings; the main link in the words chosen reflects the potential influence of the project-management style on the standards of quality expected or realized. The other main link is found in the project operating system and depends on the degree of exposure to quality principles inherent in the system.

Thus, if a project is being undertaken by a mature project-management division already existing within a large organization, the project manager could be constrained by the requirements of the existing system, particularly if the project is of a type commonly undertaken. The degree of freedom of the project manager to impose the quality standards for his particular project will be thus inhibited.

An amateur handyman, embarking on a project to construct a new garage in his own driveway, has a correspondingly higher degree of freedom in selecting and imposing quality standards on his own efforts. Yet each project may be judged by the criteria for success, measured in terms of its performance of the selected subcriteria of time, cost and quality standards.

Creating the quality environment is, therefore, seen as a function of the following:

- The management style relevant to the type of project (as above).
- The staffing of the project and the influence of the project manager on the staff's attitude and response to the quality requirements.
- The project operating environment including the quality programme available, i.e. the 'little q' described earlier in this chapter.
- The criteria for project success and the performance requirements, described in Chapter 11.

11

Performance and project management

'Performance' means one thing – meeting all the agreed requirements, no more (except at no extra expense) and no less. In the project system it is absolutely essential for the manager to know this, believe it and practise it – no more and no less. In this sense 'performance' is the same as 'total quality' – which means satisfying all the requirements of the customer in the economic as well as the functional sense.

A project is a process of change from one situation to another within a reference framework of time, cost and quality standard *baselines* relative to the objective. One criterion measures the performance of the project management – either it meets each of these baseline requirements or it does not. This is shown in Fig. 105.

The project manager, as distinct from the project coordinator, is accountable for each. Hence, as this book emphasizes, he must have control of the resources and processes to meet the particular objectives in each area, namely:

- Time – by creating and implementing practical plans so that time performance may be compared with the achievement or non-achievement of time *commitments*.
- Cost – by devising and using a practical control system so that cost performance may be compared with the use, consumption or conversion of *resources* other than time.
- Quality – by defining the standards applicable and achieving and maintaining at least those standards so that quality performance may be compared with the degree of compliance or non-compliance with the relevant *standards*.

There are no grey areas in this definition – either requirements are met or they are not met.

If performance, i.e. meeting requirements, is the essence in delivering project-management services, then all other project considerations have

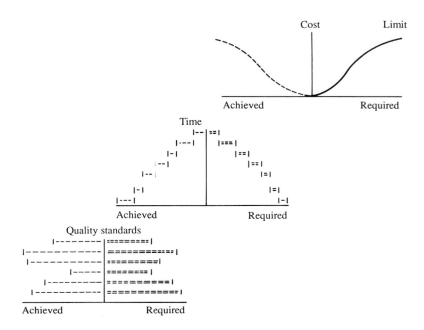

Figure 105. *Required/achieved time, cost and quality framework.*

a secondary nature from the outset. Every analysis of the project must therefore be aimed at defining the:

- Relevant requirements of time, cost and quality objectives.
- Status of the project relative to those objectives at the time of the analysis.

Failure to do this, and to review projects regularly in performance or total quality terms, is undoubtedly the biggest single reason for cost overruns, time overruns or unacceptable quality levels. The only approach which can be valid at any time in the project is that which takes into account all the relevant objectives, sets them within the relevant frame and determines and implements the strategy most appropriate to all the circumstances.

The performance policy

The project manager is responsible for finding and setting the performance policy. This does not mean that he must solve every performance problem – rather he must identify the potential for high-impact problems and adopt the response most likely to *avoid* the problem – particularly if it means changing any fundamental requirements.

This approach concentrates where the basis of results is to be found – in the attitude and thinking, in regards to performance, of all those involved in the project, including the promoter(s), project-management staff, vendors, contractors and labour.

The premise must be that every problem, whether in costs, time or quality performance can be anticipated and prevented. This must exist as a belief with the project organizers before it can be expected from the contributors. Only then can full accountability be allocated.

Thus, the performance policy must be rooted not only in fulfilment of the requirements of the project – but more positively in the exact definition and acceptance of those requirements together with the means whereby they can be fulfilled. It is axiomatic that if the requirements cannot be met, then they must be changed to those which can. This needs to be done not only at the start of the project but also on a continuous, regular basis.

Definition of all outstanding customer requirements must therefore never cease until the project is completely finished. This dictum, if applied, will ensure that the project requirements are discharged with dynamism at every phase.

Implementing the policy on performance

The performance policy is the result of strategic thinking on the definition and mutual acceptance of the project requirements between the project participants and the promoters. The strategy must then be extended to include the methods for implementation within the particular project environment.

Every project is unique. This is true even when a project is practically identical to an example already completed or still in progress. The uniqueness exists because the conditions under which a project is executed can never be repeated exactly. Consequently, the method for implementing the performance policy must be determined and incorporated in the strategic thinking and planning for each individual project.

The pre-condition for project success is that the accepted requirements on time, cost and quality can be achieved. This requires specialized knowledge to be organized and applied successfully at each and every opportunity.

The cardinal issue in implementing performance policy, therefore, lies in creating and maintaining the awareness and belief that the policy exists and is rigorously applied. This definition leaves no room for manœuvre – either the requirements are being/will be met or they are not/will not be.

Obviously, scale effects, organization history, overall project objectives and general policies must all be considered and brought into the strategic thinking. This thinking must then focus on the people and attitudes to be organized and concentrated on the project objectives and the policy generated/selected for maximum impact. More information on attitudes is given in Chapter 10. The same attitudes influence the performance of each involved party.

The baselines for the project

Project management is the management of resources in a temporary arrangement to achieve specific project objectives. By this definition, it is a service activity. A service is *performed* by discharging its liabilities and the performance can be measured by its actual *output* and *throughput* against the baselines of time, cost and quality standards which are relevant in the project. However, these baselines are open to interpretation by the various parties involved. For example, in a particular project, the three main parties could be the client, an engineer and a contractor. The baselines for the project might then be taken as the *actual* project requirements together with that combination of requirements as communicated by the client to the engineer and by the engineer to the contractor, e.g. in scopes of work. Within the environment established by these communications, and any written contractual arrangements, the possible relationships emerge as in Table 17.

This basic table shows that the meaning of performance requirements depends on the viewpoint of the observer. However, the success of the project itself demands that at least the *needs and essential requirements* of the parties meet the project needs and essential requirements, i.e. B_1 and B_2 in Table 17. This means that the convergence of interests shown in Fig. 2, Chapter 1 must cover at least the baseline needs and essential requirements of the project objectives. If this is not available, in any one of the parties, then project failure is most probable.

Table 17. Wants, needs, expectations and essential requirements.

	Wants	Needs	Expects	Essential requirements
Client	X_1	X_2	X_3	X_4
Engineer	Y_1	Y_2	Y_3	Y_4
Contractor	Z_1	Z_2	Z_3	Z_4
Contracts				A
Project		B_1		B_2

Performance of client or other top management

Project realities

The major concept in considering 'a project reality' is the *risk* assumed by the project promoters. Every project, because it is unique and a human undertaking, carries with it the element of risk and, generally, the risks need to be considered:

- in relation to the opportunities,
- in relation to each other.

Taking risks is the prime reponsibility of top management and is unavoidable. However, the risk-taking must be justified within the subsets above and may be shown as in Table 18.

Practically every organization in business, government or otherwise will have more new 'project' proposals than it can deal with. Therefore, the proposals need to be categorized according to their inherent risk and balanced against the initiating opportunity. Table 18 sets the background for management decision on whether or not to take the risks of a new project.

For example, at any given time, a large fabrication shop may have dozens of possible projects on its list, all to be priced and submitted as tenders. No two of these prospects will be identical in terms of risks versus possible rewards or, indeed, in attractiveness to the organization. In addition, each tender to be submitted will cost money, time and effort in preparation.

For these organizations, the success rate of tenders submitted/ awarded may be a key consideration with regard to their profitability.

Indeed, the estimating department (or whatever it is named) may account for a significant percentage of the total annual overhead – perhaps up to 1 or 2 per cent of the value of the tenders prepared. Consequently, they may be highly selective in managing their resources in tender preparation, and may operate a clear strategy developed solely for their tendering procedures.

In addition, of course, the organization's survival depends upon the profitability with which it can carry out any contracts awarded. Therefore the tender inquiries themselves need to be put into a 'risk

Table 18. Risks and relationships

Risks in relation to each other	Risks in relation to the project idea/opportunity
Normal risks	Everyday business risks, e.g.: Adding a new customer (is he credit-worthy, can his requirements be serviced?) Deciding on insurance options (go third party or fully comprehensive) Buying new equipment
Affordable risks	Where failure would not be disastrous, e.g. where cash is available for: Investing in new premises Investing in new technology which is tried and tested, e.g. project-management software Investing in 'normal' R&D
Not affordable risks	Where the chances of success are against the odds and failure would be disastrous, e.g.: Accepting or continuing an unviable project where failure could lead to an irrecoverable financial situation
Cannot refuse	Necessary for survival, e.g.: Leaping from the second storey of a burning building Appointing a new manager after the departure of a previous incumbent Adapting new technology which involves a step-change in productivity because the competitors are doing/have done it

versus opportunity' category and examined by top management even before any work is carried out on the tender preparation.

As another example, a contractor turning over £5 million per year in a particular service industry might have the following mix of contracts in a normal year:

four in the range £0.5 million to £2.0 million,
ten in the range £0.1 million to £0.5 million,
twenty in the range £10 000–£100 000.

Tender inquiries in the range of £10 000–£500 000 could clearly be regarded as 'normal'. Those in the range of £500 000–£2 million might be regarded as 'affordable' while an inquiry for a job worth £3 million to be completed in 6 months could be classed as a 'not affordable risk'.

The company might treat all incoming tender inquiries in this way, with a standard procedure to be followed by the estimating department according to the risk/opportunity classification.

For this organization, project reality lies in confining itself to the type of project with which the top management can feel comfortable.

Top-level decision-making is then more generally concerned with the *project viability* and the possible effects on the whole organization. Project investment decisions at this level might have to be based on an organization's policy regarding rate of return on capital, compliance with health and safety regulations, ethical considerations or a range of other factors. However, before proceeding, the organization needs the project confidence which can only be generated by analysis of the:

● project requirements,
● key factors for success,
● type of strategy needed.

Project requirements

The project as a whole must be capable of performance, i.e. the objectives must be realistic according to the time-scale, budget and the necessary standards. For example:

1 The American decision in 1963 to be able to put a man on the moon and bring him back before the end of the decade turned out to be entirely realistic. To have attempted to achieve it before 1965 would have been unrealistic. The time-scale was correct.
2 Rolls Royce's decision to proceed with development work on the RB-211 engine was unrealistic because the research and development

costs exceeded the money available to support it. The money-scale was incorrect.

3 The space-shuttle programme was very successful until one of the crafts exploded with loss of lives. The time-scale and budget were realistic, but the project at that time failed to achieve the required operational standards.

In considering whether or not to proceed with a project, therefore, the promoters need to be assured that their project has reasonable prospects for success *according to their standards*. Consequently, the initial analysis of the project must be based on the best possible decision-making information available. This means using preliminary data and information relevant to timing, budget/estimates and quality standards, etc., in a much more subjective manner than when the project is underway. Subsequent events in the project, of course, may alter the category of the project to a 'not affordable risk' and lead to project cancellation.

The key factors for success

For a project to be judged successful, the important criteria are those which exist at project completion. Technological obsolescence is a crucial factor in many project decisions. For example, those companies which developed and tried to exploit the potential markets for video playback/recording machines had two distinct choices of technology – i.e. VHS or Betamax. Those who backed the Betamax product may indeed have had many successful, individual projects en route to the market place:

1 The factories may have been constructed and made operational within record-times, within budget and to the necessary standards.
2 The machines may have been reliable, robust, well-priced and so on.

However, the total project was a relative failure because the world-market preferred the VHS format – the project failed to meet the end-criteria for success and there is no mercy in the consumer world.

On a smaller scale, there are numerous examples of project failure for one reason or another which can affect any organization. It is therefore the responsibility of the project approvers to correctly identify the key factors for success.

These can be considered broadly within the objectives of time, money and quality standards for any project in the preliminary cost estimates, budgets, forecasts, etc. However, there are always other factors which must be identified, assessed and built-into the equation. These factors may be internal or external where:

- Internal factors are under the influence or control of the organization.
- External factors exist in the environment and cannot be controlled by the organization.

Examples of how these factors are categorized are shown in Table 19. These constitute the main framework for the go/do not go decision regarding project initiation and various methods can assist the decision-making process. However, the method used is within the prerogative of top management who must consider the next step.

Table 19. Internal/external factors affecting projects.

Internal	*External*
Staffing	Government regulations
Resources/allocation	Currency/exchange rates
Management methods	Weather
Budgeting	Competition
Quality of output	New technologies

Project strategy

Projects do not just happen – they are caused. The project needs a destination before the directions can be determined, and these are the areas which require most analysis and choice with regard to the overall project strategy.

Strategic analysis and thinking must then aim at evolving an acceptable, written plan of action detailing:

- The project – budget, time-scale, quality standards and performance/total quality requirements.
- The priorities.
- How the project needs to be staffed and managed; the organization.
- How the resources will be acquired/allocated.
- How the project will be monitored and controlled.
- The contingency plan covering the main areas which can go wrong and alternative courses of action.

This approach stands the best chance of success because it:

• Identifies the main opportunities and allocates resources accordingly.
• Gives direction and sets the main objectives.
• Encourages thoroughness.
• Considers the ideas behind the project so that they can be examined for operational/economic strengths or weaknesses.
• Answers two main questions, namely:
  (a) Why do this at all?
  (b) Why do it this way?

Top-management performance

The performance of top management with regard to the projects which it undertakes can then be measured by:

1 The output, judged on the success or failure rate of the decisions reached and the projects undertaken.
2 The throughput, measured on the rate with which projects are processed through the decision-stages, allowing for external factors which speed-up or slow-down the required rate.

The performance requirements could then be related to the vision which top management has about the organization which it controls. For larger organizations, it is clear that this means that top managers must focus on the results required – not on the details of the work. Consequently, decisions made at this level will depend as much on the experience and judgement of the managers as on the actual data and information presented to them. Thus, whether the top-management performance is being considered relative to a client, a vendor or a contractor, each has its personal reasons for being involved in the project and the project will have a different effect on each organization.

It is just as necessary for a vendor or a contractor to decide correctly whether or not they undertake a particular project as it is for the client. This is especially true in the multiproject environment of many contracting organizations where the constant demands for working capital, cash flow, pressures on operating margins, etc., have to be balanced, often ruthlessly, against the time, resources and performance requirements of various ongoing projects. That they frequently succeed in the most daunting circumstances is a tribute to the organizational spirit underpinning effective project systems.

It can be seen that deficiencies in either the output or throughput of this type of decision-making can threaten the very survival of an organization and this is the major reference baseline for assessing performance at this level.

The performance of the project manager/team

The project team and the project system

The project manager/team is the executive level for delegated authority from the client or top management. As such, it is his/their responsibility to generate the capacity and responsiveness in the project system to meet the performance requirements. The project system in this context means the methods and procedures available or set up for the particular project and this is more fully explained in Chapter 12.

The performance of project tasks at each stage of the project depends crucially upon deciding which tasks are the most important *now* to bring the *total* project closer to its objectives. It follows that the tasks chosen must be the most productive in using resources and promising results from the identified areas.

These initial and continuing tasks for the project manager/team lie in establishing:

- the performance deliverables,
- the areas of production and productivity,
- the service activities for performance.

Performance deliverables

Performance has been defined as the discharge of liabilities or obligations as a service activity. Within every project, these liabilities or obligations on the project manager/team can be reduced to a series of deliverable units (throughput) with the total forming the entire project (output). These 'deliverables' could be in the form of:

- Information or data provided by the client.
- Approvals or acceptances by the client of various completed elements.
- Design drawings or tender documents produced by the engineer.
- Physical work or stages of completion generated by the contractor.
- Payments made by the client to the engineer or the contractor.

(*Conversely, the whole project could be broken into relevant management activities such as overall project management, procurement, estimating, cost and schedule control, quality, construction management and so on. While these elements are more intangible than deliverable units, they can nevertheless be assessed on a regular basis by the project managers of each participant acting jointly. This is only workable if the relevant project managers have sufficient experience of the particular industry and project type. In this case, 'performance' assessments could be realistic in spite of the subjectivity, particularly when they can be benchmarked against industry standards.*)

A total project can be expressed as a main task. However, this is the basis for working out the main subtasks and a greater number and better description of the subtasks will result in greater possibilities for sensitivity, monitoring and control of the project system throughput — its rate of production.

It is worth while examining exactly what is meant by a deliverable unit as a main subtask (sometimes referred to as a work package or cost centre). For example, consider a project for the design, construction and operation of a chemical plant. The main phases could be outlined as shown in Fig. 106. A diagram of this nature might be sufficient for top management appraisals; however, it is clearly inadequate for the general management of the project. For this purpose, the main phases must be subdivided into manageable portions and the nature, scope and

	Year 1	Year 2	Year 3
Preliminary design	———		
Management approvals	——		
Detailed design	————————		
Procurement	————————		
Construction	————————		
Commissioning	————		
Production			——

Figure 106. *Outline of main phases for construction of a chemical plant.*

timing of each portion determined as accurately as possible. For example, in the construction phase, the plant could be shown in an outline diagram as in Fig. 107. This simple layout shows the main facilities to be delivered to the client company at various stages during the course of the project. The complexity of each facility requires a time-table showing the individual delivery sequence and dates for the client to plan his necessary take-over operations in a logical and convenient way. This is shown in Fig. 108.

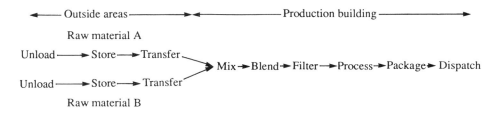

Figure 107. *Outline diagram for design and construction.*

Schedule of take-overs																
	M	A	M	J	J	A	S	O	N	D	J	F	M	A	M	J	J
Outside areas																
Raw material A																
System 1 Unloading				•												
System 2 Storage						•										
System 3 Transfer							•									
Raw material B																
System 4 Unloading									•							
System 5 Storage										•						
System 6 Transfer											•					
Production building																
System 7 Mixing										•						
System 8 Blending											•					
System 9 Filtration												•				
System 10 Processing												•				
System 11 Packaging													•			
System 12 Dispatch														•		

Figure 108. *Plan for client take-over activities.*

The 'construction' activity line from Fig. 106 has been expanded to describe twelve component 'systems' each of which constitutes a tangible unit with a definite scope of work and a fixed time for delivery – a tangible deliverable. The client in this case must be equipped with the resources to accept the units delivered to him in the sequence indicated. In many ways, this is the secret of success for both a contractor and a client – because it imposes a natural discipline which they can each recognize and work with on a joint basis. However, each of these systems needs more detail for control purposes and, for example, system 7, 'Mixing', may be expressed as in Table 20. Each element in this system must be fabricated, erected or installed according to the standard or specification for the relevant class of work. These standards can precisely describe the materials to be used in the construction, permitted methods of installation and acceptable tolerances, etc.

Table 20. Scope of work and estimated costs for a deliverable unit

Element	Material (£)	Labour (£)	Man-hours
Pipe fabrication	150 000	35 000	5 000
Pipe erection	17 800	84 000	12 000
Electrical installation	112 000	28 000	4 000
Mechanical installation	867 750	42 000	6 000
Instrumentation	47 000	14 000	2 000
Insulation	38 000	10 500	1 500
Service activities	45 000	49 000	7 000
Total	1 277 550	262 500	37 500

The time-table, showing the activity durations, start/finish dates and their interdependencies completes the description of the system as a unit of the whole project as shown in Fig. 109. This is an example of a deliverable unit from a contractor during the construction phase. The selection of unit sizes will depend on the level of detail required for control or capable of being handled by the relevant project-management system. Successful completion of each unit would be equivalent to total project success.

This sets the background for understanding of performance and total quality in relation to project deliverables. It is impossible to separate these fundamentals in the context of total project-management per-

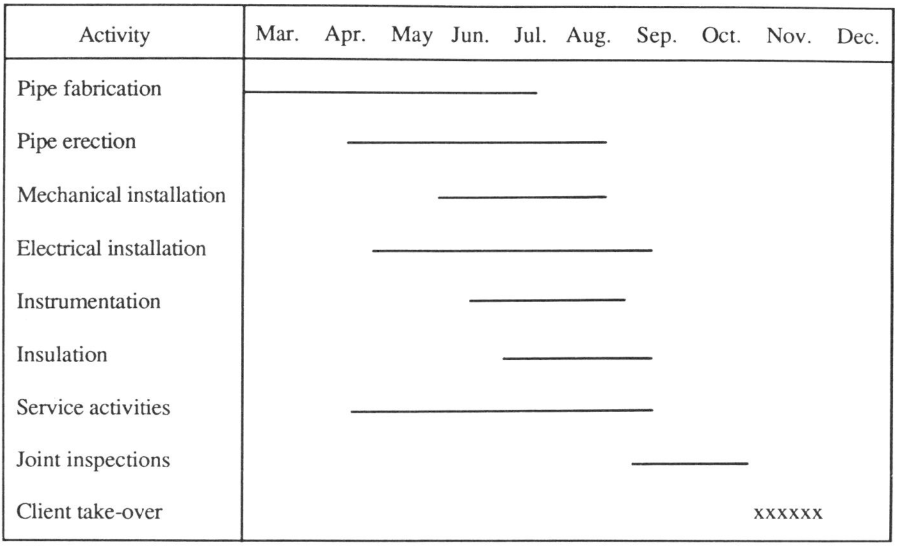

Activity	Mar.	Apr.	May	Jun.	Jul.	Aug.	Sep.	Oct.	Nov.	Dec.
Pipe fabrication	———————————									
Pipe erection			———————————							
Mechanical installation				————————						
Electrical installation			—————————————							
Instrumentation				————————						
Insulation					————————					
Service activities			—————————————							
Joint inspections						————————				
Client take-over								xxxxxx		

Figure 109. *Construction/take-over activities for mixing system.*

formance. Therefore, it can be seen that the project-management system of each party must have enough:

- Capacity to deliver its total project requirements in terms of cost and quality (output).
- Responsiveness to its circumstances as they develop in terms of delivering timely results for each identified unit (throughput).

Production and productivity

Time is the major, non-replaceable resource because, by definition, every project has a limited time-scale. Consequently, the major challenge for every project manager is in the use of time and the allocation of all other resources to make the most productive use of the available time.

Productivity in this context does not mean 'busy-ness' and it cannot therefore be measured by the impression of action. It can only be measured by the results of actions and it follows that, to produce meaningful results, the actions must be dedicated to those areas from which the results are most needed. The challenge then is to identify the one, two, three, four or five opportunities/problems with the greatest potential impact on the whole. For example, if all the thousands of craft workers on any country's space programme got together, they might never get a man to the moon and back, no matter how busy they all become in trying to do so. Not that they would work any less – paradoxically, they might work harder. The reason for failing is that they would not have the right directions. Certainly, the destination is clear enough – it is there, every night, for all to see. But the directions as to what to do to get there and back are not. They result from the discharge by the project-management team of its fundamental duty or liability – to set the direction by analysing the productive outputs required and available from the individual and combined resources.

The service activities for performance

Project management is the service activity which makes all production possible in a project, which establishes for each unit:

1 What must be done.
2 By when it must be done.
3 To what standards it must be done.
4 What resources are required for doing it.

The project manager does not actually carry out the physical tasks himself. His role is to organize and control the resources as a service activity. He must therefore recall that service activities make production possible and that these service activities in the project environment lie in the areas of:

- Agreeing the scope of work.
- Analysing and planning for performance.
- Implementing.
- Monitoring and controlling.
- Reporting and reviewing.

As such they constitute the most productive areas for project manager involvement even before he does any 'real' work and may be examined as follows:

Agreeing the scope of work

The total scope of work in a project is frequently a major source of disagreement between the parties involved. This arises because of misunderstandings or imperfect communications at the outset and it is fundamentally important that a common understanding and agreement is reached at this stage. Figure 105 and Table 17 illustrate this concept and it is further set in context in Chapter 12.

Analysing and planning for performance

A project may be divided into smaller units of manageable proportions, each with a definite scope of work, budget allocation and time-limit. These divisions can be taken as representing mini-projects in themselves because they possess all the characteristics of a project.

Consequently, the project may in fact consist of 10, 40, 100, or 1000 little projects and the capacity of the system required to perform these projects, both individually and collectively, is then the real measure of the capacity requirements for the total project performance. If this is not available, then the project cannot meet its objectives.

Analysis of the project must then be aimed at exposing the objectives and planning must account for the allocation of all the resources needed to achieve the objectives. This includes the arrangements for the management of all project-level activities such as scheduling, cost estimating/control, design, procurement, construction and commissioning management.

Implementing

The starting point for the allocation of the resources is not in the attempt to satisfy the requirements, but in deciding what the available resources can actually be made to achieve or deliver. For example, a vendor who quotes an unacceptably high delivery time is not necessarily saying:

'I am not capable of producing this item' or 'I cannot achieve the standards required'. Rather, he might be saying: 'Look here, I am aware of what you want and have taken it into consideration. However, this is what we can actually do for you in the present circumstances . . .'

This attitude is altogether preferable to that of the vendor who undertakes a particular time commitment and then cannot deliver. Similarly, the project manager/team must know and understand what they can deliver – that they are not making commitments which they cannot honour! If the analysis shows that a particular objective might not be achieved, then they must acknowledge this and cause the objective to be changed to one that they can manage.

The resources can then be deployed to deal with the project requirements in terms of:

- How they fit the sequence required. Particular resources may be plentiful or scarce. However, project planning must account for their availability to satisfy the appropriate sequence. Generally, the sequence will be determined by a 'natural order' in which events and activities declare themselves as a result of the planning considerations. In cases where unlimited resources are available, their allocation to satisfy the required sequence is totally reactive to the schedule demands. However, the more frequent case is where certain resources are constrained in one way or another and it is then necessary to become proactive by:
  (a) Manipulating the schedule to suit the resource availability.
  (b) Influencing the total demand by 'smoothing'.
  This is true not only in the project, but in many everyday activities, e.g. the flow of patients to a dental surgery is controlled by the appointments system. In that way, the dentist can treat perhaps forty cases in a day, whereas ten dentists would be required to treat them all in an hour, i.e. the schedule is manipulated to suit the resource availability. This is very important in the multi-project environment where every project, while unique in itself, has an influence on the others and the demand for resources must be constantly balanced against the supply.
- How they are phased in and out. The planning and scheduling analyses must deal not only with the total resource requirements at a particular point in the project but must also examine the relationships between the resources and the way in which they are introduced, used and withdrawn. For example:
  (a) In labour-intensive projects, histogram analysis of the scheduled activities will be necessary to ensure an efficient/effective build-up of personnel.
  (b) Availability of a key resource, such as a particular skilled person or an item of plant, will have to be considered and relevant activities rescheduled if necessary.
- The harmony in which they must work together. This is one of the key tasks of the project manager and requires an understanding of the nature of the relationships which must be developed between the resources to achieve the project objectives. The basic needs of this function are coordination and communication because the resources cannot be considered to work in isolation when they are used in pursuit of common objectives. In this respect:

(a) 'ordinate' means to arrange in ranks or classifications,
(b) 'coordinate' means to bring the parts into proper relation to each other,
(c) 'communicate' means to impart or transmit (information or instructions). These topics are dealt with in Chapter 12.

Monitoring and controlling

The progress of a project must be monitored and controlled to:

- Ensure that the analysis/plans were correct in the first instance.
- Take corrective action where necessary.
- Ensure that the balance is acceptable.
- Ensure that the standards are being achieved.

These are shown in a basic form in Fig. 110. This type of control system is known as a 'loop'. The information relevant to the performance is gathered downstream of the process and fed back to the area where action can be taken to correct deviation from the requirements. The measurements are taken in the form of data at the point where results are known and may be compared with the time, costs or other standards necessary.

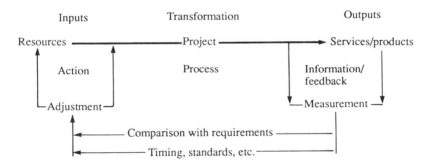

Figure 110. *Basic diagram for monitoring and control.*

The inputs (in the form of resources) are shown here to be transformed (by the project process) into outputs. The productivity of the process may be expressed as the ratio

$$\text{productivity} = \frac{\text{output}}{\text{input}}.$$

However, the units on the right have different formats, such as time or cost, and it is better to consider the productivity of the process in terms of its:

- *Efficiency*, which is about doing things right.
- *Effectiveness*, which is about doing the right things, i.e. those things which are most useful in bringing the whole project closer to its objectives.

They may be expressed in the following general ratios:

$$(1) \qquad \text{efficiency} = \frac{\text{actual output}}{\text{planned output}}.$$

For example, the cost performance index (CPI) in Chapter 9 is shown as

$$\text{CPI} = \frac{\text{budgeted cost of work performed}}{\text{actual cost of work performed}} = \frac{\text{actual output}}{\text{planned output}}$$

and is a measure of the cost *efficiency* achieved. In this case, cost efficiencies of less than 1 indicate that corrective action must be taken – otherwise a cost overrun will result.

$$(2) \qquad \text{effectiveness} = \frac{\text{actual result}}{\text{required result}}$$

and is a measure of the *validity* of actions. It is demonstrated, for example, where an urgent job is carried out to satisfy critical schedule demands regardless of costs. In this case, efficiency could be sacrificed for effectiveness. Performance may then be expressed as the ratio

$$(3) \qquad \text{performance} = \frac{\text{actual results}}{\text{optimum results}}$$

These concepts are shown in Fig. 111.

The summary in Fig. 111 suggests that resources must not be totally devoted to the concept of efficiency. In many cases it may indeed be beneficial to sacrifice efficiency in absolute terms to achieve a higher degree of effectiveness. On this basis it can be worth while to maintain resources in excess of immediate requirements if it means, for example, that schedule performance is improved. For example, on a multi-disciplinary construction project, the lowest unit costs for civil works might be achieved with a labour force of fifty people. However, if the overall schedule performance could be improved by using sixty people at the cost of some efficiency in civil unit costs, it might make more sense to take this course to achieve the total project objectives.

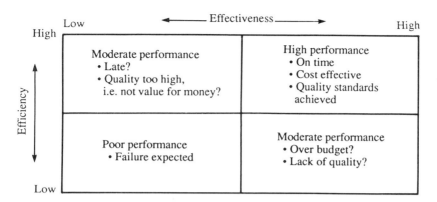

Figure 111. *The effects of efficiency versus effectiveness on performance.*

The time interval between data collection, analysis and application for either efficiency or effectiveness is clearly important and the closer one comes to a real-time system the better. However, in its absence, a trade-off is necessary between the costs and effort absorbed in the measurement/control system and the benefits realized.

The monitoring/controlling process, therefore, is not to be exclusively aimed at achieving the highest efficiencies. It better serves its purpose by identifying and maintaining a balance between doing things right and doing the right things.

Reporting and reviewing

If project planning were perfect, it should be possible to predict and write reports based on the plans in advance. However, this is not the case, even in the best-ordered projects which extend over any significant time-period. The report, therefore, must be an integral part of the project-management scheme and, as such, must be considered from a strategic viewpoint at the outset of the project.

Reports consume time, effort and money, and the output of the report must have strategic value earned in the expense of its preparation. The reporting technique must then be focused on those few issues which will have most impact on project strategy. Project reports, unlike many other management reports, are never to be considered routine.

The purpose of a project report is to communicate information which may be used as a basis for subsequent action. The nature of the report will therefore be determined by the nature of the project and the use for which the report is intended. As in planning a reporting hierarchy may be developed in three or more areas, chiefly:

- The *summary* report, presented, say, quarterly to top management, which examines the essence of the project, the initial project plans, the criteria against which the project is measured and the current status of the project in terms of those dimensions. Top management, who carry the responsibility for the overall project, must neither be kept waiting for information nor kept uninformed about any significant matter which bears on the success of the project. Consequently, this report must provide a concise, accurate review of project status backed up by unqualified data, charts and facts. Subjectivity must be kept to a minimum and the report should convey project information in a factual manner.
- The *monthly* report, which is prepared by and for the project-management team and/or the client. Its primary purpose is to refocus attention on matters of importance and to remind project staff that their day-to-day activities are subordinate to an ordered scheme. As in any form of communication, the report should be addressed to the key factors which contribute to its usefulness. The reporting format must convey the relevant information quickly and succinctly and the time/effort spent in preparation be considered on a cost/benefit basis. The report should then comprise the following:
  (a) Highlights and a brief description of project status.
  (b) The effects of any variances.
  (c) Performance analysis in terms of money, time, procurement, quality and manpower.
  (d) The current status of the project plan.
  (e) Significant events and any changes to estimates or budget.
  (f) Significant problems, options for their solution, criteria for selecting options and proposed courses of action.
- *Specific* reports which may or may not be included in monthly reports but which form part of the permanent record system, perhaps for hand-over to the client on project completion. Examples include reports from the following:
  (a) Technical or other specialists.
  (b) Quality assurance, procurement or expediting personnel.
  (c) Statutory reports or permits.

12

Organization

Project management, as defined in Chapter 1, is the control of resources in a *temporary arrangement* to achieve project objectives. The 'temporary arrangement' refers to the project organization and, in this context, means the *systematic*, effective use of human and material resources to achieve the project objectives.

The material resources include:

- money,
- time,
- space (e.g. the use of land and buildings),
- plant and equipment (for temporary use during the project life or built-in as a deliverable item).

The human resources include:

- the people involved,
- their physical/intellectual capabilities,
- their interactions and potential interactions.

The project manager, with presumed skill in managing material resources, must know how human behaviour can be channeled and made effective in an organized setting.

Organization structure

Organizing is central to getting things done efficiently and effectively. This is attained, by, for example:

- Minimizing duplication of work.
- Maximizing communications.
- Achieving relative economies of scale (by specializing in some things)

while retaining flexibility, i.e. the ability to respond to changing circumstances.

- Devising and operating efficient systems for accounting, human resources, planning, purchasing and so on.

Firms try to achieve these goals by *structuring* their organization in three basic ways, namely by:

- Function for their normal business.
- Project team or task force for projects.
- Matrix when their usual business is project-oriented.

Functional structure

A simple functional structure for a manufacturing firm is shown in Fig. 112. Firms set up in this way are typically operating in stable markets and producing a limited range of products/services. The key attributes are:

Pro	*Con*
Tasks are specialized	Each function tends to concentrate
Work is not duplicated	on its own objectives and
Territory is predetermined and	overall objectives could be
allocated to each functional	jeopardized.
group	It is hard to cut *across* the function
Each function can produce	lines for communication, etc.
economies of scale	The structure needs a stable
Simple	market and is slow to respond
Clear divisions	to change (people do not easily
	change their pattern of ways)

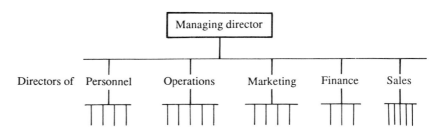

Figure 112. *Simple functional structure.*

Task-force or project-team structure

The simple functional structure in Fig. 112 can accommodate the management of small projects, with managers responsible for particular projects in addition to their normal duties. It is, however, inefficient even for such small projects and is clearly unsuitable for larger projects such as the construction of a new plant. In this case, the response is to select a task force or project team which works together during the life of the project. The task force appoints a 'project manager' and other involved staff or firms are organized under him, as shown in Fig. 113. The key attributes are:

Pro	Con
Resources are concentrated	Staff need to be committed
Team make-up can be flexible	full-time during periods of their
Minimum levels of management	assignment
for the project	Team may lack expertise/
Single contact point with	experience in project work
communications through the	
project manager	

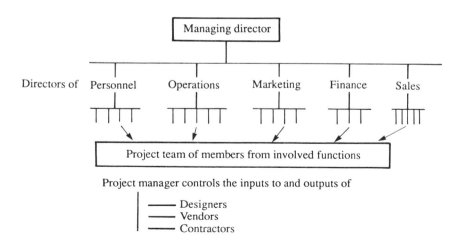

Figure 113. *Functional structure with a project team/task force for a project.*

Matrix structure

A matrix combines the task force and functional structures. It has evolved in response to the demands of multiple large-project situations. In the matrix, two 'chains of command' exist for each staff member, i.e.:

1 On the function line, where he reports to his functional manager for technical direction.
2 On the project line, where he responds to the requirements of a project manager who may be outside his functional discipline.

Matrix types might be 'weak' or 'strong'. These are shown in a simple form in Figs 114 and 115 for a design/engineering firm.

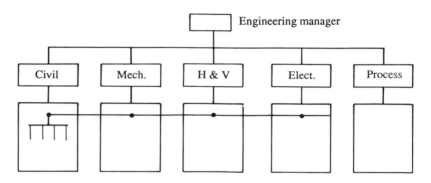

Figure 114. *Weak matrix with coordination across functions.*

The coordinator, shown in Fig. 114, crosses departmental boundaries in a 'liaising' style. As such, his direct authority for team members outside his own discipline is limited. The same weak matrix structure exists when a 'general foreman' from a particular craft has site responsibility for foremen from other crafts and Fig. 114 applies equally.

The matrix is stronger, however, when a separate group exists with direct managerial responsibility. In this case, *management* (e.g. of the design or craft effort) for each project is regarded as a distinct *function* and the project-manager's authority level is extended by the power of his position, as shown in Fig. 115.

The different departments are set up on the basis of direct line authority, with individuals allocated to each project manager as needed from time to time. The project manager has informal authority over the people involved in his project; they have dual reporting responsibilities.

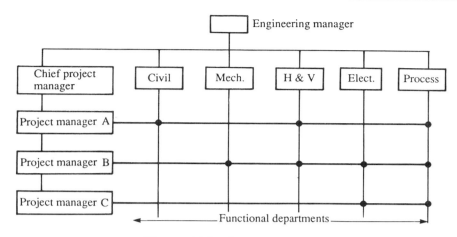

Figure 115. *Strong matrix.*

The development of this type of structure is shown in Fig. 120 for a construction organization.

Emphasis is on the performance of projects, and, to this end, the organization brings together the necessary human resources in a 'team' relationship. It is particularly relevant to the nature of project work, with expertise in a particular area as the major influence and with teams formed/reformed on the job/demand emphasis at varying stages. The key attributes are:

Pro	Con
Responsive to project needs	Dual reporting path, individuals
Flexible in use of skills/talent	have 'two bosses'
Fulfilling for staff involved in projects	Complicated resource/availability planning
Direct project communication through project manager	May induce role conflict

Project objectives and organizational roles

Project objectives, which generally derive from actual or anticipated business needs, are the desired 'products' resulting from a project. They might be, for example:

- New manufacturing plant.
- Expanded existing facilities/plants.
- Modernized or upgraded plant/equipment/buildings.
- New or revised support facilities, in areas such as warehousing, physical distribution or energy supply/conversion.

These major goals or project products are one part of the promoting organization's 'vision' of its objectives. The other parts of the vision must include:

- The operation of the project products when they are in place.
- The ways and means of ensuring that the project products are delivered on time, within the budget and to the required standards, i.e. the project control system and organization required for performance.

Clients, of any size, on industrial construction projects cannot go out and 'buy' a project; even with most 'turnkey projects' (see Chapter 14 Contract Administration) they must be intimately involved with every phase and manage the project through their own organizational efforts. Design, procurement and construction are front-line activities in this context and client organization activities precede, run parallel with and succeed these phases.

The project needs client input in knowledge during each phase (of what he wants and experience in how to get it) as much as it needs the money to pay designers, vendors and contractors. Client management organization, capability and effective control system are therefore vital issues. However, a project may succeed or fail in its objectives either because of or in spite of the client organization. For example:

- Inexperienced client project teams often cause avoidable conflict with consultants/contractors who, because of their practical experience, are pushing the project through to success – despite the client team. This is particularly relevant in cases where the client is constructing in a foreign location and is misinformed about or does not understand local practices.
- Conversely, a highly experienced client organization may run into serious difficulties if another party does not meet obligations, gets into unexpected financial difficulties or in some other way fails to translate the project goals in the client's interest.

In any event, the client takes the credit for success or failure. It is clearly essential that he appreciates the organizational roles required of each party involved in the project. These include *his own* role as well as those of consultants, contractors and vendors.

The client's role

All large organizations have formal project/construction management experiences – simply because they are involved in the continuing business process of acquiring/using/disposing of and renewing assets. However, the approach to project/construction management varies widely, for example:

- Large multinationals may have their own 'in-house' project staff covering all relevant architectural, engineering and commercial disciplines.
- Other organizations maintain a core group of experienced design/project/construction management professionals who work with external consultants/contractors.

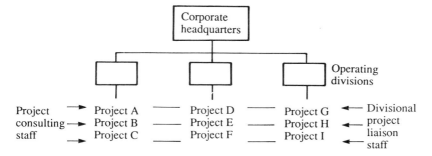

Figure 116. *Project services to operating divisions in multinationals.*

The basic function of these groups is to provide a service to the operating division or business which 'owns' the project (as shown in Fig. 116). The 'divisions' could be global businesses or single-country locations; the project consulting staff might be in a central location while the divisional 'liaison' staff will be appointed on a temporary basis for individual projects. This arrangement allows:

- The operating divisions to concentrate on their main business needs in production/operations/marketing and so on.
- The divisional project liaison staff to represent the division's interests by forming a strong link with the project consulting staff.
- The project consulting staff to develop economies of scale for project construction efforts across all divisions – these may be, for example, in standardizing project control systems or controlling corporation-wide materials procurement effort

Other client organizations are simply not equipped to manage a large project, even if they have current experience of construction. They need to bring in outside help for the specific project and appoint a project manager who may be:

1 from within the organization,
2 an individual appointed on contract,
3 an architectural or consulting engineering firm,
4 a managing contractor.

In any event, the project manager provides a service to the client for a defined project purpose and the client input in terms of defining and agreeing his requirements is a fundamental starting point. The client needs contributions from each of his functional departments during the life of the project; these contributions are both for liaison and supervision of the project-manager's activities.

For this type of client, project success may be of major strategic importance because of the relative scale of the investment. Clearly, he cannot escape from close involvement if he wants to ensure the maximum chances for a successful project.

The client project team or liaison team in these cases essentially exercises the formal role of the 'client'; the project manager is, for all project-related purposes, the client's *representative*. This is a crucial position, often characterized by responsibility without corresponding authority.

Project execution then relies most heavily on:

1 Project definition and scope of work.
2 Communications and levels of trust.
3 The 'fit' between project objectives and other involved parties, including outside designers, vendors and contractors.
4 The project control system and organizations available.

The role of professional-services organizations

Industrial construction projects are initiated and completed through a complex series of steps. Professional-services organizations could be involved at every step such as:

● Pre-feasibility studies – (a) *marketing consultants* advise on products, and their potential market demand, (b) *economists* work out prices, trends, inflation rates, capital-investment preferences, (c) *engineers/*

architects advise on site locations, services/utilities requirements, process design, capital investment costs, investment costs, resources required.

- Feasibility studies – in areas such as engineering/architectural/ process/utilities, financial matters.
- Conceptual design – producing the practical ideas for development.
- Detailed design – producing detailed drawing work.
- Procurement – preparing documents, selecting vendors, awarding/ administering contracts.
- Construction/site supervision – coordinating contractor effort on site.
- Pre-start-up/commissioning services – preparing the installed facilities for use in production.

Staff involved in any of these activities may include a high proportion of qualified professionals. Organization of this type of individual is often complicated if their primary responsibility is to their professional association rather than to their immediate employers. However, the major attribute of firms of professionals (aside from their experience/ expertise) is impartiality – they are supposed not to have any covert liaison with client competitors or monetary interest in the project outcome outside of their fee/salary structure.

Three main organizational structures are in common use in these firms, namely function, task force and matrix. Clearly, the larger firms which offer a complete range of design/procurement/construction management services must organize in a complex structure. Multiple project demands require constant manipulation/mobility of staff across project and department boundaries. This complexity is most easily accommodated through the form of a matrix.

Other professional firms which specialize in a single, main discipline, e.g. civil-engineering consultants, may be structured in departments, as shown in Fig. 117, where the partners or senior managers usually

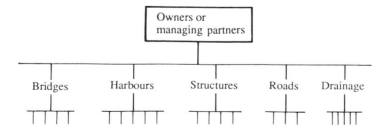

Figure 117. *Discipline structure for a design firm.*

manage particular projects. The structure works best where each department needs the minimum contact with other departments. It is clearly fine for specialized discipline projects but is not particularly suitable for the management of an industrial project with multidisciplinary requirements.

The role of management services or contracting organizations

Contractor organizations may be set up for and dedicated to specific projects. For example, a contractor could be organized with a headquarters, regional offices and site organization for each major contract. Site organization typically appears as shown in Fig. 118. The agents on several sites may be under the control of contracts managers who report to the regional offices (see Fig. 119). A contractor on a large project may have a field organization with a mixture of function and matrix, as shown in Fig. 120.

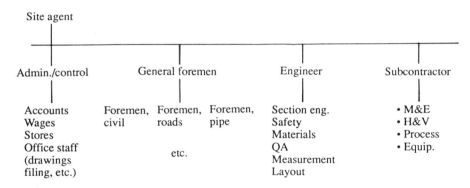

Figure 118. *Contractor's site organization.*

Figure 119. *Contractor's regional organization.*

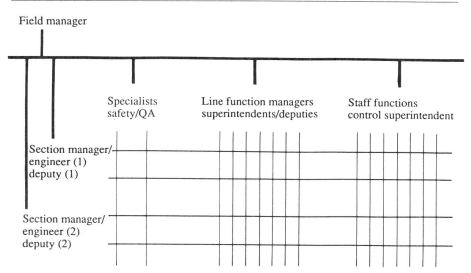

Figure 120. *Contractor's field organization – matrix.*

The role of vendor organizations

Vendors may be small firms supplying everyday services (such as security and haulage) or large, international concerns manufacturing specialist equipment. Nevertheless, each vendor has an organization with a structure and at least one contact point with the project organization.

For many situations, particularly with large orders, a special team is set up by the vendor. Or if the vendor is dealing regularly with a project organization or a large contractor, he may have a special group or internal project manager in his own organization for this purpose, e.g. as shown in Fig. 121. The main purpose of the vendor's internal project manager is to translate the client's priorities into action within the various functional departments of the manufacturer. For example, an electric-motor manufacturer may have an order schedule for a particular client as shown in Table 21. If this is repeated over a series of projects, clearly a complex situation exists even in dealing with one client. If the motor manufacturer supplies to 1000 clients, the task of satisfying all their demands all the time is enormous.

This is not an extreme case by any means. It emphasizes the fact that within the vendor organization conflicting priorities for different clients could result in later deliveries for one or a number of them – with a roll-on effect for other projects. Consequently, the client needs assurance

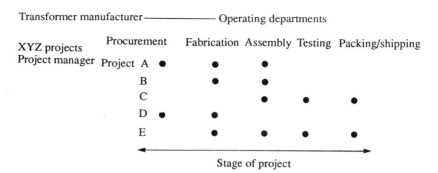

Figure 121. *Vendor organization with internal project manager.*

Table 21. Schedule of orders placed with a vendor.

Client QWE	Order placed	Motor size (hp)				Delivery promised
		½–5	5–50	50–100	100–1000	
Project AAA						
Order no. 123	12/6/89	14	18	7	3	14/11/89
127	9/7/89	56	64	19	2	12/4/90
145	8/8/89	7	80	11	7	14/6/90
Project BBB						
Order no. 665	14/6/89	9	45	18	12	15/1/90
Total		86	207	55	24	

that his orders are being progressed through the various stages from materials procurement to shipping. Regular inspection visits by senior personnel from the client organization may be warranted for particular orders as an integral part of the client's procurement process. See Chapter 13.

Organization culture

The structure of an ongoing organization is intimately related with its 'culture'. Culture generally is the set of values (and therefore behaviours) held by the organization and expected to be held by each member. These aspects of culture can show how structures develop to match different cultures – and explain how some people can fit into one organization's environment but not another's. For example, the caring staff of a nursing home would not normally be at home on a construction site, with the emphasis on performing physical tasks. Handy (see Selected reading) identifies four main culture types:

- Power culture – belonging typically to small, entrepreneurial organizations, but also to some very large ones, e.g. GEC in the UK. It is depicted as a web (Fig. 122) with the central figure(s) as the source of power and the rays spreading out from the source. This culture depends upon the politics of power, with control exercised from the centre. Rules, procedures and bureacracy are kept to a minimum, permitting a rapid response to changed circumstances or opportunities/ threats.

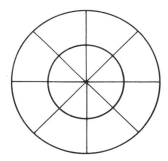

Figure 122. *The power culture – web.*

- Role culture – relying on rules and procedures underpinned by logic with tasks ordered/executed by functional specialities. It is depicted as a temple (Fig. 123) with the individual 'pillars' representing the various specialisms (crafts or design disciplines) under the coordination of senior people in the top ranks. The efficiency of this culture depends on a stable operating environment, with control of the

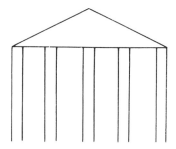

Figure 123. *The role culture – temple.*

environment and of task/outputs predictable and subject to logic, rules and procedures.

- Net/matrix culture – oriented towards a particular job or project and depicted as a net/matrix (Fig. 124). The adaptability of this type of organization is very useful where speed of reaction is important. The name 'task force' is familiar and implies the attributes of the culture. However, it is not normally found in conditions of stability because the flexible operating style favoured by team members cannot produce economies of scale or depth of expertise.

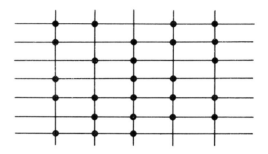

Figure 124. *The net/matrix culture.*

- Person culture is more closely analogous to a collection of individuals rather than an organization proper. It is depicted as a cluster (Fig. 125) and is associated with club-like activities, chosen by the individuals, rather than superordinate objectives. Commercial organizations could not survive with solely person cultures. However, individuals with person-culture orientation are often members of commercial organizations.

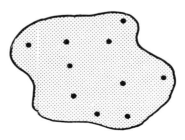

Figure 125. *The person culture – cluster.*

Cultures, projects and organizations

Cultures are not category boxes. In the project types identified in Chapter 1, for example:

- Creative projects relate to the person culture, where the individual strengths and talents achieve intrinsic importance.
- Rule-book projects relate to the role culture, where the rules and procedures take precedence.
- Team projects are the favourites of the net/matrix culture, where the expertise of the individual team members assumes importance in relation to the project needs at a particular time.
- Task projects typically employ a mix of power and role culture: power is necessary for underpinning the authority to give instruction/commands while rules and procedures dictate how the tasks are to be carried out.

Most of the organizations involved in a project will have a *dominant* culture. This dominant culture, if there is one, may be supported by others in a cultural mixture derived from and generally reflecting the organization's:

- History, ownership, size – family firms such as small contractors tend to be power oriented while publicly quoted/larger organizations tend to control activities by rules and procedures.
- Technology, goals, objectives – i.e. nature of work, where, for example, high-cost investment in automation tends to a role culture (to protect the investment or achieve/maintain quality of output) while different projects, e.g. in management consultancy, may require a net/matrix orientation.
- Operating environment – the market, location, competition and the economic situation affect cultural development. Rapid changes in products or processes require quick responses appropriate to a net/matrix culture while a stable environment will encourage a role culture.
- Employees – the dominant culture in an organization is a product of the preferences of the most influential people, although large numbers of lower-skilled workers, e.g. in bigger general contractors, will generally dictate a role orientation.

These factors push organizations, knowingly or unknowingly, to search for a 'best-fit', which is often a proportional mix rather than a single choice. For example:

- The field-construction subsidiary of a large organization behaves largely as a power/role culture; it is exclusively engaged in the management of construction-type projects. Individual crafts were developed on the basis of their depth of expertise with coordination of their output invested in a small number of supervisory engineers. The organization performs on the basis of logic, with safety and quality as overriding concerns for control by rules and procedures.
- An Irish group of construction companies is built on a power culture. The managers of each subsidiary have autonomy/freedom and their activities range from manufacturing/selling construction materials to undertaking/managing field projects.
- A firm of consulting engineers and architects shows a mix of all cultures:
  (a) Person – some of the consultants are employed on the basis of their expertise, and, in fact, carry on with activities outside the organization.
  (b) Net/matrix – the majority of their work is organized on a project-team basis.
  (c) Power – the organization is owned and controlled by a small number of individuals who form the power source.
  (d) Role – professional engineering/architectural work requires a strict adherence to the relevant codes of practice.

Organizations and systems

Organizations need systems for a 'methodical, organized' approach to any task. Details are available in other chapters of requirements for the main system elements of cost, schedule, quality and performance; other systems, such as personnel, accounting and so on are outside the scope of this book. However, for project control, the basic elements must be brought together into an *overall* system; systems, in this context, then have two main characteristics, i.e. philosophy and procedures.

System philosophy represents the received wisdom/experience of the organization which has developed a particular system. It reflects the general causes/effects which the organization has experienced to date and this explains, in part, why there is not yet a single, unified system generally available – each organization has had unique experiences and consequently develops its own philosophy. For example, government systems tend to emphasize the aspects of record-keeping because of public accountability. This discourages individualism on the part of government project managers. On the other hand, small commercial organizations can take a pragmatic approach and develop flexible responses to changing project circumstances. This means that corners are legitimately cut where possible, resulting in cost savings or schedule improvements. Unfortunately, this approach cannot often be used by larger organizations except in unusual circumstances.

These larger organizations often develop systems which operate in a series of checks and balances – designed to get the best performance at minimum risk. The systems mainly aim to reduce *uncertainty* to an acceptable level and the owners are prepared to pay for this rather than get unpleasant surprises. However, despite differences in interpretation or application, effective project-management systems have many common features, e.g.:

System feature (what is done)	System philosophy (why it is done)
Establish business/project needs early, particularly the required start-up dates	To set the clearest goal definitions at the outset – essential for project direction and as a basis for positive actions
Define the scope of work as early/completely as possible	To clarify needs, wants and wishes, to force reconciliation/ agreement on project objectives
Determine strategy as early as possible	To decide who does what, e.g. whether to use internal/external resources, employ designers/ contractors, etc.
Establish cost/schedule requirements as early as possible	To tie in the project or business needs with the resources required/available as determined from the scope and strategy
Determine work packages for each involved party. These should be based on a common cost/work-breakdown structure and numbering system	To define areas of responsibility and accountability as clearly as possible; to avoid duplication of work
Set up a communication system	To gather/distribute information from/to all involved parties and to help coordination. The communication system will be both formal (by procedure) and informal (by relationships)

System feature (what is done)	System philosophy (why it is done)
Control changes	To make change more difficult as the project progresses. The cheapest changes are at the concept/design stage and later changes become increasingly expensive
Encourage and develop a team environment	Team-working is essential (and includes openness, trust, common objectives among the organizations involved) for a successful project

System procedures on the other hand, are the 'ways of doing business' within the framework of the system's philosophy. They determine the basis for authority/accountability within the system and set the rules and regulations for the conduct of project affairs.

Larger client organizations appear to have procedures for every conceivable situation which develops. This results in volumes of written material which could become unwieldy if strictly applied or operated in an ineffective, overly bureaucratic way. However, even within systems which seem cumbersome to the outsider, effective performance can be achieved by selectively applying the relevant procedures. The procedures used by large organizations have generally been developed with many years of experience/expertise in subject areas. They are essentially in the areas of:

System feature (what is done)	System procedure (how it is done)
Determine authorizations	Define the limits, rights and duties of individuals or committees; decide who may do/sign/ authorize what, with what level of authority and under what circumstances
Establish business and project needs, define scope of works, determine strategy	Distribute available data and arrange preproject planning meetings attended by client and all those parties with sufficient, relevant authority to take

System feature (what is done)	System procedure (how it is done)
	decisions until agreement is reached on the basic objectives. The agreed scope of works is the main reference document used for building all other project elements including cost/schedule/resources/ quality requirements
Develop design concepts	Use basic data and scope of work; review at short intervals; determine and agree options; review options for best-fit on business and project needs
Estimate costs	Based on available design concepts; decide quality/type of estimate(s) required, ensure flow of estimating information in time for processing before next approval stage (if there is one)
Develop plans (e.g. for quality, cost, safety) and schedules	First based on early scope and preliminary bar charts; determine planning/ scheduling method (e.g. manual, computerized, network, etc.) according to project type, cost, complexity
Make funds available	Review business needs, scopes, cost estimates, schedules and progress. Establish major risk/ opportunity areas. Authorize fund releases at appropriate intervals – or cancel project. (Management reviews at these stages often require formal documented presentations on the main aspects of the project. For example, smaller organizations may use this type of presentation to the project bankers/financiers)

System feature (what is done)	System procedure (how it is done)
Control conceptual and detailed design	Develop the logic based on construction, commissioning and procurement requirements. It is clearly essential that design packages are available to satisfy agreed dates if the procurement, construction and commissioning schedules are not to be unduly threatened. Initiate timely, constructive client reviews to minimize (costs of) aborted design – or better still, take part in and assist design development as a team process
Control procurement	Determine sequences of procurement activities, particularly for owner-supplied or long lead-time activities or critical equipment. This means placing orders early in the project with due allowances for order cancellation costs if the project does not go ahead. Establish materials control system for inspecting, receiving, storing, issuing (see Chapter 13)
Control construction	Develop realistic schedules based on constructability reviews and agreed working methods. Break the site work into predefined, manageable areas with allocated responsibility. Tailor the construction procedures to suit the site environment, appropriate technology, local labour/resources. Measure and report progress, quality/safety/cost/schedule status.

System feature (what is done)	System procedure (how it is done)
Control start-up/commissioning	On a system by system basis rather than 'all at once'. This means ensuring that construction sequences are chosen to suit, with temporary supplies of services (steam, electricity, etc.) arranged where necessary.
Control turnover/acceptance	This may occur before start-up in cases where the client organization is responsible for this activity. Otherwise, the turnover/acceptance procedures are developed so that the client's staff have adequate inspection time/facilities to maintain a comprehensive record of accepted items/areas/facilities; this will include record drawings, spare parts and vendor documents such as operating manuals

At the more general systems/procedures levels, the main areas are:

- control of changes,
- communications and coordination,
- the team-work necessary between and within organizations.

These are developed as follows:

Systems for control of changes

All project systems rely on planned scopes, budgets and schedules for control and execution. Changes in design, materials specification, equipment requirements, building elements and so on are a feature of progressing design or construction stages which identify, e.g. possible errors or client needs/wants/wishes or improvement to design/constructability.

Unfortunately, changes in engineered designs tend not to be limited to one area or discipline – they most often affect other areas and functions, for example:

- Adding electrical control/switchgear into an existing or already built control room imposes additional load on the ventilation system; this requires a bigger air-handling unit, larger ductwork or increased air velocities, extra chilled-water supply and so on. The initial request for extra electrical equipment then influences, e.g.:
  (a) Structural design, if the larger air-handling unit needs roof-beam strengthening.
  (b) Pipework, tied into a chiller unit located hundreds of metres away from the air-handling unit.
  (c) Extra insulation for pipes and ductwork.
  (d) Larger holes in the floor than were allowed for the original ductwork.
  (e) Larger ducts in the control room already congested with overhead cable ladders and support systems.
- Relocating process equipment may require longer/shorter pipe runs, electrical power runs, instrumentation changes and so on.

Change control is clearly necessary and the system adopted must account for the interests of:

1 the project as an objective,
2 the quality of the final product,
3 the cost effects,
4 the schedule effects,
5 disruption.

Since change can affect so many areas, the approval of proposed changes needs to be endorsed by the major stakeholder or owner. A number of change areas can be identified and subject to procedural change documents, e.g.:

1 Changes in engineering design which alter the quantities or kinds of work, materials and so on
2 Changes in the field resulting from construction factors such as labour shortages, strikes, errors and so on
3 Changes requested by the client at any stage, e.g. changes in scope to meet revised project objectives.

The system of change control adopted for a particular project should suit the type of contract(s) and contract administration. More information is given in Chapter 14.

An example of a change order for construction work in the field is shown in Fig. 126. This document is known as a 'field change request' – or in the particular project system – as an 'FCR'. Major projects may encounter hundreds of these change requests, over major or minor issues, and the change-control document adapted for any system must account for their effects both financially and timewise. Changes of this nature clearly must be approved by the client project manager.

Communication and coordination

Communications

A relatively high proportion of project-staff time is spent interacting with people and groups. The majority of these interactions are concerned with the giving and receiving of information as communications. 'Communication' essentially means 'making yourself understood'; 'interaction points' can be regarded as *interfaces* or coupling points and may take the form of:

1 memos
2 telephone calls,
3 face-to-face conversations,
4 meetings (team or group),
5 electronic-mail messages,
6 letters,
7 drawings, reports or other formal documents.

These interfaces may have properties, such as:

1 good or bad (satisfy/do not satisfy requirements),
2 necessary or unnecessary,
3 mood dependent/independent,
4 helpful or unhelpful,
5 formal or informal,
6 direct/indirect,
7 customer/supplier, etc.

In any case, the interface, if it exists, should have a purpose. For example, the purpose may be to:

1 gather/receive information,
2 give information/instructions,
3 set objectives,

Project
Field Change Request

FCR no.: _____

Date: _____

Title: _____

Copy distribution:

PED

Req'd for mech. comp. _____   Effect on _____   Effect on _____
                (Yes/No)   mech. comp. (days delay)   proj. comp. (days delay)

Attachments: _____   Rev. M/C date _____   Rev. comp. date _____

Description of proposed work:

Reference drawings: _____

Reason for:

Verified with: _____
                (Name)

Estimated cost   FCR covered by
                     (check one)

                             Requested by

DA–TWC   Approvals:

Labour _____ ____ ECO
Mat'l _____
Dist. _____ ____ CCO
Total _____   Constr. approval   Date
Est. by _____
Abandoned ED ____0____   Client approval   Date
Abandoned Field Cost _____
Additional ED ____0____   Design approval   Date

Figure 126. *Change control document.*

4 make plans,
5 implement policy, etc.

Information flow and control is intimately related with authority and the flow of both is a product of the interfaces. It is clear that both the nature and quality of interfaces have a fundamental influence on the workings of an organization.

In considering 'communications' in a project, therefore, it can be helpful to carry out an analysis of interface relationships. These can be done formally, e.g. by communications surveys examining:

- Nature and frequencies of communications.
- Quality of relationships, e.g. between departments in a particular firm.
- Flow of a particular piece of written information by tracing its path from originator to file and assessing the effectiveness of the communication.
- The formal/informal network in the communication pattern.

They can also be done informally, e.g. by simply considering the flow of information

Formal requirements	*Informal requirements*
Who should/should not receive information/drawings/reports The physical links required, e.g. telephone/electronic-mail systems, radios for larger sites or security staff	Are companies/departments/ individuals kept up to date and informed of progress/ requirements? Are constructive ideas/criticisms from any source able to get a hearing? Are the levels of trust high enough to foster a good communications environment?

There are the formal project/organizational requirements including, for example:

- Agreed distribution lists for reports, documents, designs, etc.
- Agreed methods – e.g. hard copy, electronic mail, regularly scheduled meetings with notified attendees and published minutes for record purpose.

Any or all of these forms of communication take place through interfaces. The interfaces are necessarily related in a network system (where a network is anything which is connected, even loosely) and may form:

- A management information and control system in the organization context.
- A personal information and control system for individuals.

In the organizational context, the primary tools of the communication systems might be as shown in Table 22. On the personal side, the primary tools will be the media of communication, i.e.:

1 the five senses,
2 physical communication devices (telephones, etc),
3 the formal organizational system,
4 the informal network of friends and contacts.

Organizations cannot legislate for good communications. They must therefore strive to create an appropriate environment for informal networks to develop and become effective. This is extremely important in the project situation – where people and organizations which may not have previously worked together are put into a situation where they need good lines of communication.

These should, therefore, be considered in detail before the project gets going. In this sense, while it might be difficult to achieve good communications, the minimum action is to reduce potential barriers, e.g. by:

1 Anticipating potential communications difficulties and ensuring that they do not arise, e.g. physical links, such as telephones, electronic mail, computers, telexes etc. should be plentiful and well-maintained.
2 Overcoming local or national language difficulties.
3 Monitoring communication effectiveness, e.g. by timeliness and accuracy of replies for requested information.

Coordination

Diagrams of organization structures show in broad terms the division of work/tasks; cultures outline how authority and responsibility are determined and viewed by the people within the structure; systems determine the way work is performed. Elements of these features may

Table 22. Primary tools of the communication systems.

Function	Context	
	External	Internal
Gathering	Newspapers	Reporting systems
	Books	Clock/time-cards
	Journals	Meetings
	Trade statistics	
	Trade contacts	
	'Spies'	
	Letters	
Receiving	'Intelligence officers'	Supervisors
	Business analysts	Employees
	Directors	Managers
	Employees	Meetings
	Company libraries	Telephone
	Information units	
Storing	Libraries	Archives
	Databases	Filing systems
		Books of procedures/standards and specifications
		Microfilm
		Databases
		Minutes of meetings
Transmitting	Publications	Employees
	Yearly report	Notice boards
	Audited accounts	Oral messages/instructions
	Press releases	Memos
	Letters	Letters
	Purchase orders	Electronic mail
	Contracts	Drawings
	Telephone/telex	Change orders
	Facsimiles	Design notes/calculations
		Telephone/telex
		Meetings/minutes

be detected in any of the organizations involved in a project. However, in the project situation, organizations will set up temporary arrangements, each headed by a 'project manager'. Each one of these temporary organizations will need its own:

- specific objectives,
- leadership/subordinate roles (formal structure(s) of authority),
- procedures, etc.

The common feature of the overall organization charts is that they:

- Define the key tasks, e.g. function manager.
- Show who is responsible for achieving the tasks by naming the job-holder.

However, the complexity of relationships and the flows of information needed to support effective project management require 'coordination'. Coordination in this context means bringing about alignment so that individuals/groups/other resources share and act with a common purpose. It is directly affected by the amount of power or influence held by the 'coordinator'. For example, from Figs. 114 and 115 of this chapter, it is clear that the project manager in a strong matrix has more chance of effective coordination than the coordinator in the weak matrix.

Coordination as a managerial and project task is like team leadership (discussed later in this chapter) and, in particular, requires:

- Proven sources of information from both the formal and informal networks.
- Ability to integrate, e.g. fragmentary information so that the best overview is obtained; in this way, decision-making can be improved both at an individual and team level.
- Ability to use/share information and to delegate on the basis of skills and resources available against the relevant tasks.

These requirements are most often expressed in coordination meetings, set up on a regular basis. The type of coordination appropriate in a situation depends on the level, e.g.:

- Strategic – where senior management take an overview, e.g. on interorganizational coordination, selection of those who will be involved, setting overall priorities and results required, etc.
- Managerial – where individual companies are informed of events, schedules, etc., and the timing, control and coordination of their efforts directed towards satisfying the requirements in a period.

- Operational – where the day-to-day activities are controlled and coordinated by individual managers/supervisors.

The agenda and timings for these meetings normally reflect the level with, say, quarterly strategic, monthly management and weekly/daily/ hourly operational meetings depending on project circumstances.

Team management

Organizations exist because it is not possible for one person to do all the work – a manager has to work through others in nearly every managerial situation. The first line through which he acts is a group or a team and every construction project involves groups/teams at various points, e.g.:

1 A client project team or 'steering committee', representing client interests.
2 A design team, possibly led by, or certainly informed and monitored by, a project manager.
3 A construction team.

Team performance is such an important ingredient of success in every project (or other undertaking) that it has been widely researched. The research has focused on examining the patterns of behaviour of people on the premise that people working in groups or teams behave differently than as individuals. However, the individual behaviour patterns have a fundamental influence on the group/team performance. Clearly, an understanding of team performance is useful for:

1 Anticipating and minimizing the effects of negative conflict.
2 Harnessing the skills and talents of team contributors in the most productive way.

According to Tuckman (see Selected reading), groups go through the phases of:

- Forming – coming together, developing relationships.
- Norming – setting standards, agreeing work methods.
- Storming – having conflicts/disagreements/arguments and finding solutions.
- Performing – being productive.

In some situations, teams may form naturally, select a leader and get on with a task. In other situations, members are appointed under, or are selected by, an existing leader/manager. In either case, it is a distinct advantage if the leader/members are aware of team-mangement/membership roles and principles, particularly in the work environment.

A number of useful 'tools' are available for examining and influencing the composition and effectiveness of groups in the work situation. For example, Margerison and McCann (see Selected reading) have developed a practical method for relating team roles with individual preferred working styles. It is based on *team-mapping* and starts with an assessment of individual work preferences in the areas of establishing relationships, gathering data, using data and allocating time/priorities.

These are related to behaviour and team-role preferences on the axes of exploring–controlling and advising–organizing behaviour as shown in Fig. 127. These axes are used to build a 'leadership wheel' (Fig. 128). These characteristics are combined into the team-mangement sectors (shown on Fig. 128); a brief description of each sector follows:

- Reporters–advisers tend to enjoy gathering and reporting information to meetings.
- Creators–innovators enjoy generating and experimenting with creative ideas.
- Explorers–promoters typically spend a lot of time making contacts, exploring alternatives, persuading others and generating resources.
- Assessors–developers want to assess alternatives to see how they can work in practice.
- Thrusters–organizers are impatient, wanting to thrust forward to get tasks done even when others are reluctant, knocking down any barriers to get tasks done quickly and efficiently.

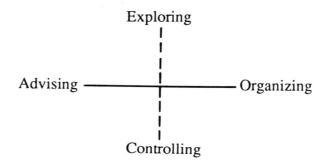

Figure 127. *The major team role preferences.*

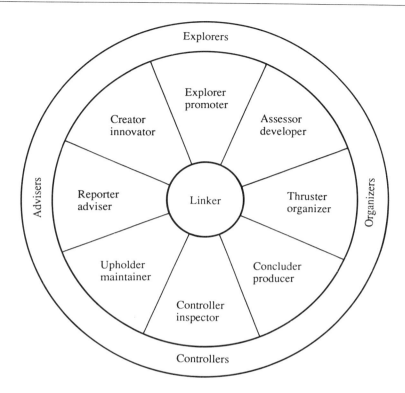

Figure 128. *The Margerison–McCann 'Team Management Wheel'.*

- Concluders–producers ensure that tasks are concluded so that plans/ideas are fulfilled. They want to run things in an orderly way so that there is a regular output where their skills can be applied.
- Controllers–inspectors exert a controlling influence on organizations to ensure that tasks are inspected, checked and done according to rules, regulations and standards.
- Upholders–maintainers strongly support friends/colleagues who believe in their ideals. They uphold the standards, values and traditions of an organization.

These roles are preferred by people with different personality types. Most people have two or three roles which they strongly prefer to exercise in teamwork.

However, for effective team performance the team members need to have a balanced mix of preferred working styles. These are determined from behaviour preferences as follows:

1 *Relating to others/establishing relationships*

Extrovert	Introvert
Prefer variety/stimulation	Think things through before communicating
Are easily bored	
Do jobs in parallel	Do jobs in sequence
Have 'open-door' policy	Prefer to work in smaller groups
Like meetings	Concentrate well over long periods
Take conversational initiatives	
	Discuss well when they know the subject and the people

2 *Gathering data/information*

Practical	Creative
Matter of fact	Imaginative
Like to touch, weigh, move things	Concentrate on 'big picture'
Prefer clear tasks	Poor at details
Like to organize physical things	Dislike routine
Prefer problems with standard solutions which can be approached on a step-by-step basis.	Individualistic
	Work in irregular patterns
Are not interested in philosophies	
Deal with specific issues – generate information which affects the outcome of a problem	
Enjoy the present, deal with the practicalities.	

3 *Making decisions/using data*

Analytical	*Belief oriented*
Evaluate information	Polarize issues
Use techniques	Have strong convictions
Like working with figures	Decide in accordance with their
Are detached about decision-making	values
Prefer evidence/data	

4 *Organizing work/allocating time and priorities*

Structured	*Flexible*
Set rules/procedures	Adapt to change
Are conscious of plans/schedules/deadlines	Gather as much information as possible before deciding
Expect others to work to systems	Dislike deadlines
Prefer neatness/tidiness	Understand the wide situation
Make decisions quickly	Prefer advising rather than controlling

The team leader

The skills and preferences of the team members are effectively harnessed through a 'linking' process practised by each team leader/project manager. The 'linking' skills are:

- Listening before deciding.
- Keeping team members up to date.
- Being available and responsive to people's problems on the job.
- Developing a balanced team of advisers, organizers, controllers and explorers.
- Allocating work to people based on their capabilities.
- Encouraging respect and understanding amongst team members.
- Delegating work which is not essential for the leader/manager to do personally.

- Setting an example and agreeing high-quality standards with the team.
- Setting achievable targets for the team but always pressing for improved performance.
- Coordinating and representing team members.
- Involving team members in problem-solving key issues.

The use of team-mapping and appropriate linking skills can help the project manager to:

- Select team members and build team-working appropriate to the project demands. For example, the commercial and time pressures of construction-site work may dictate a controlling and thruster–organizer atmosphere, with a team oriented to this area. However, it is important for the team to be balanced, as too many thrusters–organizers tend to take decisions very quickly, in their push for action, and may encounter too much conflict.
- Build on the principles required to achieve high-performance team-work. By knowing the team-management principles and putting them into action, the project manager stands a greater chance of producing a team which can deliver high performance in terms of meeting project objectives.
- Share knowledge of the preferred working roles of the team members. It is a great benefit if the team members recognize their strengths and weaknesses and understand how the roles complement each other. However, this requires a degree of openness to which many organizations aspire but do not achieve.

These principles presuppose that team members are suitably experienced/ qualified for their respective job demands. In smaller organizations, and in many normal managerial situations, it will be necessary for people to adopt roles other than their preferred ones. For example, a person who prefers to be an explorer–promoter might have to act as a thruster–organizer/concluder–producer to get jobs done; one way of doing this is to make sure that there are people on his team who are inclined to the controlling side of the wheel – otherwise, he will have to adapt the needed styles anyway.

Teams at different project phases

An industrial construction project typically follows the schematic shown in Fig. 129 from concept to completion. Teams are involved in

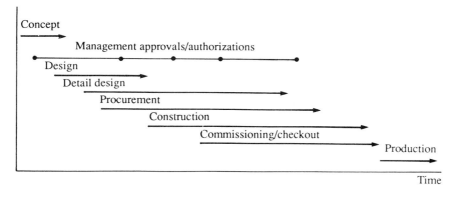

Figure 129. *Typical project phases.*

different degrees and at different overlap times. As a general concept, the teams will have the following overall responsibilities:

Client: Project strategy and execution

The main team features are:

- exploring–promoting/creating–innovating, i.e. activities which initiate the project, moving to
- controlling and inspecting – how much does it cost? what are the benefits? and
- thrusting–organizing, i.e. knocking down barriers getting the job moving.

Design: concept development, producing drawings, specifications, etc.

The main features are:

- creating–innovating/assessing–developing, i.e. activities which identify problems, devise solutions and find a practical application, moving to
- reporting–advising, for communication to the client and
- thrusting–organizing/concluding–producing, for detail drawing work where the drawing staff may be arranged according to functional disciplines.

Construction: physical execution

The main features are:

- thrusting–organizing, i.e. overcoming difficulties, moving when others are reluctant, making quick decisions, backed up by
- controlling–inspecting for cost and quality control of output and
- concluding–producing the regular output, 'punch list' items and finishes.

Commissioning/start-up: checking/accepting/running

The main features are:

- Controlling–inspecting – to ensure that everything is in place and that specifications and drawings have been followed. '
- Thrusting–organizing – pushing ahead with a tail-end schedule which finds staff overworked, stretched, new to the job/process and reluctant to accept changes in working practices involved in new facilities.

Manufacturing: operations management

The main features are:

- Concluding–producing – making the systems deliver regular output.
- All the other features needed for a balanced team in the long term.

Bringing the organizations together

Industrial construction projects range from several thousands to hundreds of millions of pounds in cost. For example, upgrading a boiler-house might cost £20 000; constructing a new power station or petro-chemical plant might be £700 million. Organizations involved in any of these projects fall into two categories, i.e. owner and others. 'Others' can be classed as 'direct' (such as engineering/contracting/vendor firms appointed by the owner) and 'indirect' (such as government, local authorities, property owners or those environmentally affected by the project – indirect involvement is outside the scope of this book). Bringing the organizations together in the most harmonious, productive atmosphere for good communications, coordination and so on is a major challenge in project execution.

Apparently, the owner with the primary project interest has the greatest stake in the project. However, this might not be so where, for example, a vendor/contractor firm has goals such as:

1 entering a new market,
2 recovering a poor reputation,
3 maintaining continuity of employment,
4 maximizing profits or generating cash flow.

It could be very important, therefore, to assess the motives of organizations before they are entrusted with project-related work.

In addition, where organizations act together for the first time, a 'learning curve' is involved, for example, on how different firms or their staff react in various circumstances. Repeated exposure and common experiences on jobs reduces the possibilities of negative conflict and leads to higher levels of trust. For example, general contractors normally have preferred subcontractors, good experiences with particular vendors makes them preferred suppliers and so on.

In the light of project circumstances, therefore, the owner initially holds the cards because he can accept or reject firms through vendor appraisal/selection. The key elements in this respect are their *ability* to deliver and their *commitment* to deliver. The first is easier to determine on the basis of order size, track record, skills/resources and so on. However, the second is more abstract and can change due to vendor priority changes during the course of the project. The owner or his representatives must therefore be prepared to monitor this commitment at regular intervals. They must also be prepared to create the circumstances which continually foster effective working relationships.

13

Procurement

Project procurement is basically about acquiring:

all the right goods, materials or services
at the right time, place and cost
in the right quantity and quality

for a particular project. (This is an extract from the generic definitions which more fully describe the process of procurement; however, it is sufficient for the purposes of this chapter.) It is different from standard industrial or general commercial procurement because:

- It is concerned with a different situation for each project (this applies even in the multiproject environment, although in that case the needs of all ongoing projects have to be considered).
- It is generally short-term (for the life of the particular project).
- The materials/services procured are generally not for resale and are bought strictly in accordance with project specifications.

Procurement is treated in a number of ways:

- The large organization will have a staff of professionals who specialize in procurement as a functional discipline; they will operate a comprehensive system including perhaps a legal/contracts section.
- The medium-sized organization may have a buyer or buying department in a functional discipline.
- The small organization has the owner or general manager who is involved in every purchase.

Procurement has a very high impact on the overall project scheme – e.g. where a promoter contracts-out as much as possible, the value to him of bought-in services/materials could exceed 90 per cent of the whole project value. Therefore, the task must be subject to strategic analysis and integrated within the physical and financial planning from the outset. In this sense, everyone involved in the project has an input to 'procurement' because the costs of his activities have to be met from project funds.

The keyword for the project manager is logistics – both the logistics of the project and of the procurement function. The mechanics of the function may be fully delegated, e.g. in the film-making industry where the producer (procurement manager) arranges all subtasks; nevertheless, accountability for the success or otherwise still lies with the director (project manager).

The nature of the project and its operating environment dictate the logistics. For example, compare the logistics of:

- Building a hospital in Birmingham, UK or Addis Ababa, Ethiopia.
- Casting for a school play or a multimillion dollar screen production.
- Preparing dinner for ten people or catering for 20 000 meals per day in an in-flight catering unit serving thirty international airlines.

Although these 'projects' are very different in nature, their success will depend on the quality (i.e. fitness for purpose and satisfaction of customer requirements) of the procurement. This quality will be measured in the results of the procurement effort and how they comply with the logistical, financial and service requirements of the project.

The major procurement functions are described under the headings of purchasing and materials management. Contract administration, which is handled as a procurement function by some organizations, is treated separately in Chapter 14.

Purchasing

In the project environment, two classes of purchasing are available, namely discretionary and non-discretionary.

- Discretionary purchasing is available where the powers or authority of the promoting company are delegated, e.g. to an individual(s) or from a head office to a local (site) administration. The delegated authority is clearly defined and limited to suit project needs. Examples are:
  (a) A project manager in a multiproject environment is entitled to initiate project-related minor works up to £5000 value without reference to head office.
  (b) A site agent on a building contract arranges with a local garage for a supply of fuels.

(c) A head-office project team on a £50 million industrial project arranges the purchase of major equipment only and requests the local contract management to purchase bulk materials and services to a gross value of £6 million.

- Non-discretionary purchasing applies where the items/services required are defined within the project scope/specifications and the approval for placing purchase orders must be referred to higher authority. Examples are:

(a) The placing of government contracts may be subject to ministerial approval.

(b) A firm of consulting engineers may produce drawings and tender documents, invite tenders, prepare bid analyses and negotiate with suppliers. However, the consultant's recommendations to the client may be accepted or rejected by him, i.e. the consultant is not allowed to place a purchase order without the client's written approval.

Categories of purchasing

Whether purchasing is discretionary or non-discretionary, it falls within the following areas:

Goods or equipment designed or specified particularly for the project

These items are distinguished by the facts that they:

- Cannot be inspected at the time of vendor selection, although similar samples may be available.
- Are not available on general price-lists and must be priced by the potential supplier on the basis of information/performance requirements.

Examples include:

1 A house designed by an architect for an owner and built by a general contractor.
2 A road designed by a local authority and built by a roadworks contractor.
3 A belt conveyor system designed by a mechanical engineer and supplied by a vendor specializing in mechanical handling.
4 Hotel seating and dining tables designed and specified by an interior designer and supplied by a furniture manufacturer.

Goods or equipment designed by a vendor and selected on the basis of suitability for the project requirements

These items are distinguished by the facts that they:

- Are built to the manufacturer's specifications (although optional extras or particular performance requirements may be available).
- Are generally available as samples.
- Are sold on the basis of catalogued prices (discounts/delivery terms may be negotiable).
- Are subject to manufacturer's warranty in regard to fitness for purpose (i.e. quality) under his specified operating conditions.
- May be tested and approved for general use by bodies such as the British Standards Institute, etc.
- May be factory-built or field-built from manufactured components.

Examples include:

1 An underwater camera selected for use in depths of 300 m.
2 An oven capable of baking 6000 Danish pastry in an hour.
3 A computer with a floppy-disc drive, 20 megabytes of hard-disc storage and a letter-quality printer.
4 A metering pump capable of accurately supplying doses of chemicals on a time/flow-rate or volumetric basis.

Bulk materials or consumables

Bulk materials are generally:

- Built-in as the project is executed.
- High-volume items such as bricks where the quantities to be purchased are calculated from drawings.

Consumables are generally:

- Used as the project is executed.
- Purchased in small quantities to suit daily, weekly, monthly needs.

Otherwise both these classes of items are generally:

- Available from a number of local suppliers or stockists.
- Standard items on catalogue/price-lists.
- Available in short delivery times from stock.
- Guaranteed by the manufacturer to conform to recognized standards.

Examples include:

1 Electrical cabling, bricks and pipes for use in an industrial project.
2 Fuels, such as propane gas, diesel oil, petrol for vehicles, equipment and heating appliances.
3 Welding-rods, nails, timber for formwork.
4 Stationery, drawing-paper.
5 Protective clothing, safety barriers.
6 Films, magnetic tape.

Services

These are distinguished by the facts that they:

- Involve applied mental or physical labour.
- May or may not result in a tangible or physical change, i.e. services may consist of consultation/advice.
- Depend upon the training and application of the servant for their quality.

Examples include:

1 Professional services such as legal, engineering, architectural, managerial, accounting, project management.
2 Trade services such as cleaning, labour supply, freight/transportation, vehicle maintenance.
3 Personal services such as hairdressing, massage.
4 Services with materials such as building, plumbing, electrical works, double-glazing, management contracts.

These describe the types of purchasing which may be required in a project. They are discharged in two main areas:

1 Liaison, where the services of the procurement function are used for project-management information and decisions.
2 The mechanics of the procurement process.

These are further elaborated as follows:

Liaison services

A procurement department could be responsible for providing liaison services which include, for project purposes:

1 Advising/informing:
   (a) Lead time between start of inquiries and delivery of items or services.
   (b) Prices available in the current market.
   (c) Tender conditions, legal clauses in conditions of contracts, purchaser's/supplier's obligations.
2 Appraising/evaluating:
   (a) Suitability of possible suppliers.
   (b) Sources of supply.
   (c) Offers, analysing bids.
3 Maintaining:
   (a) A register of current or approved suppliers, particularly where suppliers must be certified to a particular quality standard.
   (b) Current offers/prices of goods and services in common use.
   (c) Records of orders placed, status of orders.
   (d) Records of payments made, claims settled and outstanding commitments.
   (e) Catalogues of goods/services in frequent/regular demand.
4 Preparing:
   (a) Technical/legal documentation.
   (b) Purchase orders for approval signatures.
   (c) Amendments to contracts.

The mechanics of procurement

The procurement department will normally be responsible for all non-technical areas of the purchasing processes. These include, for example, commercial negotiations as well as the liaison services. Some of these are more fully described as follows:

Sourcing

Locating or identifying a vendor or source of supply, by consulting publications such as buyers' guides, by word of mouth, by seeking recommendations from other users or by investigating work.

Vendor appraisal/evaluation

Determining the suitability of a vendor for supplying particular goods or services. The aim is to select potential vendors on the basis of the results desired and this might follow a formal procedure (see Chapter 10) which establishes relevant information about the vendor such as:

1　Goods/services offered, range of expertise/experience.
2　Size of organization/sales.
3　Ownership and organization details.
4　Facilities available, including workshops, equipment, materials.
5　Methods/procedures used in engineering, design, production control, planning, quality management.
6　Staff availability.
7　Current commitments.
8　Financial stability.
9　Ability to satisfy requirements.

(The relevant standards organizations have evaluation documents for quality-assurance/vendor prequalification; these can be used/adapted in the appraisal process.)

Preparing inquiries/inviting tenders (bids)

Describing the work to be done or equipment/service required and offering potential vendors the opportunity to assess the scope of the work/equipment/service and submit prices/terms accordingly. This area covers a range of possibilities. For example:

- Tender documents for a major government project may run to many volumes and involve the work of professionals including architects, engineers, quantity surveyors, etc.
- A standard organization inquiry document may be used for common purchases. This document, which could be initially raised as a 'requisition', will normally describe the goods/service required, conditions of purchase, freight/delivery instructions, names of contact personnel for technical/administrative inquiries, etc. An example of a requisition used for both requisition and purchase is shown in Fig. 130; this form is used for distribution to a number of parties including the supplier, the receiving stores, accounts, etc.
- Oral requests for prices/terms may be used for goods/services capable of being described orally – although most organizations insist on written quotations prior to placing purchase orders.

All large organizations have their own standardized procedures for this function. The procedures are generally designed for normal commercial procurement so that the special demands of project managment may

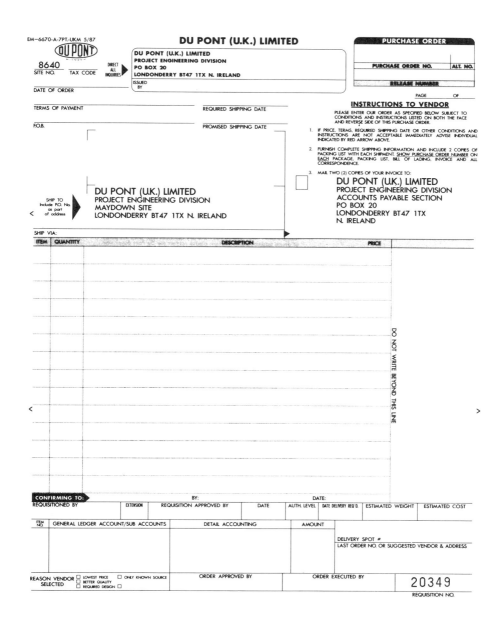

Figure 130. *Requisition form used for inquiry/purchasing.*

require temporary changes in the procedures to meet particular programme/schedule requirements. For example, a supplier may be instructed to proceed on the basis of a 'letter of intent' prior to the issue of a formal contract whose preparation may take considerable time. Conversely, a contractor or the engineering division of a large organization, will be equipped to deal with the demands of a multiproject environment and will use suitable procedures.

Analysis of bids

No two offers on an inquiry are identical in all respects. As a result, the offers must be analysed and compared. This process depends upon the nature of the inquiry.

For example:

- In large, government-type contracts, the inquiry documents are prepared by relevant professionals and offers are subject to their analyses in detailed comparison. The documents are generally presented in such a way that the lowest offer submitted has the highest chance of success (although the lowest, or any offer, is not always accepted).
- Commercial organizations will normally have more freedom in how they select from a range of offers and may analyse offers with a greater bias towards a particular vendor. The offer analysis is then used as the basis for further commercial negotiations; see Fig. 131 for 'bidder's list' and 'contractor's bid comparison' forms used commercially.

Negotiation

Negotiation with potential vendors is generally undertaken prior to placing an order or making a recommendation. The style of the negotiations depends upon the natures of the organizations involved and can range from matters of clarification only or substantial adjustment to the terms of an offer including price, delivery times, payment terms, etc. Negotiation is a wide-ranging subject and is not restricted to purchasing or procurement practices.

Negotiation means conferring, dealing or bargaining with another party in the settlement of affairs. In this context, conferring, dealing and bargaining provide the basis of agreement for the substance of the negotiation.

Bidders List

Contract Section
Project Engineering Division

Bid due date: _____ Project no.: _____ Date: _____

Type of work: _____ Lump sum: _____ Unit price: _____ T&M: _____

Name and address of bidder	Financial rating	Remarks

Recommended: _____   Approved: _____
                        Contract section   Director of construction

Contractors
Bid Comparison

Project Engineering Division

Type of work: _____ Project no.: _____ Date: _____

Estimated cost: CCE – _____ /Engineers est. _____

Contractor's name	Amount of bid			Remarks
	Lump sum	Unit price	T&M	

The above respresents a true and correct Statement of Sealed bid opened on
_____ in presence of undersigned

Award to: _____   Recommended: _____
                                                                              Contract section
Based on: _____   Approved: _____
                                                                              Director of construction

Figure 131. *'Bidder's list' and 'contractor's bid comparison' forms.*

The majority of projects either have commercial objectives or are executed by parties with commercial objectives. It is natural that these parties will, at all times, behave in a commercial manner and approach negotiations accordingly.

Procurement objectives can always be stated in terms of cost, time, performance requirements, safety, legality, etc. Thus any subobjective under possible negotiation may be examined in those terms, within the primary distinctions of the relevant material factors and the organizational/human elements, such as:

- Relevant material factors. The situation being considered will have material characteristics such as budget prices, time for commencement, time for completion, offered prices/conditions, required prices/conditions, state of the market, options, relative importance of the purchase, purchaser/supplier quality standards/requirements and so on.
- Organizational and human elements. Organizations may conduct business with each other, but the business dealings, execution of contracts, etc., will be carried out on a more personal level. In every negotiation the parties are necessarily both buying and selling at the same time, and the party which addresses the issues more professionally will normally do better.

It is essential that the procurement objectives are clearly analysed and determined in advance for any negotiation. However, not only must the purchasing party's objectives be analysed, but so must the interests and objectives of the other party. The assumption is that he will seek maximum benefits and will act accordingly.

Three general strategies are available, namely:

- competitive,
- co-operative,
- using an agent or expert.

In *competitive* negotiation, each party is concerned with gaining advantage for itself and the negotiation is structured on a win/lose basis. *Cooperative* negotiation is favoured where the conditions are such that both parties have a common interest in reaching an agreement which will bring mutual benefits – a win/win basis. *Using an agent or expert* is appropriate where a party lacks a particular skill or wants to make use of an agent's expertise in a particular market. Table 23 gives an overview of the basic differences in competitive and cooperative negotiations.

Table 23. Different features in two negotiating processes.

Feature	Cooperative negotiation	Competitive negotiation
Opening phase	Statements of interest regarding what each party wants and can offer in return	Determine needs and wants – the possible deal(s)/ option(s)
Exploring/assessing motivation, values and power	Clarify objectives	Probe for information Look for strengths and weaknesses
Behaviour	Shared purpose	Manipulate
Joint assessment	Look for creative possibilities	Identify best deal possibilities
Bidding	Offer and clarify	How much? Seek maximum concession first and obtain a commitment
Bargaining	Mutual interests Trade concession for concession	Power, time, space, manœuvrability, resistance, pressure Set deadlines, demand justification, bluff
	Call for recess?	
Closing	Mutual interests satisfied	Push for maximum concessions

Recommendations to purchase

These are required in many cases particularly where the final purchaser is using the service of professionals such as consulting engineers, architects, etc. The recommendation must generally be based upon impartial analysis of the whole tender/bid procedure, vendor offers, etc. The analysis must focus upon the facts available and keep subjectivity to a minimum. In cases where a vendor pre-qualification procedure has been used, it is very difficult to support other than the lowest bid.

Placing of orders/contracts and certifying payments

Upon acceptance of a vendor's bid, the process is formalized with a purchase order or contract. These describe the agreed aspects of the proposed transaction and contracts will, for legal purposes, bear the signatures, at least, of the representatives of the purchaser and vendor.

The purchase order/contract generally details the payment terms. These are particularly noted where the goods or services are furnished over a period of time and part payments are to be made against part deliveries. The payment terms in these cases are normally designed to protect the purchaser by making sure that the value of the goods or services received exceeds the monies paid out. Invoices submitted by the supplier are checked against the values claimed and are then certified for payment by the purchaser's representative.

A special case exists where the nature of the market or buying custom requires an advance or deposit, payable at an early stage in the transaction, against initial mobilization or other costs.

Materials management

Materials management in the project environment is concerned with the technical and commercial aspects of:

- specifications,
- quality assurance and expediting,
- reception, inspection and storage of materials,
- installation.

Specifications

Specifications are used to describe the features and performance characteristics required from or available in an item. A specification will generally contain both narrative and technical data and may be written by either the vendor or purchaser.

Many examples of vendor's specifications are freely available and include brochures and trade literature on items such as automobiles, aircraft, cameras, hi-fi equipment, boilers, pumps, etc. These specifications are used by the purchaser for comparisons with his requirements and the market availability.

Examples of cases where the purchaser may write his own specification include:

- Special computer software for particular applications.
- Engineering or building tenders which may contain both a general and a particular specification written especially for the work.
- One-off items such as transformers with special operating requirements.

The specification will contain both technical and non-technical description. Non-technical items may be related to colours, packaging, identification marks, etc. BS 4778 identifies twelve types of specifications, ranging from primary (target) specification or design brief, through all stages to eventual disposal.

Quality assurance and expediting

These take place prior to delivery of an item where relevant.

Quality assurance

Quality assurance is often concerned with the strengths and properties of materials together with the processes used and tolerances achieved during manufacture. 'Total quality' (see Chapter 10) means satisfying the customer's requirements; quality assurance guarantees that services/materials/goods conform with requirements/are fit for their intended purpose.

The extent to which quality assurance is required by the purchaser depends upon the reliability of the vendor, based on previous performance, quality-standard certification and the nature of the manufactured item. For example, even with an excellent manufacturer, the purchaser may initiate and maintain a rigorous testing and compliance programme if the required item is of particular importance. This is typical in the manufacture of special chemical-process equipment, where unusual or exotic materials are used or where exact dimensional tolerances are required. Single pieces of equipment in this category may be worth six-figure sums and the quality-assurance procedures will represent a significant cost. This type of equipment and the special procedure required will be detailed in a 'quality plan' drawn up for the particular project according to the purchaser's quality programme.

Quality-assurance procedures could also be used in areas such as steel fabrication. In this case, the purchaser may work closely with the fabricator in the initial stages of a contract to ensure that fabrication complies with requirements in terms of tolerances, accuracy of lengths cut, hole positions, etc. Once the fabricator demonstrates his capability to achieve and maintain the required quality, the quality-assurance inspections may be reduced to an occasional sampling basis.

The inspection process in these examples is largely technical and the inspectors must possess the necessary qualifications and experience. Standard testing procedures are described either in International Standards or in a particular specification. The inspector will witness these tests and certify the individual item accordingly.

In addition to the tests during manufacture, performance testing may be required on the whole equipment. For example, tests may be required on transformers or electrical switch-gear to ensure that they can carry the rated voltages and currents safely and that the overload and protection devices operate in a predefined manner. More information on quality and quality assurance is given in Chapter 10.

Expediting

Expediting is concerned with delivery schedules and is used where manufactured items are required on a predetermined date for installation or other use on the project. It does not mean 'hurry-up'. Rather, it is the task of ensuring that a vendor maintains quoted delivery dates and is not permitted, by default, to use excuses for extending the dates. The expediters' information may contribute to the basis of the project-management control system, particularly in reports of delivery schedules which are subject to change.

The expediter must, therefore, be able to work closely with the vendor through all stages of manufacturing such as design, materials specification/procurement, processes, testing programmes, commercial matters, shipping/transportation and delivery. Contact with the vendor is maintained by:

1 telephone,
2 letter/telex,
3 personal visit.

These range both in increasing effectiveness and cost. Consequently, it is necessary to consider the expediting effort from the strategic point of view and to analyse the areas where this effort will be directed for maximum benefit to the overall project.

The cost/effort/benefits available will suggest that detailed analysis and reporting for every item will not be possible, particularly on a large job. The maximum benefit, though, will generally be realized by exception reporting together with detailed sampling of relevant items on a monthly review basis. Major reviews of *all* items in the procurement process may be necessary at strategic intervals.

Reception, inspection and storage of materials

Materials for any project are not generally built-in or otherwise used immediately upon delivery. Therefore, it is necessary to make proper arrangements to receive, inspect and store in an effective manner.

Receiving generally relies upon timely advice from the vendor as to the shipping/transportation/customs-clearance sequence and estimated delivery times. Bulky items may require handling by crane or fork-lift truck and sufficient time must be allowed for arranging both the off-loading and the necessary paperwork which will be in the commercial form of a 'goods received voucher'. At this stage, the receiving agent should notify the project-management representative who will arrange for inspection.

Inspection is necessary for all goods delivered for use in the project, although the degree of inspection will vary with the nature of the item received. Inspection will generally fall into the following categories:

1 Transit damage, ascertained by visual inspection and notified for formal insurance claims.
2 Numerical count, where more than one item is delivered.
3 Condition of goods, particularly after sea journeys or where weather-exposure may have caused damage.
4 Compliance inspection, to ensure that the goods received are as ordered and as described on the vendor's documentation.

Storage facilities must be arranged where necessary. The considerations in this area may be:

● Safety, to anticipate and prevent injury to people caused by faulty stacking or unsafe storage of goods.
● Physical area or volume requirements for storage.
● Weather or other environmental damage possibilities – certain items may require dry, heated storage.

- Security, to anticipate and prevent theft.
- Fire, water and smoke damage possibilities.
- Duration of storage, where items may be in store for long or short periods or may have a limited shelf-life.
- Retrieval, to enable an orderly sequence to be maintained.

Installation or other use in the project

The materials-management aspect of the procurement process may continue after delivery, in three main areas:

- Materials in storage or being used as work in progress, for example, in an erection sequence for a large item of capital equipment.
- Performance guarantees when an item is put into service.
- Disposal after use.

In the second case, particularly, final payment may be withheld pending in-service tests. This final payment, held as 'retention money', will be settled after:

1 vendor claims for extra work
2 or owner claims for the costs of rectifying any defects.

Control of the materials after issue from stores will normally pass to installation personnel or contractors. In practice, this means that they are then responsible for any subsequent losses or damages and this must be made clear both in contractual arrangements and for insurer's liability.

The complexity of materials management requires a comprehensive system. Many computer systems are currently in use, particularly in larger organizations, which can afford to tailor software to their own requirements. However, many of the commercially available systems are not suited for multiproject environments because:

- Special interface problems exist, e.g. interaction with other project systems.
- Multi-user access is necessary to keep the data up to date; this means that a head-office computer is needed, with devices at each site and suitable 'communications protocol' (i.e. ways of communicating) for the devices.

Nevertheless, the advantages of computerization can far outweigh the costs and disadvantages – although these are sometimes hard to establish.

14

Contract administration

In addition to procurement as a commercial transaction, many projects require goods or services to be supplied under contract. A contract, which may be oral and/or written, is based on an agreement to an offer made by one party and accepted by another.

An enforceable, simple contract consists of these elements:

1 The agreement – consisting of a firm offer and acceptance, with both parties assenting to *all* the terms of the agreement.
2 The consideration – which is an exchange for something of value, generally the money to be paid when the services or goods have been delivered under the terms of the contract.
3 The intention to enter legal relations – without this intention, an agreement may exist without necessarily being a contract.
4 The capacity to contract – both parties must be free to enter into the contract. This requirement may not be realized, for example, where a company undertakes to engage in activities outside the objects clause in its memorandum of association or where the conditions of a contract contravene existing regulations within one of the parties.
5 The reality of the consent – both parties must be able to discharge their duty under the contract. For example, if a building firm agrees to construct a house with particular bricks and subsequently finds that the brick supplier has gone out of business, then the firm may claim that the contract is null and void.
6 The object of the contract must be lawful – this does not require further explanation!

Strategic considerations

Contracts are essentially communications which are legally binding. As with any form of communication, the principle should be clarity of expression so that the messsage is properly/accurately conveyed from one party to the other. The legal documents, drawings, specifications and so on which form 'the contract' are therefore vehicles for transmitting and receiving messages.

Since both parties to a contract are separate bodies, the best contracting strategy should:

- Be based on clear messages understood and agreed by each side *before* the contract is signed.
- Be fair to each side, e.g. by taking account of the nature of the work, the user's and contractor's minimum requirements and so on.
- Utilize the common interests of each side to the best advantage.
- Allocate each foreseen risk to the side best equipped to deal with it – obligations will exist on each side but it is clearly advantageous if the party with superior experience, resources and so on deals with appropriate risks.

In this way, the best type of contractual arrangement for a particular project or subproject could then be tailored to suit the circumstances. This can also take into account the fundamental motives for entering the contract. These might be:

Owner/employer	*Contractor*
Minimum cost/risk	Maximum profit/minimum risk
On time	Prestige
No accidents or injuries	Minimum disruption
Usable, maintainable products	Maximum productivity
Cooperation from contractor	Cooperation from owner
Quality standards met	Minimum 'interference'

These objectives are both conflicting and complementary. Therefore it is necessary (for the best results) for the contract to be based on both maximizing the benefits and minimizing the potential for conflict.

Types of contract

In the project procurement environment, the following are the most common types of contract:

Fixed price

These generally comprise package-deal or fixed-price/lump-sum contracts.

Package-deal contracts

The package-deal contract works best where the supplier is offering a service (or goods) in which he is regularly engaged. For example, a building contractor may offer for sale houses under construction and a purchaser may enter a package-deal contract to buy the completed product.

Similarly, a promoter could enter a package-deal contract with a supplier of steam boilers and electricity-generating equipment. Such contracts involve design, manufacture and construction work of substantial value and might require as much inspection effort on the promoter's behalf as with other forms of contract. In this case the powers of the promoter's inspection staff need to be clearly spelled out, particularly with regard to the rejection of design or workmanship. These could be covered in the quality plan for the project (see Chapter 10).

Lump-sum contracts

Lump sum contracts must, by their nature, be based upon completely detailed specifications and drawings. They are commonly used for the supply and installation of mechanical and electrical equipment but outside this type of consideration are generally applied only where:

- The contract is not of large value in relation to the whole project or
- All the work required can be precisely described so that there is complete clarity of intention.
- Risks are confined to normal business risks and no substantially innovative methods or materials are required.
- Substantial extras, deletions or variations are not expected during the course of the contract works.

Variable price

To some extent, all variable-price contracts must contain fixed prices (or elements or agreements on prices) or other considerations. The final price paid must be determinable under the agreement and this could be subject to an upper limit. Examples are:

1 Bills of quantities, used particularly in the building and civil-engineering industry. The works are described in specifications and drawings and measured in accordance with standardized rules. If the works are built exactly in accordance with the drawings, etc., then the price tendered becomes the contract sum. However, in practice, most of these contracts experience *variations*, i.e. departure from expected conditions (see Fig. 132). These can be measured in accordance with the standard procedure and alter the total price to each party's satisfaction. This type of contract is generally the fairest to each party for works of this nature.

2 Schedules of rates. This type of contract is very similar to the bills of quantities contract, except that there is no implied guarantee that any or all of the work will be carried out. Generally, quantities are not entered in the scheduled items and this is most useful where the extent of various works cannot be properly foreseen. The final price must be based upon the rates and the quantities of work measured against the items actually performed. The rates tendered and accepted are the fixed-price elements while the total price determined is variable. Contracts on this basis may also include 'time-and-materials' contracts, where, for example, hourly labour rates are in force together with a percentage mark-up for materials supplied.

3 Cost plus percentage. Used particularly for emergency works where time does not permit use of other forms of contract. The contractor is paid for actual expenditures plus an agreed percentage to cover overheads and profits. Because there is no restriction on the total cost, this type of contract is generally operated for a limited period of time.

4 Cost plus fixed fee. Usefully employed where work is of a difficult or unforeseeable nature. The contractor is reimbursed for actual costs incurred, which are variable, but is also paid an agreed sum by way of a fixed fee which might be determined by competition with other contractors.

5 Target-price contracts. This is a variation of the cost-plus contract which seeks to identify the value attached to a job. However, if risks

occur which were not included in the original target price the target might end up unfair to the contractor and lead to dispute.

Contracts for personal/professional services

These may be classified as labour only, professional briefs or management contracts. The costs are generally reimbursed on a man-hour basis or as an agreed percentage of the value of the works.

Man-hour basis

In this type of contract, the prices for labour are agreed and the costs are measured as the product of the agreed rate and the man-hours used in performing the contract. The type of labour may range from the unskilled, e.g. the building-site general operative, to the highly skilled, such as doctors, pilots, lawyers, etc.

Professional briefs

This type of contract is usually regulated by the profession involved. For architectural works, engineering design or supervision of construction, the fees and scope of work may be defined on a standard basis. Although the professional body involved may require its members to charge not less than a minimum fee or percentage of the value of works on a sliding scale, the actual fee may be negotiated between the client and the architect or engineer at a higher rate. Alternatively, fees might be fixed on a reimbursable man-hour basis. Such arrangements require differentiation regarding payments for skills, status and/or experience/expertise levels.

Generally, this type of contract relies on the integrity of the professional, whose activities are subject to the invigilation of his professional body. Nevertheless, disputes can and indeed do arise which become the subject of contract law resulting in court action.

Management contracts

These are of a more commercial nature than professional briefs and involve the performance of commercial services with measurable results.

Contract documents

Many industries have developed their own approach to the form and nature of typical contracts and contract documentation. Thus experienced contractors, who are used to bidding on the general format of the industry inquiry documents, do not expect to read every word on every inquiry.

Prior to contract, the documents are known as pre-contract, tender or inquiry documents and may be issued to potential contractors in a number of ways. These include advertising, pre-qualification and selection. The objective of the information supplied in the documents at this stage is to convey the employer's intentions on the same basis to each tenderer. Queries which arise in the tender period may be circulated to all the tenderers, together with the answer or explanation, in sufficient time to be incorporated in the offers.

Signed and submitted tender documents constitute the *offers* made by the tenderers. These offers may be comparatively analysed to select the most appropriate for the employer and this, together with any mutually agreed and accepted amendments or explanations, will normally become the basis for a contract.

Examples of documents from the construction industry include the following:

- Engineering drawings, showing the structure to be built.
- A general specification describing the quality standards for workmanship, materials, etc.
- A particular specification, drawing special attention to relevant items, such as the requirement for the contractor's quality plan.
- General conditions of contract which cover the normal liabilities of the parties, including methods of payments, insurances, etc.
- Particular conditions of contract which highlight special conditions for the contract in question.
- Bills of quantities, priced by the contractor, and set out according to standardized procedures. A section here may constitute the tender, signed by the contractor offering to carry out the works described in the documents.
- A legal agreement, signed by the employer and contractor, confirming the acceptance by the employer of the contractor's offer and their mutual intention to *contract* with each other in accordance with the documents.
- Letters of explanation or clarification agreed and accepted by both parties during the tender period.

These documents are normally prepared by the engineering personnel involved, although procurement, commercial and legal staff might be involved in relevant issues.

Discharge of contracts

Under a properly constituted contract, the parties have rights and obligations, which are discharged by performance, agreement or frustration.

Discharge by performance

Performance implies execution or implementation and requires that the parties perform *precisely* (i.e. definitely, meticulously, rigorously) all the terms of the contract. Not surprisingly, it is in this area of contracts administration where most disputes arise.

It is envisaged that when parties enter into contract, both intend to perform precisely their respective obligations and to exercise their rights in accordance with the performance of the other. In simple contracts, such as for the sale of goods, strict interpretation of the conditions of contract may be obvious and respected by the parties. However, in more complex cases, ambiguity in wording may give rise to various forms of interpretation or misinterpretation. Such contracts will generally contain provisions for the settlement of disputes by court action or by reference to third-party arbitration.

Prior to this stage, one party may make a *claim* against the other. A claim in this context is a statement of position regarding the interpretation of the contract in the circumstances which have arisen and is expressed as a *demand as of right*. The claims may be treated by the parties as:

- valid,
- invalid,
- partially valid,
- disputed,

and the settlement of the claims handled as follows:

Contractors' claims

Contractors are generally interested in maximizing the value of a contract to their benefit. Therefore, typical contractors' claims are for extra payments (as opposed to any other consideration) or the granting of extra time to avoid paying penalty charges.

The claims usually arise from:

1 Additional work, which will fall into the categories of:
   (a) Work essential to the performance of the contract. For this type of claim, a distinction must be made regarding the nature of the contract in that no consideration may be allowed for lump-sum contracts, where it is deemed that the tender included for all work necessary to perform the contract. For other types of contract, which are valued according to the actual work done, the essential extra work may be costed and paid for by measurement of the quantities involved and the rates determined according to the terms of the contract.
   (b) Work chosen by the employer which the contractor is obliged to carry out and for which he has the right to be paid.
   (c) Work which arose due to the costs of overcoming unforeseeable conditions. While contracts may contain a clause relating to the sufficiency of the tender, covering the entire body of the works described in the documents, it may happen that conditions or obstructions arise which could not reasonably have been foreseen at the time of the tender. In this case, the contractor may claim for the costs incurred in overcoming the condition or obstruction, although the payment would not include profit to the contractor, and would be based only on the actual costs of the work arising.

2 Increases in the costs of labour or materials. Many contracts contain clauses which state that the tender is based upon the prices ruling at the date of the tender submission and that subsequent increases will be borne by the employer. This is particularly so where the contract period may be lengthy, although some contracts may call for the contractor to bear all such increases and this will be reflected in the tender prices.

3 Delay in the execution of the contract. Delays might affect all or part of the performance of a contract and could be complete or partial. In general, extra payment may only be claimed where:
   (a) Delay actually occurred.

(b) The cause was outside the contractor's liabilities in terms of the contract.

(c) Loss to the contractor actually arose and has not otherwise been reimbursed under the contract.

Delay claims, particularly those arising from the direct actions of the employer, can be particularly expensive. However, the value of the claim is restricted to the loss actually incurred by the contractor. The onus is on the contractor to prove his loss. Claims for the extension of contract time may or may not involve claims for extra payments.

Employers' claims

Employers, on the other hand, assuming that they actually want the work done or the terms of the contract honoured, are more likely to claim against a contractor for unsatisfactory workmanship, materials or time for performance.

Claims typically fall into the following areas:

1 Part performance. Where, for example, a contractor fails to complete work, it must be first considered whether or not the employer is free to accept or reject the work. If he accepts it, then the contractor must be paid to the value of the work done. If he rejects it, then he is not obliged to pay for it. A special case arises when the employer has no option but to accept the work (e.g. because of immediate danger to life or property or because of nuisance) in which case he may not be obliged to pay for it.

2 Substantial performance. Where an employer claims that a contractor did not *precisely* perform all the terms of a contract, he must be aware of the doctrine of substantial performance. This allows that where a contractor has performed the most part of a contract to an acceptable degree, he is entitled to be paid the full contract price less an allowance for defective items or those which do not fully comply with the contract.

3 Time taken for performance. Many contracts are awarded on the basis of a contractor's promise to complete the works or make delivery within a specified time. In general, a party who does not discharge his obligations within the specified time is liable for damages. However, if the substance of the contract is not affected by the time limits and the employer has not suffered materially, he will have no claim. This is because time is not regarded as the essence of a contract unless:

(a) This condition is clearly provided for or
(b) notice is given to perform within a reasonable time or
(c) it is clearly essential that time limits are to be observed, e.g. where follow-on contracts or weather-windows are involved.

Some contracts make specific provision for *remedies* in the event of a *breach* of contract due to a contractor's failure to perform. A breach of contract is a 'breaking or neglect of the rules' and the remedies are intended to make good any resulting loss or damage. They may be termed 'penalties' or 'liquidated damages' and are distinguished as follows:

- Liquidated damages are a *genuine pre-estimate of losses* which would occur in the event of a breach of contract. They are based on a fixed sum per day or per week by which the time limit is broken and may generally be recovered without having to prove actual loss.
- Penalties are designed to be held over the head of a party to force him to perform. However, penalties cannot be enforced if they are not of proportion to the actual loss which occurred or may have occurred and should be considered accordingly; they may generally be considered invalid.

Discharge by agreement

The most common form of this type of discharge is where an existing contract is varied *on agreement* by both parties. Generally, the agreement must be in written form to be enforceable and typical variations may be as follows:

- Addition or deletion of items affecting the value of the contract.
- Alteration or substitution of items or the quality of items or standards of workmanship.
- Changes in completion or delivery dates.

These are typically recorded as 'contract variation orders' as shown in Fig. 132.

A special case exists where an employer wishes to delete a major item to the contractor's dissatisfaction. In such a case, the contractor may be entitled to recover his anticipated profit as if he had actually supplied the major item.

Waivers are a particular form of discharge by agreement and arise where one party gives up a right for precise performance from the other, to be replaced by another time or method of performance.

Variation Order   No. _____

Project _____

Contract _____

Contractor _____

You are hereby instructed to execute/omit* the following in accordance with and subject to the conditions of the contract:

Description

Price increase/decrease*_____

Net effect on contract price payable

Total of previous variation orders (increase/decrease)*_____

This variation order (increase/decrease)*_____

Total (increase/decrease)*_____

* delete as appropriate

Signed:

_____   _____

for employer   for contractor

Dated   _____   _____

Figure 132. *Contract variation order.*

Discharge by frustration

This type of discharge will only arise where it becomes impossible to perform the contract by reason of:

- Physical conditions arising during the course of the contract which make *impossible* either the object of the contract or a stipulated method of performance.
- A subsequent change in the law which renders the performance of the contract illegal (the object of a contract must be lawful).
- Removal of the basis of the contract.

It goes without saying that if one party deliberately creates the frustrating circumstances, then he cannot claim discharge by frustration. However, the onus is on the other party to disprove the claim.

Selected reading

Note: These selected books and articles cover project, construction and general management topics. They are not presented in either order of importance or recommendation. Many of them contain further good reading lists or bibliographies.

Project Management

Harrison, F. L. (1981). *Advanced Project Management*. Gower Publishing.

Humphreys, K. K. (ed.) (1984). *Project & Cost Engineers Handbook*. Marcel Dekker, Inc.

Kerzner, Harold (1984). *Project Management: A Systems Approach to Planning, Scheduling and Controlling*. Van Nostrand Reinhold.

Kharbanda, O. P. *et al.* (1980). *Project Cost Control in Action*. Gower Publishing.

Lock, Dennis (1986). *Project Management*. Gower Publishing.

Lock, Dennis (1987). *Project Management Handbook*. Gower Publishing.

Rase, Howard F. and Barrow, M. H. (1957). *Project Engineering of Process Plants*. John Wiley.

Riggs, James L. *What's the Score?*. The Military Engineer, vol. 77, no. 503, pp. 496–9 September/October 1985.

Rosenau, Milton D. Jr. (1984). *Project Management for Engineers*. Van Nostrand Reinhold.

Stallworthy, E. A. and Kharbanda, O. P. (1983). *Total Project Management*. Gower Publishing.

Turner, W. S. III (1980). *Project Auditing Methodology*. North-Holland Publishing.

Construction management

Bureau of Engineering Research (1989). *Project Control for Construction*. The University of Texas at Austin *CII Publication* No. 6-5, September.

The Business Roundtable (1983). *More Construction for the Money*. Summary report of the Construction Industry Cost Effectiveness Committee.

Constructability: A Primer. CII Publication No. 3-1 July 1986.

Construction Industry Institute Model Plant. CII Publication No. 2-1 October 1986.

Impact of Various Construction Contract Types and Clauses. CII Publication No. 5-1 1986.

Davis, Kent and Ledbetter, W. B. (1987). *Measuring Design and Construction Quality Costs*. A report to the Construction Industry Institute, The University of Texas at Austin from the Civil Engineering Department, Clemson University, Clemson, South Carolina.

Davis, Belfield and Everest (eds) (1988). *Spon's Mechanical and Electrical Services Price Book*. In *Spon's Price Book Series*. E & FN Spons.

Evaluation of Design Effectiveness. CII Publication No. 8-1 July 1986.

Maclay, Ian (1985). *Made in the USA*. Report of a visit to the Engineering, Construction and Process Plant Industry in the North Eastern United States in Autumn by the Secretary of Economic Construction and Process Plant EDCs. NEDO Publication.

How Flexible is Construction? (1978). A study of resources and participants in the construction process by Building and Civil Engineering EDCs. NEDO Publication.

Oxley, R. and Poskitt, J. (1980). *Management Techniques Applied to the Construction Industry*. Granada Publishing.

Pilcher, Roy (1976). *Principles of Construction Management*. McGraw-Hill.

Pilcher, Roy. (1985). *Cost Control in Construction*. Collins.

Twort, A. C. (1966). *Civil Engineering, Supervision and Management*. Edward Arnold.

Woodward, J. F. (1975). *Quantitative Methods in Construction Management and Design*. Macmillan.

General management

Ansoff, Igor (1987). *Corporate Strategy*. Penguin.

Armstrong, Michael (1987). *Handbook of Personnel Management*. Kogan Page.

Bailey, F. G. (1985). *Strategems and Spoils – A Social Anthropology of Politics*. Basil Blackwell.

Beer, S. (1972). *The Brain of the Firm*. Allen Lane.

Beer, S. *et al.* (1984). *Managing Human Assets*. Free Press.

Boisot, Max (1987). *Information and Organizations – The Manager as Anthropologist*. Fontana.

Crosby, Philip B. (1980). *Quality is Free – The Art of making Quality Certain*.

Drucker, Peter (1970). *The Effective Executive*. Pan Books.

Handy, Charles B. (1986). *Understanding Organizations*. Penguin.

Juran, J. M. (1988). *Juran on Planning for Quality*. Free Press.

Kelly, Joe (1980). *How Managers Manage*. Prentice-Hall.

Kepner, Charles M. and Tregoe, Benjamin (1985). *The New Rational Manager*. McGraw-Hill.

Knott, Geoffrey (1985). *Understanding Financial Management*. Pan.

Margerison-McCann (1986). *Team Management Resource*. MCB University Press.

Marsh, Peter (1984). *Contract Negotiations Handbook*. Gower.

Meidan, Arthur. *Handbook of Business Policy*. MCB University Press.

Quality and Value for Money (1985). A Report to the National Economic Council by the Task Force on Quality and Standards. NEDO Publications.

Ohmae, Kenichi (1984). *The Mind of the Strategist*. Penguin.

Pascale, R. T. and Athos, A. G. (1988). *The Art of Japanese Management*. Penguin.

Peters, Thomas J. and Waterman, Robert M. Jr. (1982). *In Search of Excellence*. Harper and Row.

Price, Frank (1984). *Right First Time*. Gower.

Sykes, J. B. *Concise Oxford Dictionary*, 7th ed. Oxford University Press.

Tuckman, B. W. (1965). *Developmental sequence in small groups. Psychological Bulletin*.

Twiss, Brian (1987). *Management of Technological Innovation*. 3rd ed. Longman.

Weston and Brigham (1979). *Managerial Finance*. Holt, Rinehart and Winston.

Wheelan, T. and Hunger, J. D. (1986). *Strategic Management and Business Policy* 2nd ed. Addison-Wesley.

Wild, Ray (ed.) (1983). *How to Manage*. Pan.

Wills, Kennedy, Cheese and Rushton (1986). *Maximising Marketing Effectiveness*. MCB University Press.

Index